SHAME, IMAGES OF GOD AND THE CYCLE OF VIOLENCE

in Adults Who Experienced Childhood Corporal Punishment

Jeanette Anderson Good

University Press of America,® Inc.
Lanham • New York • Oxford

Copyright © 1999 by
University Press of America,® Inc.
4720 Boston Way
Lanham, Maryland 20706

12 Hid's Copse Rd.
Cumnor Hill, Oxford OX2 9JJ

Library of Congress Cataloging-in-Publication Data

Good, Jeanette Anderson.
Shame, images of God, and the cycle of violence in adults who experienced
childhood corporal punishment / Jeanette Anderson Good.
p.   cm.
Includes bibliographical references and index.
1. Violence. 2. Shame. 3. Children and violence.
4. Corporal punishment. I. Title.
HM1116.G66   1999   303.6—dc21   99—37777 CIP

ISBN 0-7618-1483-3 (cloth: alk. ppr.)

The paper used in this publication meets the minimum
requirements of American National Standard for Information
Sciences—Permanence of Paper for Printed Library Materials,
ANSI Z39.48—1984

I dedicate this book to future children that their spirits may never be broken by the humiliation of childhood corporal punishment.

CONTENTS

LIST OF TABLES

FOREWORD

Violence has emerged as one the most daunting problems facing our society as we reach the year 2000. Children kill children in schools and playgrounds, husbands batter and murder wives, and sick and shamed individuals target marginalized groups in hate crimes. We have not found healthy and creative ways to deal with difference. Racial differences, gender differences, class differences, religious differences offer potential opportunities for great growth; instead they frequently become excuses for aggression and the exercise of dominance by one group or one individual over another. While violence has taken a tremendous toll on our society, few have made a serious effort to draw a comprehensive picture of the forces that contribute to this alarming state of affairs.

Psychologists are often turned to for solutions in the wake of violent outbursts. And yet, I believe, the field of psychology has contributed to some of our collective passivity in the face of aggression and violence by suggesting that humans are innately aggressive and self-serving. The "boys will be boys" argument is often invoked when aggression erupts on the playing fields of adolescence. Our basic need for connection, the desire to love and serve others, to form and contribute to community has been overshadowed in the prevailing psychological theories that suggest babies are born self-centered, that at our core we are basically aggressive. Accepting that human beings are basically aggressive leads to a sense of resignation and a failure of imagination in trying to understand and possibly intervene at the source of the most troubling causes of violence.

Jeanette Good has beautifully reviewed and outlined several important antecedents of violence, adult shame, depression and suicidality. Looking at the childrearing practice of corporal punishment, all too often accepted without question, she traces some of the ominous threads from childhood corporal punishment to later violence. The long-term consequences of corporal punishment are real and costly...for individuals and for our society. Jeanette Good's timely research indicates that corporal punishment, hitting children, leads to adult violence, suicidality and depression. Those who are hit by caretakers also develop high levels of pathological shame. Childhood corporal punishment increases the likelihood that one will be a victim or perpetrator of adult partner violence. Yet many people (38% of the group studied here) agreed that disciplining a child sometimes necessitates a "good hard spanking."

We need to educate the public about the long-term consequences of hitting children. While supporters of corporal punishment suggest it works to stop undesirable behavior, it yields a Pyrrhic victory. The long-range outcome is more violence. We need to help those people who were hit as children so they can break the intergenerational cycle of violence and abuse. We need to develop empathic awareness of the hurt that occurs when children are hit. Studies have shown that mothers who break the intergenerational cycle of abuse were aware of the hurt they experienced as children when they were hit and did not wish to inflict this pain on their children (Egeland and Sussman-Stillman, 1996). This is the kind of empathy we need to be developing in all people who have been punished with hitting and beating: self empathy and empathy with others. We also need to be teaching what I call "anti-shame strategies" to those victims of corporal punishment who are vulnerable to humiliation and rage and who are in danger of turning their own shame into aggression against others.

Jeanette Good has given us a solid piece of scholarship on the complicated topics of corporal punishment, shame, images of God and violence. Her writing is grounded, clear and relevant to the crises we face as a culture around the looming threats of violence. Yet as I read this sober, complex book, I found myself feeling hope and a call to action. This book inspires a sense that we can do something significant about violence in our culture. We can educate rather than moralize; we can move toward empathy and courage in the place of shame and isolation. We can create communities of understanding and encouragement and we can begin to question a pessimistic worldview that says human beings are simply aggressive and selfish by nature. There is a way out of shame: through empathic attunement and engagement in growth fostering relationships.

Judith V. Jordan, Ph.D.
Stone Center
Wellesley College

ACKNOWLEDGEMENTS

Writing a book can be a lonely process because hours must be spent in solitary thought, reflection, prayer, writing, and re-writing. I have been graced along this journey with numbers of colleagues and friends who have served as my "community of encouragement."

I want to express my deepest heart-felt gratitude to the following people:

Murray Straus who agreed early on, in the formative stages of this project, to meet with me in his office at the University of New Hampshire; he has encouraged my work in the area of shame and corporal punishment of children.

Kathy Kendall-Tackett, research consultant at the University of New Hampshire Family Research Laboratory, who has served as mentor and friend during this long process.

The University of New Hampshire Family Research Laboratory team under the direction of Murray Straus and David Finkelhor, who analyzed and gave my dissertation proposal poignant feedback.

Luke Johnson who reminded me to listen to the passions of my heart as the energizer and sustainer of my faith and vocational calling. Luke carefully read the first draft of my proposal and encouraged me to study the shame/honor system of the Mediterranean world.

James Gilligan who generously and compassionately spent two hours with me in his library discussing shame, childhood corporal punishment and violence.

The Stone Center for giving me the opportunity to spend an academic year reflecting on their relational and cultural theory and especially for Judith Jordan and her inspirational work on shame.

Carrie Doehring who has been a superb advisor at Boston University: steady, encouraging, guiding, while allowing me to claim my own voice and spirit in this project.

Chris Schlauch who as second reader of my dissertation—the basis of this book—continually re-fined this project. Whereas Carrie helped me design and build a piece of fine furniture, Chris was the one who encouraged the laborious finishing touches. Even when I thought the sanding had been done, Chris said, "how about a little more sanding, and another coat of finish?" Sometimes it takes the finished product to appreciate the hard work.

John Houlihan whose research enthusiasm was contagious.

Ben Crosby and support staff of the New Hampshire Conference, United Church of Christ, and especially Lynda Colbert who was always on call for my computer emergencies. Ben encouraged me to enter into the computer age and Lynda kept me in it.

Ken and Sue Henderson who lovingly and selflessly came to my rescue as I was trying to learn how to do an index.

The three small churches I have served as Interim Pastor during my Ph.D. studies: Harrisville Community and Salisbury Congregational UCC in New Hampshire and the First Church of Danvers Congregational UCC in Massachusetts all of whom have helped me re-fine my reflections on what it means to be a "community of encouragement."

My parents, Dorathy and Vinal Good, who have been convinced of the importance of this work.

Fred B. Craddock who has been a steadfast, spirit-filled mentor for over a decade. More than anyone else, he has spent hours reflecting with me about my calling to address violence issues within both church and society. He introduced me to David deSilva's work which has profoundly influenced this book. I am absolutely grateful for Dr. Craddock's sensitivity to abuse and trauma issues and his insightful ability to encourage, inspire and lift the human spirit.

Carole Carlson and her family who have endlessly and steadfastly supported this work and my Ph.D. studies. Without Carole and Fred Craddock I may never have pursued this project.

For those who have helped me stay fully alive during this wearying project; I am particularly grateful for the gift of Andrea Bocelli's music and walks by the sea.

Excerpts from James Fowler, <u>Faithful Change: The Personal and Public Challenges of Postmodern Life</u>, copyright © 1996 by Abingdon Press, are reprinted by permission of the publisher.

Excerpts from Iona and Peter Opie, Editors, <u>A Family Book of Nursery Rhymes</u> copyright © Iona and Peter Opie, 1963, are reprinted by permission of Oxford University Press.

The excerpt from Maya Angelou, <u>I Know Why the Caged Bird Sings</u>, copyright © 1969 by Maya Angelou, is reprinted by permission of Random House, Inc.

The excerpt from Kenneth Wooden, <u>Weeping In the Playtime of Others</u>, copyright © 1976 by McGraw-Hill, are reprinted by permission of the publisher.

Excerpts from David A. deSilva, <u>Despising Shame: Honor Discourse and Community Maintenance in the Epistle to the Hebrews</u>, copyright © 1995 by The Society of Biblical Literature, are reprinted by permission of the publisher.

Excerpts from Jerome H. Neyrey, <u>The Social World of Luke-Acts: Models for Interpretation copyright,</u> © 1991 by Hendrickson Publishers, are reprinted by permission of the publisher.

The entire Research Packet used in this study can be obtained by ordering the original dissertation of this work: <u>Shame, Images of God and the Cycle of Violence in Adults Who Experienced Childhood Corporal Punishment</u>, © 1998 by Jeanette Anderson Good by contacting:

UMI Dissertation Services
300 North Zeeb Road
P.O. Box 1346
Ann Arbor, Michigan 48106-1346
1-800-521-0600
734-761-4700
http://www.umi.com

The order number is 9911902

CHAPTER 1

Shame, Images of God and the Cycle of Violence in Adults Who Experienced Childhood Corporal Punishment:

An Introduction

Jeanette Anderson Good

> ...better to die of hunger than of shame
> Elie Wiesel, Memoirs—All Rivers Run to the Sea

> Most of the seriously violent inmates were in prison because they had been so humiliated and shamed by the whole human world that they had undergone what I can only call 'a death of the self.' (Fain, The Boston Globe, April 17, 1996)

Statement of the Problem

The purpose of this book is to investigate factors which may promote as well as mitigate the expression of violence in adults. Previous research has indicated that shame, a history of childhood corporal punishment, and certain religious beliefs may be major factors in the intergenerational cycle of violence.[1] The question of how human behavior and personality are related to violence has been both an historical and contemporary concern of religious, theological and social

---

[1] For instance, this study examines the relationship between severity of childhood corporal punishment and adult partner violence.

scientific literature. Drawing upon these diverse and rich bodies of literature, this study asks how three factors—shame, images of God and childhood corporal punishment—are related with a fourth factor, adult violence.

Background of the Problem

With the advent of modern psychology there had been great hopes that the twentieth century would be a century different from all other centuries. Psychology had become "a 'science' that seemed to promise prediction and control of human affairs" (Koch, 1992, p. 22). According to Sigmund Koch, the twentieth century was to be the psychological century. At last there was a discipline that could save humankind; religion couldn't, scientific psychology could!

By mid century humankind had developed instruments of mass destruction capable of annihilating all life on earth. In retrospect the twentieth century has been among the bloodiest and most violent; a century so horrific in its magnitude of human suffering that even theology has been shaken to its core (Blumenthal, 1993, p. xi). With the advent of weapons of mass destruction, our century potentially may be the most destructive century known by humankind (Greven, 1990, 1992, p. 8; Scheff and Retzinger, 1991, p. xvii).

Why is violence so rampant? What are the roots of violence? Is there an intergenerational cycle of violence? Are there theological, religious, and philosophical as well as sociological, psychological and even physiological roots of violence? Prominent scholars in the study of violence ask the question which has become a question of our time "Is there any hope of understanding the causes of violence" (Scheff and Retzinger, 1991, p. xvii)? This study not only attempts to understand factors related to violence (for example, shame, guilt, images of God and history of childhood corporal punishment) but it also examines the age old question of how to impede if not stop the continuation of violence from generation to generation.

While corporal punishment has been an accepted practice in many cultures, recent research has shown that corporal punishment of children contributes to an intergenerational cycle of violence (Straus, 1991, p. 96). For instance, being corporally punished as a teenager increases the likelihood that one will corporally punish and/or physically abuse one's own children (p. 95). Furthermore, corporal punishment legitimizes "other forms of violence" such as partner abuse (p. 9). One learns as a child that "if someone is doing something outrageous and other methods of getting the person to listen to reason have failed, it is ok to use physical violence" (p. 9). According to Straus, this learned pattern of using physical violence in childhood to negotiate conflict is frequently repeated in adulthood. Straus (1994b), Greven (1990, 1992) and Hyman (1997) are of the opinion that corporal punishment of children is one of the major factors in the cycle of violence in our world. By examining possible correlations among shame, images of God and violence in adults who were corporally punished as children, this study may be able to differentiate those adults who are more likely to continue the cycle of violence from those who are more likely to break it. Thus this study hopes to ascertain whether shame, guilt and certain images of God contribute to or potentially mitigate or minimize violence in adults who were corporally punished as children.

This book critically reviews certain emerging biblical literatures on the shame/honor system and its relationship to violence primarily in the first-century eastern Mediterranean world.[2] As this book will emphasize, the task at hand is not to transport the present into the past or to import the past into the present. But rather the point of such a methodology is to place this emerging biblical literature on the shame/honor system of the first-century eastern Mediterranean world in dialogue with contemporary pastoral theological and social scientific research while at the same time critically reviewing such a project. Bridging such a conversation between the biblical world and contemporary life should enable us to determine if there are clues which might be helpful as we proceed today in mitigating and preventing violence.[3]

For instance, recent research (deSilva, 1995) has indicated that the early Christian community, as depicted in the Epistle to the Hebrews, resisted the shaming tactics of the dominant culture (Greco-Roman society) by maintaining a mutually supportive, encouraging and esteeming community. Social scientific research (Gelles and Straus, 1988) indicates that the greater the support (communal and personal) the lower the rates of violence. People who are socially isolated tend to be more violent. In fact, research also indicates that those parents who break the cycle of violence tend to be parents who share certain characteristics in common:

> These nonabusive parents had more extensive social support.... The parents also displayed more open anger about their own abusive experience and were able to describe these traumas more freely. If they had been abused, it was by one parent, while the other parent served as a supportive life raft in a sea of trouble and pain. (p. 122)

---

[2] This study acknowledges the Greco-Roman Empire as the context and dominant culture in which early Christianity struggled to find its identity. Meeks (1986) makes this point by writing, "The Christians...we are trying to understand lived in the world of the early Roman empire, and that world also lived in them: in their thinking, in their language, in their relationships" (p. 13). That is to say that the Greco-Roman Empire was a pervasive presence and force inherent in this first-century eastern Mediterranean world (Johnson, 1986, p. 43).

[3] An example of an interdisciplinary approach to understanding the first-century eastern Mediterranean culture is seen in the works of New Testament scholars Bruce J. Malina and Jerome H. Neyrey (1991a, 1991b, 1991c). Neyrey (1991) states that in 1986 a group of scholars known as the "The Context Group, formed a seminar to apply the social sciences for interpretation of biblical texts. Although trained in the contemporary historical-critical method of biblical studies and working with the standard texts, they chose to do something quite different. Far from abandoning the historical-critical method, they enlarged it by calling attention to the use of the social sciences in the task of understanding biblical texts in their full cultural context" (p.ix).

An interdisciplinary research methodology consisting of three steps will be employed in this study. In the first step, a revised correlational method is used to understand how various literatures on shame, violence, corporal punishment, and images of God (i.e., pastoral theological perspectives on shame; biblical/theological perspectives on shame, honor and images of God; social scientific perspectives on shame, violence, images of God) are related to each other. In the second step, an empirical research design is employed to test the statistical significance of correlations of measures among shame, guilt, violence and images of God. In the third step, these empirical findings are brought into dialogue with the cross-disciplinary review of literature undertaken in the first step, in order to elaborate the meaning of the findings. These elaborated meanings will ultimately be related to practice (i.e., clinical and pastoral practice).

Significance of the Study

This study is of significance in its unique examination of shame, images of God and the cycle of violence in adults who experienced childhood corporal punishment. There are no current empirical studies that integrate religious, theological and social scientific literatures with the intent of better understanding the possible relationships among shame, images of God and the cycle of violence in adults who experienced childhood corporal punishment. This study is also unique in its interdisciplinary, multi-method research methodology. This research should be of special interest to the fields of pastoral psychology, religion and the social sciences because it provides a model of how to do such interdisciplinary, multi-method research. Such research moves beyond the specialized knowledge of each discipline and provides ways of bridging these disciplines. Finally, this study is of special significance to practitioners whether they are clinicians, trauma specialists and/or pastors.

Research Significance

Loder (1990) states that no "single methodology" is adequate in bridging the fields of psychology and theology. Therefore, in examining the question of how human personality is related to violence, I have developed a comprehensive interdisciplinary, multi-method model that investigates how shame and images of God are related to the cycle of violence in adults who have experienced childhood corporal punishment.

This interdisciplinary and multi-method research model consists of three steps or "moments." The first moment consists of comprehensive interdisciplinary research, employing a "revised correlational methodology" (Browning, 1991; Tracy, 1983; Tillich, 1951) which coordinates the questions and findings of diverse areas of inquiry: religious, theological and psychological resources (both theoretical and empirical).

The second moment consists of an empirical study, which draws upon a more limited literature and only indirectly builds upon and extends the diverse and comprehensive literature of the first moment. This second moment is "mono-method," employing only one methodology: the empirical method.

The third moment of research is once again not only interdisciplinary and comprehensive but also pragmatic and practical (Chopp, 1995; Browning, 1991). This third moment employs what Browning calls a "practice-theory-practice"[4] model meaning that the findings of the second moment (empirical research) address and influence the questions, issues and concerns formulated in the first moment. The revision progresses from step to step. Furthermore, this third moment involves a practical "emancipatory praxis,"(Chopp, 1995) which envisions a present and future world in which the expression of violence in adults is minimized.

Thus this study employs contemporary empirical research and theoretical writings as well as historical biblical materials. For example, Capps (1990) suggests that the field of pastoral theology recover what Ricoeur (1971) calls the "disclosive power" of the biblical text, meaning that the text does not so much reveal something hidden, as much as it discloses a "world," providing "a new way of looking at things" (p. 558).

Ricoeur's theoretical hermeneutical model lends itself well to examining shame and images of God in the biblical texts as "a new way of looking at" the cycle of violence in our contemporary society and also looking at ways of minimizing its effects. Therefore, methodologically, I have utilized a first-century eastern Mediterranean view of shame/honor as a means of more clearly understanding the relationships among shame, images of God and the cycle of violence. To this end, I have explored to what extent the shame/honor system of the first-century eastern Mediterranean world was directly related to violence and thus may contribute to our contemporary understanding of violence, not only providing "a new way of looking at things" (Ricoeur, 1971, p. 558), but also providing insight into how the cycle of violence can be broken today.

Cross-Disciplinary Methodology

I have used a cross-disciplinary methodology bringing a biblical understanding of shame, images of God, and the cycle of violence into conversation with a more contemporary pastoral theological and psychological understanding of shame, images of God and violence. This study has explored whether certain insights from the shame/honor system of the early Christian community (deSilva, pp. 286-287) and the Hebrew scriptures (Huber, 1983) could serve as a contemporary model for understanding the role of shame and images of God in maintaining or breaking a cycle of violence.

---

[4] Practice is always theory laden and theory is always practically based.

Significance for Pastoral Psychology and the Study of Religion

The interdisciplinary and multi-method research methodology employed in this study is significant to the fields of religious and theological studies, pastoral psychology, practical theology and the social sciences. In a unique manner this research demonstrates how theory and practice (Browning, 1991; Freire, 1973; Schlauch, 1995) are interrelated; how religious and theological studies as well as psychological studies play an integral role in articulating the research question(s); how these questions give rise to a more focused empirical study and how the findings of such an empirical study are related to religious and theological writings and influence the interdisciplinary formulation of research question(s).

This study's cross-disciplinary methodology relating biblical studies with psychology is of significance to pastoral theologians (Albers, 1995; Patton, 1985; Fowler, 1993; Burton, 1988, 1991; Capps, 1993; Schneider; 1977, Johnson, E.L. 1992; and Thompson, E. 1996) and biblical scholars who have written about the shame/honor system of the Mediterranean world (Huber, 1983; deSilva 1995; Malina and Neyrey 1991a, 1991b, 1991c, and Crossan, 1992).

Significance for Social/Scientific Studies

Using a cross-disciplinary model to interpret this study's empirical findings concerning shame, guilt, images of God and violence in adults who have experienced childhood corporal punishment will also be of interest to sociologists of emotions (Scheff and Retzinger, 1991), criminologists (Braithwaite, 1989, 1993), prison psychiatrists (Gilligan, 1996), trauma theorists (Lansky, 1984, 1987; Herman 1992; Linehan, 1993; van der Kolk, 1987), violence researchers (Straus, 1994b, Straus and Gelles, 1990) and "self-in relationship" theorists (Jordan, 1989; Jordan et al. 1991) in their search to decrease violence and heal trauma.

Clinical Significance

In recent years there has been a growing interest in finding effective clinical treatment modalities for adults who have experienced and/or witnessed violence in childhood (Herman, 1992, Linehan, 1993, van der Kolk, McFarlane and Weisaeth, 1996). Trauma theorists such as Bessel A. van der Kolk and Alexander C. McFarlane (1996) acknowledge that "reenactment of victimization is a major cause of violence in society"(p. 11). Even though recent studies have documented relationships among adult violence and a history of childhood physical and/or sexual abuse, (p. 11) there are still few studies that examine a possible relationship between adult violence and a history of childhood corporal punishment. Thus, this study is of clinical/pastoral significance in understanding how images of God are related to the presence or absence of shame and violence in adults who have experienced childhood corporal punishment (Gorsuch, 1968; Greven, 1977, 1991; Doehring, 1993). Moreover this study is of significance to clinicians and pastors since it asks the question whether corporal punishment of children is reenacted from generation to generation and is related to adult shame, violence and images of God.

Knowing how shame, images of God and a history of childhood corporal punishment are related to the presence or absence of adult violence will be helpful especially to violence researchers, to clinicians and trauma specialists who work both with adults who experienced childhood corporal punishment and with offenders of violent behavior. This study will also be helpful to faith communities concerned about breaking the cycle of violence. This study is of special relevance to trauma theorists. For instance, is Helen Block Lewis's (1971) understanding of the cognitive processing of "bypassed shame" similar to the processing of trauma memories? Lewis (1971, 1987a) points out that people who experience "bypassed shame" have difficulty integrating affect with cognition. Likewise trauma survivors, especially those with full blown Post Traumatic Stress Disorder, frequently experience difficulty in integrating "affective experience with the cognitive structuring of experience" (van der Kolk, 1996, p. 234).

Definition of the Terms

Shame

This study recognizes two forms of shame: healthy and unhealthy. Healthy shame has a "protective function for the self" (Thompson, 1996, p. 314) and can serve as a form of conscience (Fowler, 1993). Unhealthy shame can have a debilitating effect upon human functioning (Schneider, 1977, pp. 18-28; Fowler, 1993; Thompson, 1996, p. 314) and be a stimulus for violence (Gilligan, 1996; Scheff and Retzinger, 1991).

For investigative purposes the operational definition of shame used in this study is that of David R. Cook, author of the Internalized Shame Scale. For Cook (1994) shame is operationally defined as frequent feelings of "worthlessness, failure, and alienation from yourself" (p. 62). Shame is further "understood as a primary human affect" (Cook, 1994, p. 13) which can trigger an entire constellation of related feelings: incompetence, inferiority, defectiveness, unworthiness, threats of exposure, emptiness, alienation, and self-contempt, among others (p. 15). For purposes of this study, shame is feeling bad about oneself because of one's perceived identity.

Research has indicated that a conceptual distinction between shame and guilt is frequently difficult to ascertain (Cook, 1994). In this study guilt will be examined as an exploratory question, not only to differentiate shame from guilt but also to facilitate a discussion of healthy shame (Schneider, 1977; Fowler, 1994; Thompson, 1996), i.e., shame that serves not only as a form of conscience but also inhibits violence.

This study employs the following definition of guilt:

...some behavior or set of behaviors that has transgressed a moral standard (or, on the fantasy level, would transgress one if enacted), and that generates feelings of regret, remorse, and/or concern (sometimes extreme) for an injured party. (Harder, 1995, p. 370)

In contrast to shame, guilt is feeling bad about oneself because of what one has done or failed to do, either in reality or in fantasy.

Violence

Violence is operationally defined by Straus and Gelles (1988), whose instrument will be used to measure partner violence:

Violence is defined as an act carried out with the intention, or perceived intention, of causing physical pain or injury to another person. This definition is synonymous with the legal concept of 'assault' and the concept of 'physical aggression' used in social psychology. (p. 15)

Corporal Punishment

This study will use the definition employed by Murray Straus (1994b):

Corporal punishment is the use of physical force with the intention of causing a child to experience pain, but not injury, for the purpose of correction or control of the child's behavior. (p. 4)

This definition is differentiated from physical abuse which includes physically injuring a child (p. 4).

Cycle of Violence

The cycle of violence will be understood as the human tendency to repeat violence from generation to generation (see Greven, 1990, 1992).

Images of God

The traditional definition of Image of God (Imago Dei) based on Genesis 1:26-27 as the "divine endowment by which human persons are said to bear the 'image and likeness' of God" (Anderson, 1990, p. 571). For investigative purposes this study defines God image as one's experiential and conceptual understanding of God (Brokaw and Edwards, 1994, p. 357). God image and self image are intricately interrelated, meaning that one's conscious self image is intimately tied to one's conscious God image (Lawrence, 1996). Conscious and unconscious images of

God can come not only from interpersonal relationships, but also from many sources (Sandler and Rosenblatt, 1962). Thus this study acknowledges that a person's images of God can have conscious and unconscious parental as well as Biblical roots.

Limitations of the Study

The first limitation concerns the a-historical, non-contextual descriptions of much of the shame and corporal punishment literature. These preliminary broad characterizations of shame are helpful in beginning to understand what shame is about and how it is related to levels of childhood corporal punishment, violence and images of God. However, more contextually sensitive descriptions might have gleaned more data of how these factors are actually related.

The second limitation concerns the other forms of violence that often accompany corporal punishment. It is not unusual for a child who is corporally punished also to have been verbally, physically, and sexually abused (Herman, 1992; van der Kolk, 1987; Linehan, 1993; Straus, 1994b). Furthermore, it is not easy to disentangle "the effects of corporal punishment from the effects of other aversive behaviors that usually goes [sic] with corporal punishment, such as verbal attacks on the child, the lack of warmth or support, and the failure to set clear standards" (Straus, p. 195). In this study, I will gather limited data on other experiences of childhood trauma beyond corporal punishment, thus making it difficult to determine the confounding role of such traumatic experiences.

A third limitation concerns the retrospective dimension of this study. In the demographic questionnaire I ask adult participants how often and at what ages they were corporally punished. However, recall and memory are problematic (Straus, 1994b, p. 199). Early childhood memories most likely will not be recalled (p. 200). Furthermore, if one carries high levels of shame at having been corporally punished, one may be reticent to disclose such painful memories.

A fourth limitation concerns nature versus nurture. This study will not be able to determine if an adult is violent because he or she was corporally punished or because of a "biologically based predisposition to aggression" (Straus, 1994b, p. 195).

A fifth limitation is methodological. One might question the feasibility of bridging a conversation between the biblical world and contemporary life pertaining to the issues of shame/honor, images of God and violence. It is, indeed, questionable that a contemporary person can ever totally see, value and understand life in the ancient world. There is a risk in making such broad generalizations about the shame/honor system of the ancient Mediterranean world that this entire ancient culture is viewed through the lens or axis of shame and honor (deSilva, 1995) without sensitivity to particular cultural contexts.

Finally, the quantitative instruments employed in this study can only yield conscious data.

Summary

The ultimate purpose of this cross-disciplinary multi method approach is to discover effective ways to mitigate or minimize violence in adults who were corporally punished as children in hopes of stopping the cycle of intergenerational violence.

CHAPTER 2

Review of the Literature

There Was A Little Girl

There was a little girl, and she had a little curl
Right in the middle of her forehead;
When she was good she was very, very good,
But when she was bad she was horrid.

She stood on her head, on her little truckle-bed,
With nobody by for to hinder;
She screamed and she squalled, she yelled and she bawled,
And drummed her little heels against the winder.

Her mother heard the noise and thought it was the boys,
A-kicking up a rumpus in the attic;
But when she climbed the stair, and saw Jemima there,
She took her and did whip her most emphatic.
[A Mother Goose rhyme in Opie and Opie, 1964]

Introduction

This old and familiar nursery rhyme, read and recited countless times to little children at bedtime the world over, provides the haunting profile of an abused child. We have the portrait of a traumatized child who has an image of herself as being very, very good at times, but at other times as being so bad that she is horrid. As Gelles and Straus' (1988) classic study on family violence has noted, abused children display a number of characteristics including symptoms such as: "…poor self-concept, a tendency to withdraw and become isolated, and a pattern of hyperactivity and tantrums" (p. 125). The little girl with a curl right in the middle of her forehead displays all the above symptoms of childhood abuse. She is withdrawn, is isolated, has an intermittent poor self-concept and has a pattern of hyperactivity and tantrums. Her mother eventually whips her because of her horrid behavior. And with such whippings most likely the intergenerational cycle of violence is continued.

In the past three decades there has been a growing interest in the study of shame and violence from a divergent number of fields (psychology, sociology, criminology, anthropology and law.) Simultaneously there has been a growing interest in a pastoral theological understanding of shame (Patton, 1985; Fowler, 1993; Huber, 1983; Burton, 1988, 1991; Capps, 1993; Schneider, 1977). A possible correlation between shame and violence has only become a locus of interest since the mid 1980s, and the theological literature on a correlation between shame and violence is virtually non-existent except for peripheral references by Huber (1983), Patton (1985) and Fowler (1993, 1996).

This review of the literature is divided into three major sections. Part I examines various aspects of shame, shame and violence, and violence prevention from a psychological perspective. Part II examines shame and corporal punishment from a religious perspective. Part III examines various aspects of shame, images of God, and violence from a religious and biblical/theological perspective.

Part I: Psychological Literature

Part I of the literature review examines the psychological literature related to shame, shame and violence and violence prevention. This part will be divided into three sections. The first section examines psychoanalytic literature on shame beginning with the contributions of Sigmund Freud and proceeding to those of Erik Erikson. Included in this section is a review of relational/feminist models as well as the works of Nathanson as they relate to shame and affect theory.

Section two specifically focuses on shame and violence literature, providing the theoretical basis for this dissertation. Finally the work of Donald C. Klein is examined as a possible psychological model for violence prevention.

1. Psychological Literature: Shame

Seminal psychological literature on shame comes from a variety of theoretical perspectives: psychoanalytic, Adlerian, self-in-relation, self-psychology, family systems, and developmental. Key works are those of Alfred Adler (1931); Karen Horney (1945, 1950); Helen Lynd (1958); Heinz Kohut (1971a, 1977, 1978a, 1978b, 1984); Donald Nathanson (1987, 1992); Donald Klein (1991a, 1991b, 1992); Judith Jordan (1989); Fossum and Masson (1986); Helen Block Lewis (1971, 1976, 1981, 1987a); Piers and Singer (1953/1971); Erik Erikson (1958, 1968, 1969), and Leon Wurmser (1981).

Freud and Shame

In recent years the psychological literature on shame has been heavily influenced by the psychoanalytic community (Schneider, 1977). However, this influence has not always been the case. Lewis (1981) argues that Freud neglected the affective states of shame (p. 202-203), focusing on guilt and anxiety but virtually ignoring shame (Lewis, 1987a, p. 2; Scheff and Retzinger, 1991, p. 12). In fact, Freud had no theory of shame (Gilligan, 1996, p. 213), forcing him to rely on his "instinct" theory to explain violence (p. 213). Freud did not see shame as a major factor in peoples' psychological lives or as a stimulating affect of violence. Furthermore, Schneider (1977) points out that Freud showed little sensitivity to his "patients' desire to hide their secrets, their embarrassment, and their shame about their thoughts, feelings, and actions" (Scheff and Retzinger, 1991, p. 12). Scheff and Retzinger (1991) believe that one of the key flaws of orthodox psychoanalytic theory and practice has been, in fact, the downplaying of shame (p. 12). Schneider (1977) saw this key flaw:

> Freud was shameless (in the sense of being disrespectful) in his relentless attack on what he thought of as the patient's 'resistances' to knowing themselves. (p. 12)

In fact, Lewis (1987) points out that Freud's cases were filled with incidents of people experiencing shame and guilt in relation to others (p. 24). Toward the end of her life, Helen Block Lewis began to view resistance as "a misnomer for shame and guilt" (p. 24).

Freud, with his individualistic, intrapsychic focus (Schlauch, 1995, p. 62), seemed to have missed the relational dynamics of shame. In fact, Helen Block Lewis concludes that the traditional and non-relational structure of psychoanalysis can contribute to shame:

> The therapist's minimal expression of empathy and total withholding of his or her own psychic struggles can make the therapeutic relation itself a source of shame. (Fowler, 1993, p. 817)

Erikson and Shame

Erik H. Erikson expanded Freud's individualistic orientation by emphasizing the importance of a person's psychosocial history as informing and influencing a person's life. Core to Erikson's developmental theory are his "Eight Ages of Man [sic]" in which he reframes and expands upon Freud's stages of psychosexual development (Fowler, 1996, p. 107). Whereas Freud had four phases, Erikson has eight stages. It is Erikson's second stage, "autonomy versus shame and doubt," that this study re-examines in relationship to corporal punishment. This second stage corresponds in time frame to Freud's second stage which he called the "anal phase," roughly between the ages of one and three.

Erikson's second psychosocial stage is not only critical to understanding the formation of shame in the development of the self (Fowler, 1996, p. 107), but also critical to understanding the link between corporal punishment and shame. Erikson rightly named this second stage "autonomy versus shame and doubt," since it is during this age frame—18 months to three years—that one can observe the struggle of wills between parent and toddler. Frequently this struggle of wills is settled by a "spanking,"[5] (which instills in the child not only shame but also self-doubt.) It is an argument of this study that spanking contributes to a sense of shame and self-doubt.

Erikson built on Freud's theory of psychosexual development. Freud introduced his life-cycle theory in 1905 in Three Essays on the Theory of Sexuality. Freud saw childhood development through the lens of his libido theory:

> According to Freud, childhood phases of development correspond to successive shifts in the investment of sexual energy to areas of the body usually associated with eroticism: the mouth, the anus, and the genitalia. (Kaplan, Sadock, Grebb, 1994, p. 16)

In fact, according to Nathanson (1992) Freud's psychosexual development viewed "all shame as either vaguely or specifically sexual" (p. 195).

The critiques of Freud's treatment of trauma are helpful for understanding his limited perspectives on shame. For instance, in studying the history of trauma theory (Herman, 1992, p. 13, van der Kolk, Weisaeth and van der Hart, 1996, pp. 53-56), it is commonly accepted today that Freud's sexually driven psychoanalytic theory was both a method of seeing and a method of not seeing, a method of "selective inattention" (Straus, 1994, p. 68). Psychoanalysis for Erikson was a "method of observation" (Erikson, 1958, p. 17), a "way of looking at things" (Erikson, 1950, p. 359). Yet methods of observation, as we will continue to note, can be problematic. Methods of observation imply that we see through a certain lens, from a certain perspective. Methods are also like maps that serve as guides enabling us to visit certain sites while deciding not to visit others. Chris Schlauch (1996) insightfully reminds us that maps both reveal and hide, foregrounding certain material while backgrounding other material which becomes invisible or goes underground (Scheff and Retzinger, 1991).

Initially Freud saw childhood sexual trauma as the root cause of his female patients' adult "hysteria" (Breuer and Freud, 1893-1895, 259-260). Freud at first seemed certain about what he had observed: "I therefore put forward the thesis that at the bottom of every case of hysteria there are one or more occurrences of premature sexual experience..." (Herman, p. 13). When Freud's colleagues turned against him because of his new theory on the etiology of hysteria, he suffered from public shame and began to doubt and question his perceptions, losing the autonomy of his vision (Gay, 1988, pp. 93-96).

---

[5] Murray Straus (1994b) claims that at least 90 percent of toddlers are hit.

Relational/Feminist Models and Shame

In recent years relational/feminist theoretical models of human personality have brought a broader and more inclusive perspective to the understanding of shame. While contemporary western personality theories have seen "separation and autonomy" as the hallmark of mental health (Hartling, 1995; Gilligan, 1982; Jordan, Kaplan, Miller, Stiver, & Surrey, 1991; Miller, 1987; Surrey, 1985), relational therapies have put greater emphasis on the self in relationship. Shame is experienced in relationship: one can experience shame either in relationship to oneself "falling short of the internalized ego ideal" (Piers and Singer, 1953/1971) or in relationship to the other (Erikson, 1963, p. 253). For Helen Block Lewis (1987a) the focus of shame is always relational: the "self-in-the eyes-of-the-other" and the self "devaluing the self" (p. 15). The new self-in-relationship therapeutic model of the Stone Center with its awareness of gender issues, power dynamics, the role of connection and separation, and cultural issues is broadening psychologists' understanding of shame and its relationship to violence.

The Stone Center at Wellesley College is an internationally known research and education center whose unique mission is the prevention of psychological problems, the enhancement of well-being, and the search for a comprehensive understanding of human development. To this end, the Stone Center understands gender as inter-related with other contextual variables such as race, class and sexual orientation. Their relational and cultural theory is based on a pluralistic perspective, representing the experiences of women of diverse cultural backgrounds and sexual orientations, particularly lesbian women. Currently the Stone Center pays particular attention to the experience of women, children, and families across culturally diverse populations. This group of psychotherapists first focused on gender and paid attention to how women grow most fully "through growth fostering relationships" (Jordan, 1997, p. 3). As their relational and cultural theory and practice evolved they began to emphasize the importance of understanding the self as being in relationship (not only for women, but also for every human being.) Thus the contextual perspective (Doehring, 1998, in press) is critical to their work. They look at the ways that gender interacts with other contextual factors (racial, socioeconomic, sexual orientation) within cultural systems that may value or devalue people because of these contextual factors.

The relational model being developed at the Stone Center in Wellesley is straightforward. Jordan (1997) argues that connections and relationships are central to women's lives. The source of most human suffering is disconnection. And women grow most fully "through growth fostering relationships" (Jordan, p. 3). Even though shame has a relational dynamic, shame according to Judith Jordan (1989; seminar lecture—The Stone Center, 2/7/96) is the experience of being disconnected, what Jean Baker Miller would call "condemned isolation" or "being locked out of the possibility of human connection" (Miller, 1988). Unlike western personality theories which have seen "separation and autonomy" as the hallmark of mental health, the relational model emphasizes relationships with "increasing empathic responsiveness" as the primary feature to deepening life enhancing connections (Jordan, 1997, p. 15). From a Stone Center perspective one might argue that empathy is to connection as shame is to isolation.

Jordan (1997) argues that empathy ("the dynamic cognitive—affective process of joining with and understanding another's subjective experience") is central to the relational theory (p. 15). In fact, Jordan (1997) argues that empathy challenges the psychological notion of a separate self since empathic responsiveness encourages a person to experience life from the other's perspective: "In true empathic exchange, each is both object and subject, mutually engaged in affecting and being affected, knowing and being known" (p. 15).

A relational therapeutic model based on connection through empathy deepens a sense of personal conscience. We become more concerned about the consequences of our actions and behaviors on others. One might argue that such a model enhances both healthy shame and guilt. Healthy shame and guilt, which is stimulated by empathy, bring us into fuller connection with others. Healthy shame is a form of conscience, which can prevent one from doing harmful actions. Healthy guilt is a deep concern about how one's behavior has hurt others.

The relational theorists emphasize that traditional western white male psychology has worn perceptual "blinders" to aspects of women's experience and to the differences that gender makes. While confessing their past blind spots (Jordan, 1997, p. 1), these same relational theorists (equipped with a new multicultural perspective) argue that they are broadening the lens through which human psychological development is perceived and understood. Jordan (1997) argues that western culture has held an unexamined bias: valuing individuality over and above relationships (p. 3); Jordan goes on to state that "western culture has devalued women's skills in empathy and our capacity and motivation to foster growth in others" (p. 3). Jordan further argues that the self-in-relation theoretical model represents "a major paradigm shift in all of western psychology...from a psychology of the separate self to a psychology of relational being" (p. 3).

Jordan (1989) argues that the "need for connection and emotional joining is our primary need" with empathy serving this need (p. 5). Jordan (1989) feels that the group of people who have the most difficult time connecting with others are narcissistic people (p. 6). When wounded in interpersonal connections, those with narcissistic problems can explode into what Kohut (1978a) has called "narcissistic rage" (Jordan, 1989, p. 6). Jordan would argue that the rage response in narcissistic individuals has to do with the inadequacy they experience in their failed attempts to connect.

Jordan (1989) argues that shame is frequently considered to be "the opposite of narcissistic pride, the loss of self-respect or self-esteem" (p. 6). She suggests in her seminal 1989 work on shame that "there may be sex differences in the experience of shame" (p. 6). Thus Jordan (1989) explicitly states that she is describing shame in women (p. 6). Jordan (1997) views shame as a core issue in women's lives as well as in the lives of marginalized groups of people: "Shame involves a profound sense of longing for connection and feeling unworthy to be in connection;..." (p. 5). But in essence shame is the experience par excellence of disconnection.

I would like to suggest that shame is most importantly a felt sense of unworthiness to be in connection, a deep sense of unlovability, with the ongoing awareness of how very much one wants to connect with others. While shame involves extreme self-consciousness, it also signals powerful relational longings and awareness of the other's response. There is a loss of the sense of empathic possibility, others are not experienced as empathic, and the capacity for self-empathy is lost. One feels unworthy of love, not because of some discrete actions, which would be the cause for guilt, but because one is defective or flawed in some essential way. (Jordan, 1987, p. 6)

Jordan (1989) cites Nathanson (1987) as also viewing shame as an experience of disconnection: "During mutual gaze we feel attached. In the moment of shame, we feel shorn not just from the other but from all possible others" ([1987, p. 9] p. 6).

Jordan (1989) emphasizes that the experience of merely being different at times can be a source of shame (p. 6). Frequently one's perceptions of reality and one's very being (if different than that of the dominant culture) are devalued and viewed as defective or inadequate by those in power and in control (p. 6). Thus the act of shaming people is often used as a weapon to silence, control, intimidate and discredit nondominant and marginalized peoples' perceptions of reality (Jordan, 1997, p. 5). Jordan (1989) emphasizes that the effect of such shaming tactics can be "global and immobilizing" (p. 6).

Jordan notes that the ultimate weapon in shaming a person or group of people is to act as if they don't exist. This punitive shaming tactic not only produces a sense of paralyzing despair but also can fuel rage and potential violence. To illustrate, Jordan (1989) cites William James:

No more fiendish punishment could be devised, were such a thing physically possible, than that one should be turned loose in society and remain absolutely unnoticed by all the members thereof. If none turned around when we entered, answered when we spoke, or minded what we did, but if every person we met 'cut us dead,' and acted as if we were nonexistent things, a kind of rage and impotent despair would ere long well up in us. (James, 1890,1968, p. 42)

What is most interesting is Jordan's (1989) interpretation of James (1890/1968, p. 42). Jordan (1989) reflects on the difference between an intrapsychic, self-psychology response versus a relational perspective response to what such a person might need therapeutically:

An intrapsychic, self-psychology rendering of this might suggest the person needs to be adored, acknowledged, admired; a relational perspective views the essential injury here to a sense of connection and, hence, to vitality. (p. 7)

One school (self-psychology) emphasizes the "narcissistic injury" and the primary need of mirroring. The other school (relational) emphasizes the "disconnection injury" and the primary human need of connection. Both schools acknowledge the rage factor: narcissistic injury produces rage; disconnection (being made to feel that one doesn't exist or maybe shouldn't exist) also produces intense rage.

There is continually strong criticism of the Stone Center's relational therapeutic model. Sources find the theory too simplistic. Sources have complained that the relational therapeutic model is elitist—a group of white heterosexual privileged women claiming to name the female experience for all women (Miller, Jordan, Kaplan, Stiver and Surrey, 1997). While others have argued that the Stone Center's relational approach tends to idealize women and relationships (Miller et al. 1997). Still others (Manning, 1997)—as noted in a recent book review in The New York Times Book Review—have questioned the relational therapeutic model's emphasis on connection which some believe downplays the importance of autonomy, individuality and self-sufficiency in the lives of women.

The relational and cultural theorists at the Stone Center view theory and practice as a work in progress. To their credit they have acknowledged their critics by seeking "to address more explicitly the differences that exist among many women from different backgrounds, be they racial, cultural, socioeconomic, or involving sexual orientation" (Jordan, 1997, p. 1). For instance, Jean Baker Miller (Miller et al., 1997) has addressed critiques that the Stone Center's relational theory idealizes women and relationships. Furthermore, the Stone Center theorists have openly acknowledged that their initial work was biased and had blindspots by representing primarily a "white, middle-class, well-educated heterosexual experience" (Jordan, 1997, p. 1).

Nathanson, Shame and Affect Theory

A major theorist in the study of shame has been psychoanalyst and psychiatrist Donald L. Nathanson (1987, 1992, 1996). Educated as a research biologist, a physician, an endocrinologist and only later as a psychiatrist (1966, p. xii), Nathanson has attempted to bridge the field of psychoanalysis and affect theory. Rather than viewing emotions "as something that interferes with rational, mature, neocortical thinking," (p. 4) Nathanson suggests that intense emotions such as shame can be the doorway to the "dynamic unconscious" (p. 3). Building on the affect theory of Silvan Tomkins, Nathanson has inspired the conceptual base for the empirical research of David R. Cook, author of the Internalized Shame Scale (ISS) (Cook, 1994, p. 13).

Nathanson (1987, 1992) has "expanded and interpreted" Silvan Tomkins's affect theory. Tomkins, an experimental psychologist, developed what he called the affect system in the 1940s (1992, p. 57). Nathanson defines affect as "the strictly biological portion of emotion"(p.49) meaning the physiological aspect of emotion whereas feeling is the conscious awareness of affect.[6] Tomkins asserts that he discovered nine innate affects, which he believed were "hard-wired" and

---

[6] Nathanson differentiates feeling from affect by using Michael Franz Basch's definition.

preprogrammed within all human beings (pp. 58-59). He divided these affects into three groups: 1. Positive 2. Neutral and 3. Negative affects. There are two positive affects: 1. Interest-excitement and 2. enjoyment-joy. There is one neutral affect: surprise-startle. There are five negative affects: 1. Fear-terror, 2. Distress-anguish, 3. Anger-rage, 4. Dismell-disgust (sic) and 5. Shame-humiliation. In Tomkins's affect theory each affect consists of two words which go from mildest to the most intense form of affect.

Critical to this study is Nathanson's central argument based on Tomkins's affect theory "that the function of any affect is to amplify the highly specific stimulus that set it in motion" (1992, p. 59). This study examines most closely the correlation between shame-humiliation and anger-rage. Building on Tomkins, Nathanson asserts that affect is not only contagious (p. 62) and urgent (p. 65) but it is also the engine that drives us, "making good things better and bad things worse" (p. 59).

The affect shame-humiliation for Tomkins and Nathanson is intimately tied to interest-excitement, enjoyment-joy. Nathanson describes this tie: "Shame feels so miserable because it interrupts what feels best in life" (1992, p. 73). In essence, shame-humiliation impedes or interferes with other positive affects (pp. 134-135):

> Shame interrupts, halts, takes over, inconveniences, trips up, makes incompetent anything that had previously been interesting or enjoyable. (1992, p. 209)

In fact, he asserts that shame exists only in relationship to other affects (p. 136). For instance, shame can impede the positive affects: 1) interest-excitement and 2) enjoyment-joy (p. 139). Shame not only can impede positive affects it can also fuel negative affects such as anger and rage. According to Tomkins as translated by Nathanson it is the coassemblies of affects that can heighten their effect:

> The coassembly of an affect with any drive, with cognition, with memory, with another affect, or with any combination of the above, produces powerful amplification of the preexisting function. In other words, affect is the amplifier that brings motivation to drive, to memory, or to any human activity. Wherever there is urgency it has been achieved through such amplification. The affects can be intensely rewarding, as in the case of the positive affects, or intensely punishing,…(1987, p. 15)

To explain his shame theory Nathanson organized what he calls "The Compass of Shame" (1992, p. 312). The compass of shame consists of four strategies to handle shame: 1. Withdrawal, 2. Avoidance, 3. Attack self and 4. Attack others (p. 312). According to Nathanson withdrawal is swift and total and is the coping mechanism used by certain individuals in the attempt to heal and repair from humiliating and shaming incidences (p. 319). Avoidance is slower and one might argue that it is similar to the constriction frequently experienced by trauma survivors (Herman, 1992). The attack self and the attack others are the violence quadrants. Attack self is the coping strategy used by people who feel helpless and isolated because of shame. Attack others is a way that people protect themselves from feeling inferior. Nathanson argues that people have a fundamental need not to feel lower than others do and violence stimulated by shame is an attempt at times to elevate the self: "someone must be made lower than I" (p. 314). Nathanson sees a powerful correlation between shame and violence:

> Every incident of domestic violence, of graffiti, of public vandalism, of schoolyard fighting, of put-down, ridicule, contempt, and intentional public humiliation can be traced to activity around this locus of reaction to shame affect. (1992, p. 314)

Nathanson like many other shame theorists (Scheff and Retzinger, 1991; Tangney, 1995a) builds on the seminal work of Helen Block Lewis (1971) especially her notion of "bypassed shame." Nathanson (1992) states that throughout his book he will claim that "the shame mechanism is triggered often in situations that we do not recognize as embarrassing, painful circumstances when our attention is drawn from whatever had attracted us and we are momentarily ill at ease" (p. 145).

Similarly to Helen Lynd (1958), another seminal shame author, Nathanson (1992) sees a tie between shame and identity: "Shame is intimately tied to identity, to our very concept of ourselves as human" (p. 149).[7] He further argues that self-concept has to do with shame and healthy pride (p. 83-84). Healthy pride is affiliative—bringing people together—whereas shame is alienating and isolating (p. 187). Shame is "associated with some perceived deficiency in the self..."(p. 196) and pride is "pleasure associated with an elevation in the sense of self" (p. 196).

Controversial to Nathanson's theory is his hypothesis albeit untested that there is a neurochemical basis for the shame affect:

> Shame affect involves a neurochemical, a substance secreted in the ancient subcortical portion of the brain, a compound that causes sudden widening or dilatation of the blood vessels in the brain. (p. 141)

Nathanson with his biological focus on shame participates in a method of "selective inattention," focusing on the biological nature of affects without envisioning a broader social/environmental understanding of the roots of shame.[8] For instance, Nathanson (1987, 1992) asserts that there is a neurochemical basis for shame. In fact, he suggests that one day it might be possible "to develop medications that counter the effect of shame in those who are oversensitive to it for developmental or genetic reasons" (1987, p. 27). However, Nathanson's visional field of other important factors that can lead to shame experiences seems at times quite limited. For instance, he is highly critical of Helen Block Lewis's relational understanding

---

[7] Ironically, Nathanson (1987, 1992) barely cites Lynd.

[8] Nathanson's tendency not to fully examine social and environmental factors related to shame is what Elaine L. Graham (1996) calls biological determinism and reductionism (p. 86).

of shame and seems to have little insight into what James Fowler (1996) calls "shame due to enforced minority status" (p. 121).[9]

Even though Nathanson is highly critical of psychodynamic theory he does not question the prevalent psychodynamic view that shame is correlated with genital and anal awareness (1987, p. 6). In fact, he sees a powerful linkage between genitalia and shame. Nathanson (1987) cites Amsterdam and Levitt (1980) as "defining shame as a painful form of self-awareness...between 18 and 24 months of age" when "the infant becomes capable of painful self-awareness on exposure to a mirror" (p. 39).

It is not as if Nathanson sees no correlations between emotions and the body. He points out that in its study of "hysteria paralysis," that "psychoanalysis was initially a method of studying the effects of emotion on cognition and bodily function" (p. 25). Yet Nathanson rejects Freud's "drive theory" (p. 119) arguing that "its theoretical base in drive theory is simply outdated, a relic of a physiology long ago disconfirmed" (p. 45). However, he does hypothesize that shame may be the border between the inner and outer worlds, in other words shame is linked with the unconscious: "Some have gone so far as to say that there would be no unconscious were it not for shame" (p. 149). Throughout his work Nathanson (1992) remains critical of psychoanalysis, especially Freudian drive theory. Nonetheless, he asserts that affect theory may be the hidden link between neurobiology and intrapsychic life "for which Freud searched so tenaciously" (1987, p. 17).

In fairness to Nathanson there has been an evolution in Nathanson's understanding of the interactional/relational aspect of shame. Nathanson in Shame and Pride (1992) acknowledges that shame can be "triggered in the context of social relationships" (p. 214). However, his earlier work (1987) shows little awareness of the interactional/relational aspect of shame especially in relationship to women. In fact, one of Nathanson's strong criticisms of Helen Block Lewis's research was her interactional/relational understanding of shame, the fact that she viewed both shame and guilt as "inherently social affects...that serve to repair lost affectionate bonds" (1987, p. 9). Nathanson writes, "...Helen Block Lewis, felt that the human is intrinsically social, that the infant is born social" (1992, p. 218). In contrast, Nathanson (1992) holds a view of human beings as separate and individual from the day of conception (p. 223). For Nathanson it is our affective experiences that link us to others:

---

[9] Fowler (1996) asserts that "shame due to enforced minority status" has been long ignored in the shame literature. Fowler seems to be arguing against a method of selective inattention as regards the potentially multivaried roots of shame: "This variant of shame cannot be healed without attention to issues of economic and political justice, equality, and the effective affirmation of inclusiveness in societies" (p. 121).

> Love would be viewed as the name we give the most powerful positive form of this connection...shame would then be regarded as an affect that returns the individual to its state of primary isolation. (1992, p. 234)

Nonetheless, biologically oriented Nathanson (1992) criticizes Lewis's relational view of guilt and shame:

> Both emotions are viewed only in terms of the way they affect our membership in social networks, and for this reason her work must now be considered inadequate to explain all the phenomenology of shame. (p. 218)

Nathanson, especially in his earlier writings, seemed not to comprehend why Helen Block Lewis (1971) claimed that women were more sensitive to shame than men (1987, p. 42). He doesn't seem to understand that women have frequently been treated as second class citizens and that this treatment is in and of itself shaming as stated by Helen Block Lewis in her 1987 article on "The Role of Shame in Depression over the Life Span":

> In brief, I have suggested that their second-class status in the world of power, increase their tendency to the experience of shame. (Lewis, 1987c, p. 29)

Summary

The above review of the psychological literature explores one of the major flaws of orthodox psychoanalytic theory and practice—the downplaying of shame. In fact, Freud had no shame theory and was forced to rely on his "instinct" theory to explain violence. Likewise, Freud neglected the affective states of shame (Schneider, pp. 202-203) and failed to see a relationship between shame and what psychoanalysis has called resistance.

For Erikson psychoanalysis was the quintessential "method of observation." Yet as a child of both psychoanalysis and a culture supportive of corporal punishment, Erikson failed to examine a possible relationship between shame and childhood corporal punishment in his developmental theory.

Relational/feminist theoretical models of human personality have broadened our understanding of shame. Stone Center theorist Judith Jordan emphasizes that shame is primarily the experience of being disconnected. Such self-in-relation theorists argue that the source of most human suffering is disconnection. Jordan states that dominant cultures frequently use shaming tactics as a way to silence, control, discredit, immobilize and isolate non-dominant and minority groups. In this study I argue that shame and violence are both experiences of disconnection and isolation.

Building on the affect theory of Silvan Tomkins, Nathanson suggests that intense emotions like shame can be the doorway to the dynamic unconscious. Nathanson sees affects as the primary engine that drive human beings. It is the coassembly of affects that amplifies or stifles human interaction. Shame, for instance, can fuel negative affects such as anger and rage or it can impede positive affects such as joy and excitement. Critical to this study is Nathanson's theory that affects can be intensely rewarding or intensely punishing.

Nathanson's Compass of Shame explains different strategies people use to cope with shame: withdrawal, avoidance, attack self, attack others. His biological orientation impedes him from understanding more of the relational and cultural dynamics of shame, especially what James Fowler (1996) refers to as "shame due to enforced minority status" (p. 121).

2. Psychological Literature: Shame and Violence

Core to this study is Helen Block Lewis's understanding of bypassed and unacknowledged shame, Scheff and Retzinger's understanding of a shame/rage spiral (Scheff and Retzinger, 1991), Tangney et al.'s empirical studies on shame/guilt, anger and hostility (Tangney, 1995a; Tangney, Wagner, Barlow, Marschall, & Gramzow, 1994; Tangney, Wagner, Fletcher, & Gramzow, 1992), Gilligan's (1996) theoretical work on shame and violence, and Klein's (1991a, 1992b) preventative approach to a humiliation/rage spiral.

Helen Block Lewis and Humiliated Fury

Helen Block Lewis (1971), a pioneer in our understanding of shame (Fowler, 1993, p. 817) and its relationship to rage and violence first observed a tie between "shame and anger (or humiliated fury) in her clinical case studies" (Tangney, 1995a, p. 1139). Lewis, a trained psychoanalyst and research psychologist at Yale, came to the conclusion that "analytic situations themselves, in structure and often in dynamics" (Fowler, 1993, p. 817) can produce shame/humiliation and ultimately anger/rage.

> In analysis one adult comes to another—the latter a stranger, who maintains an analytic distance and avoids self-disclosure—verbalizes the most painful and humiliating concerns. The therapist's minimal expressions of empathy and total withholding of his or her own psychic struggles can make the therapeutic relation itself a source of shame. (Fowler, 1993, p. 817)

For Lewis (1971) "shame is a state of self-devaluation" which "is about the whole self" and can affect the entire self (p. 312). Lewis (1987a) describes the phenomenology of shame as a painful experience that makes us want to hide, to avert our gaze or hang our heads, die on the spot or crawl into a hole (p. 1). Ironically, at the same time that a person experiencing shame feels small and wants to disappear, "the self may be dealing with an excess of autonomic stimulation— blushing, or sweating or diffuse rage, experienced as a 'flood' of sensations" (p. 18).

Critical to Lewis's work is the concept of affectless or bypassed shame and unidentified or unacknowledged shame (Lewis, 1971, pp. 233-250). Her theory suggests that it is the hidden, unacknowledged aspects of shame that can become the most destructive; affectless or bypassed shame is shame that is cognitively experienced but with little or no feeling (Thompson, 1996). For instance, in the therapeutic hour a patient may feel wounded by something a therapist says or fails to say. The first reaction of the patient is a "'wince' or 'jolt' or wordless 'shock' in feeling," (Lewis, 1971, p. 233), the patient withdraws by becoming silent or hesitant in speech, this withdrawal is followed by a "lighting-speed sequence" (Lewis, 1987a, p. xi) of feelings: initial anger at the therapist; guilt that one is angry at the very person who is trying to be helpful, namely, the therapist; and depression and intensified shame as the feelings of anger are turned toward the self (Fowler, 1993, p. 817).

Thompson (1996) states that "with unacknowledged shame the feeling of shame is 'available to consciousness' and the person manifests some physical signs of shame such as blushing, but the individual 'will not or cannot identify it' (Lewis, p. 196) or misnames or disguises it (Scheff & Retzinger, 1991, p. 28)" (pp.313-314). For instance, unacknowledged shame within therapists frequently inhibits them from being empathetically attuned to the shame of their clients (Fowler, 1993, p. 817). When shame is bypassed and unacknowledged it can turn into a shame/rage spiral exploding into "humiliated fury" (Lewis, 1971, p. 87), thus leading to aggression and acts of violence.

Hartling (1995) states that for Lewis (1971, 1987a) humiliation is a variant of shame, which is distinguished by its particular mixture of hostility and guilt (p. 50). Lewis in turn uses the term "humiliated fury" to describe the sequence of events that happen after a shame experience (p. 50). Hartling argues that for Lewis "humiliated fury is a distinct form of anger" that occurs when shame is evoked and not dispelled, leading to retaliation and eventually resulting in guilt (p. 50).

Helen Block Lewis saw shame as fundamentally relational (Morrison, 1989, p. 52) and as part of the human attachment system (Lewis, 1987a, p. xi). Even though Lewis (1987a) acknowledged that shame is about the self, she is critical of those who have viewed shame as simply a narcissistic reaction and human nature as essentially individualistic (p. 30):

> Shame, although it catches the self 'at the quick,' to use Lynd's (1958) term is also quintessentially other connected as well. (Lewis, 1987c, p.30)

Thus for Lewis shame represents "a failure of the central attachment bond" (Lewis, 1987a, p. 19).

The self-in-the-eyes-of-the-other is the focus of shame (Lewis, 1987a, p. 15). Not only is there an evaluative component to shame (i.e., other peoples' real or imagined negative opinions), shame elicits the intense fear of losing the "other" (Lewis, p. 4). Lewis (1987a) argues that there is a relationship between "humiliated fury" and the threat of lost love. Shame becomes a means by which people try to preserve their loving relationships to others" (p. 2). Lewis (1987a) even suggests that shame with its autonomic reactions: sweating, blushing, increased heart rate "is an emergency response to threatened affectional ties" (pp. 16-17). In fact, when attachment bonds with loving relationships are threatened, Lewis argues that "shame is an inevitable human response to loss of love, whether in early childhood or in old age" (p. 30). From this relational perspective, the "other" is a powerful force in the experience of shame (Lewis, 1987a, p. 19). For shame to occur there must be an emotional relationship between the person and the 'other' such that the person cares what the other thinks or feels about the self. In this affective tie the self does not feel autonomous or independent, but dependent and vulnerable to rejection. Shame is a vicarious experience of the significant other's scorn (Lewis, 1971a, p. 42).

According to Lewis (1971) in intimate relationships there is often what she calls a "righting tendency," meaning that the one shamed tries to shame or humiliate the other by a "turning of the tables" (p. 42). In fact, in many cultures shaming has been used as a severe form of punishment (Lewis, 1987a, p. 2). These hostile feelings are "easily redirected outward toward others who may be held in part responsible for the ugly feeling of shame" (Tangney, 1995a, p. 1139). But humiliating, shaming or devaluing a loved one can make a person feel guilty because of his or her aggressive tendencies. Lewis (1971) argues that "shame-based rage is readily turned back against the self, both because the self is in a passive position vis-a-vis the 'other' and because the self values the 'other'" (p. 42).

Scheff and Retzinger and Shame/Rage Spiral

Thomas Scheff and Susan Retzinger (1991) were the first social scientists to do an in-depth non-empirical study on the correlation between violence and shame. In fact, in Emotions and Violence (1991) they set out to propose an explanation of the roots of human violence (p. 3). Building on the works of Lewis (1971, 1976, 1981) in both theory and method, Scheff and Retzinger (1991) describe a shame/rage spiral in which unacknowledged shame leads to anger and then to aggression (p. ix).

Scheff and Retzinger (1991) argue that there is a "sequence of emotion" underlying "all destructive aggression," namely evoked shame leads to rage and then to violence (p. 3). Expanding upon Lewis's concept of "humiliated fury," Scheff (1987, p. 111), Scheff and Retzinger (1991, xi) describe what they call "shame-rage spirals." Citing Lewis (1971), Scheff (1987) argues that "when shame is evoked and not dispelled, it usually touches off a sequence of emotions in rapid succession" (p. 111). This sequence of emotions is what Scheff and Retzinger (1991) call "shame-rage spirals" (p. xi). In essence, the sequence is shame followed by anger followed by guilt (Scheff, 1987, p. 111). Scheff (1987) develops Helen Block Lewis's (1987a) notion that "shame is a feeling trap" (p. 2). A person can feel trapped in an emotional spiral which not only is intense and overwhelming but seems to go on in an unending fashion. Scheff (1987) describes such a feeling trap as "the phenomenon of having emotional reactions to one's emotional reactions, which may become a closed loop" (pp. 111-112). These interpersonal reactions not only snowball while continuing to gather rapid momentum; but there is often an obsessive intensity (Lewis, 1987a, p. 23) that leads Scheff (1987) to describe the protracted nature of such potentially violent arguments as "the interminable quarrel" (p. 112). The shame-rage spirals are described as a series of loops:

> Within each individual there is a series of loops of shame (as being ashamed of being ashamed causes further shame). Between the individuals there is a downward spiral into disrespect and interminable anger as the failure to confront escalating shame erects a wall separating them. (pp. xi-ix)

Scheff (1987) argues that Lewis's concept of unacknowledged shame is not only the central aspect of her theory but is also a key to understanding the relationship between shame and violence (p. 109). Scheff and Retzinger (1991) argue that shame is both ignored and denied in modern society (p. 19). Scheff and Retzinger (1991) see shame as the master emotion, meaning that shame may exert a triggering effect on other emotions such as fear, grief, anger etc (p. ix):

> The major emotions—like shame, fear, grief, and anger—all have an instinctual basis; they are part of our genetic inheritance. But shame may interfere with the effective management of these emotions; we are often ashamed of our emotions. As we will suggest, under some conditions shame can inhibit, and under other conditions amplify, emotion. (p. xix)

Thus for Scheff and Retzinger (1991), not only is shame "the Master Emotion" whose presence or absence can either prevent or stimulate violence (p.xix), but also there are forms of shame that can stimulate violence and forms of shame that can prevent violence (p.x). John Braithwaite suggests that the fundamental question remains how to differentiate forms of shame that can fuel violence from forms of shame that can prevent it (p. x).

Similarly to Lewis, Scheff and Retzinger (1991) see shame as a relational dynamic. Building on Lewis's theory, Scheff and Retzinger (1991) argue that shame causes aggression when it is not acknowledged (p. x) and when it is communicated disrespectfully (xii). Respectful shaming protects the interpersonal connection by shaming a deed or action "which is perceived as wrong while refraining from rejecting the wrongdoer as a person" (p. xii).

Furthermore, they argue that when people experience attunement, a sense of being connected interpersonally, it is easier to acknowledge shame (p. x). It is the combination of unacknowledged or repressed alienation and shame that leads to violence. In fact, they argue that for prolonged violence to occur there must be two basic conditions:

> One, the parties to the conflict are alienated from each other and are in a state of shame: and two, their state of alienation and their shame go unacknowledged. (p. xix)

Other shame and violence theorists have argued that there are relationships among shame, violence and alienation, disconnection, separation, lack of bonding, abandonment and disengagement (Fain, J. 1996, p. 57; Jordan, 1989, p. 7; Retzinger, 1991, pp. 38-39; Straus, 1994a, p. 143; Straus & Hill, 1997, p. 3; Huber, 1983, p. 148; Gilligan, 1996, p. 96). According to shame theorists, when a person is shamed, the individual experiences emotional separation or at least the threat of separation or abandonment. In this threatened state a person can become enraged (Retzinger, 1991a).

One can clearly question Scheff and Retzinger's (1991) biblical interpretations of shame and guilt. They argue that the writers of the Hebrew scripture (Old Testament) were part of "shame cultures" whereas the writers of the New Testament were part of a society in which "the social control of adults involved guilt" (p. 5):

> The interpretation proposes that there is external control, through shame, in traditional societies, and internal control through guilt,...(p. 5)

This differentiation between shame and guilt cultures in relationship to the writings of the Hebrew scriptures (Old Testament) and the New Testament is contrary to much current biblical research. Their argument that the writers of the Hebrew scriptures were part of a traditional society in which social control was maintained by shame, whereas the writers of the New Testament were members of a society transitioning to modernity where social control was maintained by guilt rather than shame, simply does not hold up. All the biblical writings were part of the ancient Mediterranean world in which shame and honor were dominant cultural forces of social control.

Tangney and Shame/ Guilt Distinctions and Violence

June Price Tangney (1995a) builds her theory primarily on the works of Helen Block Lewis (1971). According to Tangney, Lewis in her landmark book <u>Shame and Guilt in Neurosis</u> (1971) presented "a radically different conceptualization of shame and guilt" (p. 1134). Core to this new conceptualization was the role of the self. According to Tangney, Lewis's critical differentiation between shame and guilt centers on the role of the self in certain experiences:

> The experience of shame is directly about the <u>self</u>, which is the focus of evaluation. In guilt, the self is not the central object of negative evaluation, but rather the <u>thing</u> done or undone is the focus. In guilt, the self is negatively evaluated in connection with something but is not itself the focus of the experiences. ([Lewis, 1971, p. 30], Tangney, 1995a, p. 1134)

For purposes of this study Tangney is most helpful in differentiating between guilt and shame. Tangney (1995a) differentiates shame from guilt in the following way:

Shame is an acutely painful emotion that is typically accompanied by a sense of shrinking or of 'being small' and by a sense of worthlessness and powerlessness.... Although shame does not necessarily involve an actual observing audience, present to witness one's shortcoming, there is often the imagery of how one's defective self would appear to others. (pp. 1134-1135)

In contrast, guilt is generally a less painful and devastating experience than shame because, in guilt, our primary concern is with a particular behavior, somewhat apart from the self. So guilt does not affect one's core identity. Feelings of guilt can be painful, nonetheless. Guilt involves a sense of tension, remorse, and regret over the 'bad thing done.' People in the midst of a guilt experience often report a nagging focus or preoccupation with the transgression—thinking of it over and over, wishing they had behaved differently or could somehow undo the deed. (p. 1135)

Tangney (1995a) cites numerous quantitative and qualitative studies (Ferguson, Stegge, & Damhuis, 1990, 1991; Ferguson & Stegge, 1995; Lindsay-Hartz, 1984; Lindsay-Hartz, de Rivera, & Mascolo, 1995; Tangney, 1993; Tangney, Marschall, et al., 1994; Tangney, Miller, et al., 1995; Wicker, Payne, & Morgan, 1983) to support her distinction between shame and guilt (p. 1135). In two recent studies (Tangney, 1993; Tangney, Miller, et al., 1995) young adults were asked to rate phenomenological dimensions of shame and guilt. In both independent studies shame experiences were rated as significantly more intense and painful than guilt experiences.

When shamed, people felt physically smaller and more inferior to others. Shame experiences were more likely to involve a sense of exposure and a preoccupation with others' opinions. And when feeling shame, people were more compelled to hide and less inclined to admit what they had done. (p. 1135)

David W. Harder (1995) is quite critical of Tangney's differentiation between shame and guilt. He argues that she has taken one aspect of Lewis's (1971) shame-guilt distinction and made it the only distinction (p. 382). Furthermore, Harder disagrees with Tangney's "tendency to consider almost all negative self-evaluations as shame, and to restrict guilt to specific actions unconnected with negative self-judgements," (p. 383). He feels that this same definitional distinction has led other shame theorists such as Michael Lewis (1992, p. 101) "to conclude that a student who feels it is his fault that his father died (because he did not visit during a holiday) is experiencing shame, not guilt, and that a disturbed man who believes he brought on his mother's severe headaches (because of his noise) is likewise experiencing shame, not guilt" (p. 383).

Harder is of the opinion that guilt feelings can also have a global negative affect upon the self (p. 382). It is evident that Harder holds a much more traditional clinical definition of the differentiation between shame and guilt which focuses more on the primary locus of self-evaluation: "whether it is the view of the 'other' (shame) or one's internal standards, irrespective of others' opinions (guilt)" (p. 383).

Citing diverse research studies, Tangney (1995a) does not view shame and guilt as equally moral emotions (p. 1136). She clearly views guilt as the more moral of the two, having an adaptive function, meaning guilt encourages a person to make amends, correct misdeeds (Harder, 1995, p. 381), "confess, apologize, and/or repair the damage that was done" (Tangney, 1995a, p. 1138). Whereas a person experiencing shame may tend to withdraw within the self, thus removing one's attention from the distressed other. Citing numerous studies (Eisenberg, 1986; Hoffman, 1982; Tangney, Marschall, et al., 1994; Zahn-Waxler & Robinson, 1995) Tangney argues a correlation between guilt and empathy:

> In focusing on an offending behavior (as opposed to an offending self), the person experiencing guilt is relatively free of the egocentric, self-involved process of shame. Rather, because the focus on the specific behavior is likely to highlight the consequences of that behavior for a distressed other, guilt serves to foster a continued other-oriented empathic connection. (p. 1137)

Tangney et al.'s research strongly supports the tie between other-oriented empathy and guilt. Her findings also support the link between shame-proneness and "self-oriented" personal distress which in turn can negatively impact one's ability to be empathic toward others (Tangney, 1995a, p. 1141). She cites an extensive body of literature, which indicates that empathy apart from being endowed with other positive characteristics, such as altruism, inhibits interpersonal aggression (p. 1137). Wiehe's (1997) recent review of the research literature on aggression substantiates Tangney's findings that empathy is a moderating variable in the display of aggression (Wiehe, 1997, p. 1191).

In recent years much of the research by Tangney (1995a) has focused "on the relationship of shame and guilt to anger-related processes" (p. 1139). Expanding upon the theoretical works of Lewis (1971), Scheff (1977, 1995) and Retzinger (1987), Tangney et al. in a series of empirical studies (Tangney, 1995b; Tangney, Wagner, Barlow, Marschall, & Gramzow, 1994; Tangney, Wagner, Fletcher, & Gramzow, 1992) have "found that individuals prone to the ugly feeling of shame are also prone to feelings of outwardly directed anger and hostility"(Tangney, 1995a, p. 1140). They have found that guilt, which is relatively "shame-free," is generally associated with one's ability to manage hostility and anger in a constructive manner. These studies have shown that shame-prone individuals are not only more prone to anger, but once angry they have more difficulty in managing their anger than those who experience "shame-free" guilt (p. 1140).

Gilligan and Shame and Violence

James Gilligan (1996) does not build on the works of Helen Block Lewis, Scheff and Retzinger, and Tangney. In fact, these core shame and violence theorists are never mentioned. After years of working with the violent male prisoner and with the criminally insane, Gilligan argues from his experience that the most deadly emotion of all is shame.

Gilligan's work is an attempt to develop a theory which identifies the root causes of violent behavior of men who end up in prison (p. 31). Gilligan argues that this violence is relational (p. 6) and it is always an attempt to achieve justice (p. 11).

Gilligan uses metaphorical language to argue that violent offenders have undergone a "death of the self" (p. 38). For some men, murder becomes an attempt to bring back to life one's dead self (p. 41). Self-mutilation frequently becomes a way for people who have experienced "soul death" to feel alive again (p. 39). In fact, Gilligan states that "the suicide rates among men who have just committed murder is several hundred times greater than it is among ordinary men of the same age, sex, and race, in this country and elsewhere" (p. 41). Gilligan views such violent men as being spiritually dead, and that the "death of their souls" has roots in histories of childhood abuse including corporal punishment (p. 43). For Gilligan corporal punishment is humiliating and can kill a person's sense of self. In fact, for Gilligan physical "violence is the ultimate humiliation," (p. 54) causing the self to "die" (p. 48).

Among this population of men, Gilligan correlates shame with an insufficiency of self-love. In essence, violence is for many such men the "ultimate means of communicating the absence of love" (p. 47). For Gilligan shame is the absence or deficiency of self-love. And similarly to Heinz Kohut, Gilligan states that human beings cannot exist without love:

> The soul needs love as vitally and urgently as the lungs need oxygen; without it the soul dies, just as the body does without oxygen. (p. 51)

Gilligan views violent offenders as extremely sensitive to insult (p. 60). In fact, at the root of grotesque violence is what Gilligan calls "the logic of shame" (p. 65). Building on the works of Erik Erikson (1950,1963) Gilligan argues that shame can make a person feel uncomfortably exposed, stared at without one's consent, violated. Gilligan's logic of shame is a form of magical thinking in which the violent offender rationally says to him or herself: "'If I kill this person in this way, I will kill shame—I will be able to protect myself from being exposed and vulnerable to and potentially overwhelmed by the feeling of shame'"(pp. 65-66).

Having worked with this prison population, Gilligan is conscious of the power dynamics implicit in shame. Shame makes a person feel powerless and inferior, whereas violence can make a person feel powerful and possibly superior (p. 276). Shame is at the root of violence because the most common reason for engaging in violence is to replace chronic feelings of inferiority with feelings of pride and self-esteem (p. 81).

Gilligan has used his experience with violent offenders to develop what he calls the "germ theory" of violence (p. 103). Gilligan treats violence as a public health issue, identifying "shame" as the most lethal emotional pathogen of our time (p. 104). In fact, Gilligan broadly states that "the emotion shame is the ultimate cause of all violence whether toward others or toward the self" (p. 110). Shame makes certain people feel dishonored and disrespected, and certain individuals according to Gilligan choose death over dishonor:

I have yet to see a serious act of violence that was not provoked by the experience of feeling shamed and humiliated, disrespected and ridiculed, and that did not represent the attempt to prevent or undo this 'loss of face'—no no matter how severe the punishment, even if it includes death. (p. 110)

Not only does shame make certain people feel dishonored and disrespected, shame can also degrade a person so completely that their former identity is totally destroyed (pp. 152-153).

Gilligan is of the opinion that many in our society live by an unstated code of honor (p. 267). Some of these individuals will kill if they feel their honor, or that of a loved one is at stake. For instance, urban street gangs live by "codes of honor" and "to be 'dis'ed' is literally a mortal insult" (p. 263) which many believe must be avenged. In essence, Gilligan seems to be arguing that there is a hidden, unacknowledged code of honor and shame system in many cultural groups which not only generates but also obligates male violence (p. 267).

In Gilligan's "germ" theory of violence, a central precondition for violence among the men he has treated as a prison psychiatrist has been overwhelming shame combined with the absence of love and or guilt (pp. 113-114). Furthermore, a precondition for such violence is punishment:

Punishment stimulates shame and diminishes guilt, and shame stimulates violence, especially when it is not inhibited by guilt. (p. 187)

Shame stimulates rage and a rage/violence spiral. Love and/ or guilt is necessary to inhibit violent impulses.

Gilligan points out that Freud believed that guilt stimulates the need for punishment given the fact that punishment can relieve uncomfortable guilt feelings (p. 113). Furthermore, Gilligan from his psychodynamic perspective emphasizes that Freud had no theory of shame. According to Gilligan corporal punishment can increase feelings of shame while decreasing feelings of guilt. In essence, corporal punishment can absolve guilt.

Based on his work with violent offenders Gilligan argues that we need to assess psychologically peoples' levels of shame. Shame should be a marker for the potential of violence (p. 249). Gilligan further argues that people who are overwhelmed with shame can feel dead and numb inside. Because they feel so dead and numb they may not feel remorse over their behavior (p. 256).

Klein: Humiliation and Violence Prevention

Donald C. Klein (1991b) building on the works of Helen Block Lewis (1971,1976) and Thomas Scheff (1987) acknowledges that humiliation can turn into destructive rage in which people or even nations inflict violence on self- and/ or others (pp. 115, 118).

Klein points out that Lewis (1976) saw humiliation as part of a "shame state" which encompassed feelings of ridicule, mortification, embarrassment, chagrin, and dishonor along with humiliation (Klein, 1991b, p. 117). Quoting directly from Susan Miller (1988) Klein differentiates humiliation from shame by stating that the core difference has to do with power dynamics: "'humiliation involves being put into a lowly, debased, and powerless position by someone who has, at that moment, greater power than oneself,' whereas 'shame involves reflection upon the self by the self'" (Klein, 1991b, p. 117).

Even though one could clearly debate definitions and argue that he has too narrowly defined shame, Klein (1991b, 1992) presents a model to minimize the destructive impact of shame/humiliation in personal and societal relationships.

Klein suggests that humiliation-prone people need to learn to immunize themselves psychologically to the destructive impact of humiliation. This is done both by refusing to assume the role of victim and also by consciously redefining one's identity (1992, p. 255). Klein describes such an immunizing approach used by marginalized groups within society:

> Members of victimized groups in our society—among them women, African-Americans, and homosexuals—independently have described going through a very similar period of consciousness-raising in which a previously introjected self-image of inferiority is almost literally 'vomited out' to be replaced in successive stages by a period of creating a separate, self-sustaining culture of one's own kind, and finally, being prepared to enter into an interdependent relationship of equal power with one's former oppressors. (Klein, 1992, p. 257)

He goes on to suggest the necessity of creating "humiliation-free institutions" (1992, p. 255) as well as envisioning a humiliation-free society and world (p. 256). Since Klein directly sees a link between humiliation and violence, he argues that sensitivity to humiliation dynamics could have broad international consequences for peace. Klein (1991b, 1992) writing for the Journal of Primary Prevention outlines two tactics to prevent the destructive impact of humiliation. First, people need to learn how to become psychologically immunized to the destructive impact of humiliating insults. Second, Klein seeing an intimate relationship between humiliation and violence, argues that it is critical to create a global society in which public ridicule and collective humiliation are outlawed (1992, p. 257). Klein's approach could be strengthened if he included the almost universal experience of humiliation, that of childhood corporal punishment.

Summary

Helen Block Lewis (1971) is a pioneer in our understanding of shame and its relationship to rage and violence. As a psychoanalyst she acknowledged that the structure of analysis with its analytic distance can be a source of shame. Her theory of bypassed and unacknowledged shame stresses that it is the hidden, unconscious aspects of shame which can be most destructive and lead to what she calls "humiliated fury." For Lewis shame is fundamentally relational. Critical to this study is her understanding that shaming can be used as a form of punishment. She refers to this shaming/punishment cycle as a "righting tendency," meaning that the one shamed tries to shame or humiliate the other.

Scheff and Retzinger, (1991) building on the works of Lewis, theoretically describe a shame/rage spiral in which unacknowledged shame leads to anger and then to aggression (p. ix). They view shame as the master emotion, meaning that it can interfere with the effective management of other intense emotions such as fear, grief and anger. Shame can at times inhibit emotion and at other times can amplify emotion. Similarly to Lewis they see shame as a relational dynamic. Shaming can isolate, alienate and separate. They argue that it is the combination of unacknowledged or repressed alienation and shame that leads to violence.

Building on the works of Lewis, June Price Tangney (1995) differentiates between guilt and shame. The focus of shame is on the self whereas the focus of guilt is on the thing done or left undone. Moreover, Tangney (1995) argues that shame and guilt are not equally moral emotions. According to her research, guilt is the more moral of the two, having an adaptive function, meaning guilt encourages a person to make amends and/or correct misdeeds. Shame-prone people withdraw from others and display more difficulty in managing their anger. Tangney et al.'s research supports a relationship between guilt and empathy. According to current research empathy can inhibit violence.

Based upon his work with violent offenders James Gilligan (1996) argues that there is an intimate tie between violence and shame. In fact, he states that shame can be the most deadly of all human emotions and is at the root of violence. He sees a relational dimension to both shame and violence. Violence, according to Gilligan, is always an attempt to achieve justice and replace chronic feelings of inferiority with feelings of pride and self-esteem. Gilligan's "germ" theory of violence holds as a central tenet the belief that a precondition for violence is overwhelming shame combined with an absence of love and or guilt. For Gilligan corporal punishment is not only humiliating and can kill a person's sense of self, but it also can increase feelings of shame while decreasing feelings of guilt. In the area of violence prevention Gilligan argues shame should be a marker for potential violence.

Finally, Donald C. Klein (1991b) presents a model for violence prevention. Klein, building on Lewis (1971, 1976) and Thomas Scheff (1987), acknowledges a tie between humiliation and violence. Klein suggests that humiliation-prone people need to learn psychologically to immunize themselves to the destructive impact of humiliation by redefining their identify and refusing to assume the role of victim.

Part II will examine the more specific issues related to shame, corporal punishment and religion.

Part II: Shame and Corporal Punishment and Religion

Introduction

Selective Inattention of Corporal Punishment

As stated earlier, toward the end of her life Helen Block Lewis began to see a relationship between resistance in psychotherapy and deep-seated feelings of shame and guilt. Thus one might "turn the tables" (Lewis, 1987a) on Freud and argue that he was resistant to both the dynamics of shame and the reality of childhood physical abuse in the lives of his adult clients. Straus (1994b) supports Greven's (1990, 1992) argument that Freud has "perceptual blinders" in relationship to corporal punishment of children because of his own personal history:

> Greven (1991) argues that Freud could not bring himself to acknowledge the legitimate experiential basis for the fantasies of being beaten because he himself was a product of corporal punishment and had internalized its values. (Straus, 1994b, p. 263)

The values that Freud internalized were most likely the unquestioned societal necessity of childhood corporal punishment, its harmless nature, and an unacknowledged shame related to his own history of corporal punishment.

Greven (1990, 1992) states that Freud tragically failed to see a link between the experience of childhood punishment and adult depression (p. 130). In "Mourning and Melancholia" (1917) Freud describes depression as culminating in a "delusional expectation of punishment" (p. 130). Today social scientific research has documented a correlation between childhood physical punishment/abuse and adult major depression and even suicide (Straus, 1994b; Fergusson and Lynskey, 1997; Straus, Sugarman, Giles-Sims, 1997). Furthermore, in the essay "A Child Is Being Beaten: A Contribution to the Study of the Origin of Sexual Perversions" (1919), Freud interpreted his adults' revelations about childhood beatings as fantasies (p. 131). Ironically, Straus (1994b) has years later documented a correlation between childhood corporal punishment and masochistic sex (Straus, 1994b).

This foregrounding of certain material while backgrounding other is what Murray Straus (1994b), pre-eminent researcher in the area of family violence, calls "selective inattention" (p. 68). Until the women's movement there was a "selective inattention" to wife beating. And even today Straus (1994b) suggests that most people view hitting a woman as a worse act than hitting a child. Like Freud not only do we not see the detrimental effects of childhood corporal punishment, but as Straus points out, the "authors of textbooks on child development and advice books for parents almost totally ignore the research on corporal punishment" thus participating in a kind of "conspiracy of silence" (p. 82). This study explores the reasons behind this conspiracy of silence regarding childhood corporal punishment.

Murray Straus (1994b) states that Philip Greven explains the selective inattention to the potential detrimental effects of childhood corporal punishment by stating that society at large wears "perceptual blinders" because early childhood corporal punishment is such a universal experience. Thus society at large participates in a conspiracy of silence, denying the potential detrimental effects of such punitive childrearing practices. In fact, Straus states that "90 percent of Americans hit toddlers" and probably 50 percent of infants are hit (p. 3). Straus believes that corporal punishment is a significant factor in the "psychological development of almost all American children" (p. 4).

Part II is divided into two sections, both of which will focus on the selective inattention of corporal punishment. Section I presents a number of core theorists who argue that religion has been used to justify and support the use of childhood corporal punishment. Section II focuses on corporal punishment and the cycle of violence.

1. Religion Justifying Corporal Punishment and Child Abuse

Alice Miller, Corporal Punishment and a Conspiracy of Denial

Alice Miller (1984), a psychoanalyst and prolific writer has linked child abuse and intergenerational violence. She has also come to view psychoanalysis as an impediment to the uncovering of childhood abuse histories. Furthermore, she has theorized a link between perpetuation of childhood abuse and religion.

Miller (1984) emphasizes not only the extent to which childhood can influence adult life, but also the extent to which unexamined abuse in childhood can be repeated in adulthood. It is her conviction that "childhood is the key to understanding a person's later life" (p. 6). Psychoanalysis for Miller should be a creative form of consciousness-raising about the truth of one's childhood (p. 5). Yet a "conspiracy of denial" of childhood pain keeps adults from being aware of the poisonous effects of their childhood.

Miller (1983, 1984) universally refers to past child-rearing practices as "poisonous pedagogy"[10] which she considers a form of child abuse:

> An enormous amount can be done to a child in the first two years: he or she can be molded, dominated, taught good habits, scolded, and punished—without any repercussions for the person raising the child and without the child taking revenge. (pp. 6-7)

Miller states her position that young children should be allowed to defend themselves by expressing their pain and anger:

---

[10] Miller (1984) defines "poisonous pedagogy" as "that tradition of child-rearing which attempts to suppress all vitality, creativity and feeling in the child and maintain the autocratic, godlike position of the parents at all costs" (p. 18).

If he [sic] is prevented from reacting in his [sic] own way because the parents cannot tolerate his [sic] reactions (crying, sadness, rage) and forbid them by means of looks or other pedagogical methods, then the child will learn to be silent. (p. 7)

According to Miller (1983, 1984) traditionally all young children have been silenced to some degree, forcing their emotional lives to go underground (p. 6). Thus virtually all children learn at an early age about a "conspiracy of silence" (Straus, 1994b), a deep denial of pain, surrounding child abuse. The fact that children are not allowed to voice their sense of injustice or to emotionally express their pain, anger and humiliation leads to repression (p. 7). In a sense, Miller is expressing a sequence of humiliation and anger similar to Helen Block Lewis's description of "bypassed shame," shame that goes underground (Scheff and Retzinger, 1991) because it is not affectively acknowledged and if triggered can lead to humiliated fury.

Core to Miller's theory is how traditional childrearing techniques and theories have been used to effectively crush "the spontaneous feelings of children" (1983, 1984, p. 7). Key to "poisonous pedagogy" is the belief that parents must be advised of the necessity of breaking the will of the child and doing so without expressing anger. This technique was especially encouraged within Protestantism (Greven, 1990, 1992). Thus the non-emotional parent models for the child how to punish and to receive punishment without the expression of intense emotions and affect:

If the child persists in responding emotionally to a spanking or other reprimand, by getting angry or by crying, the parent threatens the child with another spanking as punishment for the child's emotional reaction to the original spanking. The goal is to eliminate feeling from the act of punishment and from the child's response to it. (Capps, 1995, p. 7)

Thus emotions are repressed, forced underground (Scheff and Retzinger, 1991), and most likely remain underground until some humiliating event triggers the old repressed childhood feelings of powerlessness, rage and anger.

Pastoral theologian Donald Capps (1995) has noted an evolution in Miller's writings. In her first three books: The Drama of the Gifted Child, For Your Own Good, and Thou Shalt Not Be Aware, Miller saw no conflict between her views on child abuse and psychoanalysis (p. 3). Capps argues that by the late 1980s and early 1990s Miller had already begun to make her break with psychoanalysis arguing that "psychoanalysis and the recovery of childhood trauma" (p. 3) were incompatible. In essence, she argued that psychoanalysis gave her "perceptual blinders" not only to her own abuse as a child but also to the childhood abuse in the lives of her patients (Capps, 1995, p. 3).

In contradiction to Capps's reading of Miller, this author is of the opinion that Miller was discovering a deep incompatibility between classical psychoanalysis and the uncovering of childhood abuse as early as 1984. In Thou Shalt Not Be Aware—Society's Betrayal of the Child, Miller (1984) takes exception to Freudian drive theory as related to infantile sexuality. She argues that classical analytic practice has tended "to regard everything patients tell about their childhood as fantasy and as their own desires projected onto the external world. Thus, in terms of drive theory, parents do not actually abuse their children in order to fulfill their own needs but children supposedly fantasize this abuse" (Miller, 1984, p. 4). According to Miller, (1984) Freudian drive theory encourages adults to deny (conceal rather than reveal) their childhood trauma and ultimately blame themselves.

Miller (1984) asks the most important question as to why "many analysts" haven't addressed the impact of childhood abuse on adult life (p. 7). Trying not to single out psychoanalysis as the sole culprit, Miller admits that people from many disciplines wear "perceptual blinders" (p. 11) to the traumatization of childhood. Core to this denial system is "the unspoken commandment to spare the parents and blame the child" (p. 19) which has become part of our cultural fabric. Miller asserts that at the heart of the denial of childhood abuse and trauma is religion. In particular, our Judeo-Christian heritage has supported "poisonous pedagogical" child rearing practices (p. 94) by emphasizing the Fourth Commandment (p. 22). No matter what, a child is to honor his or her father and mother. This is the supreme commandment and if one has to deny childhood abuse and its ensuing humiliation, so be it. Thus those adults who have not dealt with their own histories of childhood trauma and humiliation tend to be those who most vehemently deny and cover-up childhood trauma in an attempt to protect one's parents (p. 22). But behind the Fourth Commandment is still another commandment older than the Ten Commandments—"Thou shalt not be aware" (p. 95). It is this command "not to be aware" that enables our society to wear "perceptual blinders" to the impact of childhood corporal punishment on adulthood.

Miller (1983, 1984) clearly sees the tie between childhood corporal punishment/abuse and humiliation. In general "poisonous pedagogical" child-rearing practices are humiliating because of the power differentials that make the child feel helpless and powerless. In regard to corporal punishment Miller (1983, 1984) argues that the boundary between "spanking" and "beating" a child is at best a tenuous one (p. ix). But for Miller the level of humiliation is the same:

> But even when a spanking is a gentler form of physical violence, the psychic pain and humiliation and the need to repress these feelings are the same as in the case of more severe punishment. (p. ix)

It is in her work <u>For Your Own Good—Hidden Cruelty in Child-Rearing and the Roots of Violence</u> that Miller (1983, 1984) most fully addresses the tie between childhood corporal punishment/abuse and intergenerational violence. She cautions the reader not to feel "exempt from the consequences of child beating" if all they have ever done is "spank" their children (p. ix). The greatest harm we can do to the next generation, she argues, is to claim that such punishment is not harmful:

> When people who have been beaten or spanked as children attempt to play down the consequences by setting themselves up as examples, even claiming it was good for them, they are inevitably contributing to the continuation of cruelty in the world by this refusal to take their childhood tragedies seriously. Taking over this attitude, their children, pupils, and students will

in turn beat their own children, citing their parents, teachers, and professors as authorities. (1983, p. x)

For purposes of this study, what is of most value in Miller's work is her theory of intergenerational abuse and violence and the link between interpersonal violence and societal violence. Capps (1995) interprets Miller:

> Miller lives for the eradication of child abuse, and believes that it could in fact be eradicated if one generation of humans were enlightened enough not to do it, for child abuse is a learned behavior—one learned from our parents—and could therefore, in her view, become one of the many behaviors that humans, in the course of their evolution, have managed to unlearn. (Capps, 1995, p. 4)

Most pertinent to this study is Miller's concern with the intergenerational affects of child abuse. She argues in virtually all of her writings that adults who have not affectively and cognitively come to grips with their own histories of child abuse are likely to repeat this abuse with their own children: "This is because whatever was repressed in their own childhood comes to overt expression in their behavior as adults" (Capps, 1995, p. 15). One might argue that Alice Miller has identified what one could call "bypassed child abuse," child abuse that was affectively repressed in childhood, and is overtly expressed emotionally and physically in the behavior of adults against their own children (p. 15).

Some have criticized Miller's work as being too repetitive (Capps, 1995, p. 4). Others have criticized Miller as being naive about human nature, but Capps (1995) regards Miller's apparent optimistic and hopeful views about human nature as positive and constructive. In fact, he offers little criticism of her work. A more challenging critique comes from Dixon, Underwood, Hoeft and Roth (1996).

Dixon et al. (1996) argue that Miller offers an important critique of psychoanalysis and religion, but her claims are simply too broad, global and universalistic. Ironically, Dixon et al. (1996) maintain that through the years Miller—the premier advocate of awareness—seems to have become "increasingly blind to the potential limitations of her own perspective" (p. 192). For instance, Miller seems to categorically dismiss psychoanalysis without perceiving its helpfulness for some people. Furthermore, Miller holds only a negative view of religion. Miller participates in a kind of "whole-sale censure of religion" viewing it not only as obsolete but also as pernicious. Dixon et al. (1996) thus caution uncritical reliance on her work:

> The limitations of her understanding of religion and its role in both culture and psyche could prove a major stumbling block to wider acceptance and use of her work in religious circles. (p. 193)

In fact, it is Miller's universal claims about religion that Dixon et al. (1996) signal as most problematic. Miller seems to wear her only perceptual blinders in relationship to Freudian theory and fails to examine to what extent her views on religion are quite Freudian (p. 192). Dixon et al. note that Miller fails to acknowledge that religion has also provided for many people over the centuries a catalyst for social justice and human fulfillment:

> It has been and continues to be a source of healing as well as harm, a force for liberation as well as repression. Thus we criticize her for operating with a narrow, limited, and reductionistic theory of religion. (p. 193)

Dixon et al. (1996) also question Miller's utopian vision about human nature. They note that Miller assumes that children raised in a nurturing and accepting environment will produce human good both personally and societally. Dixon et al. (1996) raise the nurture versus nature debate by pointing out that Miller's theory is based on the unexamined assumption that every child born with a good-natured soul and "raised free of abuse, trauma, and disrespect will have only good intentions towards others" (p. 193).

Furthermore, from a post-modern, post-structuralist perspective one might argue that Miller's theory is not contextual enough. Dixon et al. (1996) argue that Miller fails to expand her power analysis of abuse "beyond parent and child to other structures of domination and subordination" (p. 195). For instance, she does not examine the interrelationships between "hierarchical structures of gender, race, class, or sexual orientation" (p. 195). Finally, Dixon et al. (1996) argue that Miller tends to carry on what they call the psychoanalytic tradition of "mother-blaming" and "woman-blaming" (p. 195).

Nonetheless, Dixon et al. (1996) feel that Miller's theories are important in that they point the readers in the direction of examining the possible interrelationships between individual trauma and social ills. However as Dixon et al. (1996) point out Miller's theory is limited by her "poorly conceptualized theory of the interactions between individuals and society," her mother/woman blaming, her unexamined assumptions about human nature, and her seemingly "simplistic understanding of religion as nothing but 'poisonous pedagogy'" (p. 196).

Philip Greven—The Use of Religion To Legitimize Corporal Punishment

Building on the work of Alice Miller (1984), Philip Greven (1990, 1992) believes that historically religion has been used in the Western world to justify the use of corporal punishment and other forms of violence (p. 94). Greven argues that Protestant evangelicals, fundamentalists and Pentecostals have further condoned the use of childhood corporal punishment as a way of instilling divine obedience in children. He states that the theological rationale is that children's wills are inherently evil (Straus, 1994b, p. 68) and innately opposed to the will of God (Capps, 1995, p. 51). Parents are God's representatives on earth. When children disobey parental authority, their wills must be conquered, subdued and broken in order to save their souls (Capps, 1995, p. 51). A child who disobeys his or her parents will ultimately disobey God (Greven, 1990, 1992, p. 21). Thus physical punishment, divine obedience, and salvation are all interrelated.

Greven (1990, 1992) writes as an insider, acknowledging that he was physically punished as a child and as a parent has on several occasions corporally punished his own children. Greven holds the conviction, although not tested empirically, that corporal punishment is related to the violent apocalyptic impulse in Protestantism, meaning "the desire for the world's end and for the salvation of the few at the expense of the many" (p. xiv). He argues that this apocalyptic expectation of the end of history within one's lifetime is related to the intense pain caused by childhood physical punishments (p. 8). In this apocalyptic belief system the adult who was painfully corporally punished in childhood will be saved or rescued while others will not. Greven further argues that the childhood experience of punishment has influenced Christian theology, which has been heavily rooted in the threat of punishment (p. 8).

Greven shares the same conviction with Alice Miller that the breeding ground for public societal violence is personal violence (p. 9). Our society has learned how to be violent within our families of origin. He adamantly argues that all forms of violence against children are harmful and hurtful (p. 9). Core to this study is the notion that such childhood hurt and pain is frequently denied, repressed and ultimately forgotten. One can argue that the pain and hurt of childhood corporal punishment is bypassed, meaning it is not cognitively and affectively remembered only to resurface at times in highly destructive ways in one's adulthood. Greven in essence suggests that such pain and or memory goes underground:

> The feelings generated by the pain caused by adults' assaults against children are mostly repressed, forgotten, and denied, but they actually never disappear. Everything remains recorded in our innermost beings, and the effects of punishment permeate our lives, our thoughts, our culture, and our world. (p. 10)

He strongly argues that our past effects our present and future. Recent research in child abuse indicates that it is the lack of memories of childhood abuse that can be most destructive in adult behavior. Thus for Greven the destructive effects of childhood corporal punishment remain invisible to us. He argues that once the invisible becomes visible that the entire issue of childhood corporal punishment and its relationship to societal violence will be perceived in a totally different light (p. 10).

Theoretically Greven sees a relationship between childhood corporal punishment and dissociation:

> Dissociation is one of the most basic means of survival for many children, who learn early in life to distance themselves, or parts of themselves, from experiences too painful or frightening to bear. Traumas, both physical and emotional, are often coped with by denial and repression of the feelings they generate. The dissociative process is rooted, it appears, in the ability of so many children and adults to hypnotize themselves, to render unconscious aspects of their feelings and experiences that, for whatever reasons, they find unbearable or unacceptable. (Capps, 1992, p. 8)

Donald Capps—"Religion and Child Abuse: Perfect Together"

Pastoral theologian Donald Capps (1992, 1995) has built specifically on the works of Alice Miller and Philip Greven. Capps (1993) has also written extensively on shame and on Erik Erikson's developmental theory (Capps, 1983). Recently he has examined the religious abuse of children (Capps, 1995).

In his earliest work on religion and child abuse, Capps (1992) argues that children have frequently "been betrayed, exploited, and abused" in the name of religion (p. 2). In this earliest work he attempts a very difficult methodological strategy, namely that of examining the issue of child abuse from the vantagepoint of the adult remembering his or her childhood. This study uses in part this kind of a methodology in that adults are asked to remember certain aspects of their childhood especially related to corporal punishment.

Capps argues that there is a certain collusion between religion and child abuse, meaning that religion justifies child abuse. Basing his argument on that of Phililp Greven, Capps (1990) notes that there is a religious conviction that views children as entering the world with a wayward will which needs to be broken (p. 3). He paraphrases Greven's work:

> It is therefore the responsibility of parents to break, or at least so successfully to challenge and frustrate the child's natural will that he or she will then be able to respond to parental guidance and live in conformity with the superior will of God. (p. 3)

Capps (1992) integrates Greven (1990, 1992) and Miller (1993) by arguing that the "very idea of 'breaking the child's will' is an instance of what Alice Miller (1983) has called 'poisonous pedagogy'" (p. 3). Thus parents have a kind of religious mandate to break the child's will by inflicting physical punishment (p. 3). The physical pain is further denied by the expressed parental justification that such physical pain is actually for the child's own good and for their spiritual well-being (p. 4). Capps (1992) emphasizes that parents often feel that they are acting on behalf of God—disciplining their disobedient children in a similar fashion to how God will discipline them in adulthood if and when they are disobedient adults. Thus childhood corporal punishment for religious reasons becomes the church school of child obedience training.

Yet such corporal punishment did not always convince children that God was on their parents' side or that God was working through the pain inflicted upon them through a hickory stick, a yardstick, a belt or a parental hand. The life of Aimee Sample McPherson is a case in point:

> Like all other restless youngsters, I was constantly getting into dilemmas and difficulties. After similar outrages to the dignity of my household, I would be banished to my room and told that in exactly one-half an hour I would be spanked. I was thoroughly familiar with those whippings. They were not gentle love pats, and my parents never stopped till I was a thoroughly chastised girl. The time of waiting

for the footsteps on the stair, the opening of the door, and the descending palm was the worst of all. On one such occasion I stood looking wildly about for a way out of the dilemma. No earthly recourse was nigh. Taught as I was about heavenly intervention, I thought of prayer. Dropping to my knees on the side of my bed, I began to pray, loudly, earnestly. 'Oh, God, don't let mama whip me! Oh, God, dear, kind, sweet God, don't let mama spank me !'(Capps, 1992, p. 4)

Childhood corporal punishment not only initiates children into the use of violence to resolve conflict but also teaches them how to use power to control, intimidate and humiliate.

Ellison and Sherkat: Conservative Protestants and Corporal Punishment

A significant empirical study exploring the relationship between religion and corporal punishment is that of Ellison and Sherkat (1993). Using data from the General Social Survey they found that Conservative Protestants disproportionately supported the use of corporal punishment. They theorized that the Conservative Protestant support for corporal punishment was because of three aspects of their religious ideology: (1) literal interpretation of the bible, (2) the conviction that human nature (including children) is inherently sinful, (3) and the belief that sinful human nature demands punishment (including children) (p. 131). Because of the hierarchical nature of Catholicism and its authoritarian values, Ellison and Sherkat investigated whether Catholics would be "especially supportive of physical discipline" (p. 136). Congruent with the earlier study by Alwin (1986), they found that "Catholics do not disproportionately support corporal punishment" (p. 136).

The 1988 General Social Survey (GSS) consisted of a national cross-sectional sample of approximately 1,500 U.S. adults (p. 134). Ellison and Sherkat (1993) found that Conservative Protestants were twice as likely to interpret the bible literally as individuals with comparable backgrounds. Belief in a literal interpretation of the bible is the "strongest predictor of negative beliefs about human nature" (p. 137). Finally, the combination of beliefs—biblical literalism and the belief that human nature is fundamentally corrupt "concur strongly with the proposition that 'sinners against God must be punished'"(p. 137). There was also a very interesting gender factor in this study:

Females are 50 percent more likely than males to accept biblical literalism, but they are also significantly more optimistic regarding the inherent goodness of human nature. (p. 138)

Finally most significant for this study was the relationship between a person's views of human nature, punishment of sin and support for corporal punishment:

Individuals who feel that human nature is sinful and corrupt and that sinful behavior should be punished express strong support for the principle of corporal punishment. (p. 139)

The study also found that educational attainment has a negative impact on support for corporal punishment, meaning the more education one attains the less one favors corporal punishment. Ellison and Sherkat (1993) interpreted this finding to mean that educational attainment lessens the likelihood of a belief in the literal interpretation of the bible. This study did not examine the intergenerational use of corporal punishment. More empirical research examining the relationship between religion and the support of corporal punishment is necessary. It is important not to label Conservative Protestants as the sole religious supporters of childhood corporal punishment and thus making them the religious "fall guy" around this important societal issue.

Summary

As the literature suggests there is a long history of societal denial regarding the detrimental impact of childhood corporal punishment. Not only has Miller (1984) strongly linked child abuse and intergenerational violence, but she has also viewed psychoanalysis as an impediment to the uncovering of childhood abuse histories. Furthermore, she emphasizes that religion is at the heart of the denial of childhood abuse.

Philip Greven (1990, 1992) argues that historically religion has been used in the western world to legitimize the use of corporal punishment and other forms of violence (p. 94). In fact, he suggests that the childhood experience of punishment has influenced Christian theology, which has been heavily rooted in the threat of punishment (p. 8). Like others, Greven (1990, 1992) shares the conviction that the breeding ground for public societal violence is interpersonal violence (p. 9).

Donald Capps building on the works of Miller and Greven suggests that there is a collusion between religion and child abuse. Not only does religion give its stamp of approval to child abuse, Capps argues that religion, in fact, promotes child abuse (Capps, 1995, p. ix). An expert on the writings of Erik Erikson, Capps (1983, 1992, 1995) could have expanded his theory on child abuse and religion by examining a possible relationship between childhood corporal punishment and shame.

Ellison and Sherkat's (1993) important study found that Conservative Protestants disproportionately support the use of corporal punishment. In fact, their study found that there was a relationship between the conviction that human nature is sinful and corrupt, the belief that it is necessary to punish sinful behavior and the support for corporal punishment.

Section II examines the relationship between corporal punishment and the cycle of violence or intergenerational violence.

2. Corporal Punishment and the Cycle of Violence

Murray Straus—The Family—The Cradle of Violence

Social scientist Murray Straus (1994b) expands the theoretical works of Philip Greven (1990, 1992) and Alice Miller (1984). Similarly to Greven (1990, 1992), Straus (1994b) believes that corporal punishment of children is one of the major factors in the cycle of violence in our world today. Straus (1994b) in fact begins his landmark book by writing,

> 'Beating the devil out of him,' is just a hyperbola for spanking. Not long ago it also had a religious meaning based on the ideas of original sin and being possessed by the devil. (p. 3)

Even though Straus acknowledges that certain religious groups continue to justify corporal punishment on religious grounds, he does not generally write about the religious meaning that corporal punishment might have for the general population. This study examines to what extent corporal punishment still has religious meaning based on one's image of God, one's beliefs about the innate goodness or badness of human nature, and the development of conscience seen in the form of "discretionary shame" and guilt.

Straus (1994b) cites the works of Guarendi and Eich (1990) Back to the Family: How to Encourage Traditional Values in Complicated Times, and Dobson (1970 and 1988), Dare to Discipline and The Strong-Willed Child. Straus notes that these authors like the general population are against child abuse, but that they like "more than 80 percent of the population" believe that "hitting a 'willfully disobedient' child is an act of love and concern, not abuse" (p. 15). According to Straus these Conservative Protestant authors ardently reject the notion that corporal punishment is a form of violence against children. Straus further states that the position taken by Dobson and Guarendi differs from most Americans because of their religious justification of corporal punishment. Straus interprets their position by stating:

> They believe hitting a child is an obligation imposed by God, just as God expects parents to love and nurture children...The child must come to understand that he or she is being hit as an act of love. Fundamentalist Protestants typically cite scriptures to show that children are inherently evil. (p. 15)

Straus (1994b) builds on Greven's (1990, 1992) and Ellison and Sherkat's (1993) notion that Fundamentalist Protestants not only typically believe that it is the responsibility of parents to shape and mold the wills of children, but they also cite scripture to demonstrate that children are inherently evil. Corporal punishment thus becomes a religious tool not only to shape and mold the wills of children, but also a way of beating out their innate evilness. Straus has not researched images of God and their relationship to corporal punishment. However, he does cite Lambert, Triandis, and Wolf's (1959) study in which they found a relationship between the use of corporal punishment in nonliterate societies and religious systems which hold images of punitive deities (p. 191).

Straus (1994b) strongly challenges the position of hitting children for their own good (Miller, 1984) or as a God ordained expression of love (Greven, 1990, 1992). Straus contends that the fact that children are so often hit out of love and concern is one of the most damaging effects of corporal punishment (p. 16). In fact, one could expand Straus's argument and suggest that corporal punishment out of love and concern can be a form of traumatic bonding (Dutton and Painter, 1981). Traumatic bonding is a term originally coined by Dutton and Painter (1981) to describe the intense bonding between victim and victimizer which happens in the context of intermittent maltreatment combined with "either intense dependency or loving connection" (Saunders and Arnold, 1991, p. 5).

Straus's empirical research has shown that corporal punishment of children is related to the transmission of intergenerational violence:

> At the inter-generational level of analysis, corporal punishment increases the chance that when the child is an adult he or she will approve of interpersonal violence, be in a violent marriage, and be depressed. (p. 96)

Straus (1994b) also claims along with (Greven, 1990, 1992; Miller, 1984) that there is a correlation between family violence and societal violence:

> ...The family is the 'cradle of violence' and that a reduction in the largely taken for granted family violence called spanking is one of the most important steps we can make toward achieving a less violent world. (p. xiii)

Straus (1994b) has almost stood alone in his belief that spanking children— childhood corporal punishment—is a major psychological and social problem (p. ix) (and one might add a religious problem) when the effects upon the development of conscience are examined. In fact, in the early to mid 1980s Straus was practically denounced by some feminists because of his theory that corporal punishment or what one might call "ordinary spanking" is one of the causes of "wife beating" and his personal belief that hitting children is as unacceptable as hitting wives (p. ix).

In recent studies Straus has shown that even small amounts of corporal punishment are harmful (Straus, Sugarman, & Giles-Sims, 1997). Straus (1994b) argues that most social scientists are of the opinion that corporal punishment itself is not the problem, but rather the problem is incompetent and harsh parenting (p. xiii). Yet Straus has consistently argued that the harmful effects of corporal punishment show up later in life (p.xi). Straus's consistent thesis is "that corporal punishment by itself, has harmful psychological side effects for children and hurts the society as a whole" (p. xii).

How is society hurt? According to Straus (1994b), the classic study by Sears, Maccoby, and Levin's (1957) <u>Patterns of Child Rearing</u> showed that not only do children who are spanked tend to be more aggressive, but they also tend to have less fully developed consciences (p. 100). Straus interprets these findings by stating that corporal punishment may force people to conform to the rules; however, such forced conformity may interfere with the internalized development of conscience (p. 144). In a more recent study (Straus, Sugarman, & Giles-Sims, 1997), Straus et al. found that "when parents use corporal punishment to reduce antisocial behavior (ASB), the long-term effect tends to be the opposite," meaning there is increased physical aggression in the children as well as other forms of antisocial behavior (p. 761).

In Straus et al.'s (1997) most recent study, the use of corporal punishment is a "significant predictor of ASB 2 years later" even when controlling for the effects of parental behaviors and socioeconomic variables (p. 765). In fact, the increase in antisocial behavior started with children who were spanked by their mothers only once during the week prior to the survey (p.765). Straus cautions the public in its interpretation of this data:

> However, one must keep in mind that even frequent CP does not necessarily lead to ASB, just as frequent smoking does not necessarily lead to death from a smoking-related disease. At age 65 years, two thirds of frequent smokers can point out that they smoked more than a pack of cigarettes a day all of their lives and have not died from cancer or other smoking-related diseases. [42] Similarly, most adults who experienced frequent CP can say, 'I was spanked and I am OK.' (p. 765)

In short, Straus argues that a reduction or elimination of corporal punishment by non-violent forms of discipline would not only reduce the risk of antisocial behavior in children but would also decrease the levels of violence in American society (Straus et al., 1997, p. 1) and ultimately create a far less violent and punitive world (Straus, 1994b, p. xiii).

Corporal Punishment—Public Pressure, Degradation and Humiliation

Corporal punishment of children is often done in public and a child can experience a double dose of shame: shame/humiliation because one is corporally punished and shame/humiliation because others witness the punishment. Because of the power imbalance between adults and children, children have little recourse to restore their sense of honor or self-worth.

Davis and Kii's (1997) study focused on the naturalistic observations of 250 children hit by adult caretakers in public settings. They emphasize that the detrimental impact of childhood corporal punishment in noneducational public settings has not been adequately explored (p. 4). They surmise that public childhood corporal punishment may affect children differently than being hit in private in that children are more prone to feel humiliated when hit in a public setting (p. 21). Furthermore, they suggest that parents may be "quicker to hit in public than in private" (p.20) to avoid being publicly embarrassed and/or humiliated by the behavior of their children and similarly to avoid giving the impression that they are not in control of their children.

Likewise, those who publicly witness corporal punishment collude in the culturally sanctioned mandate to hit by not intervening. Davis and Kii (1997) note that in their study of children who were corporally punished in public noneducational settings that witnesses distanced themselves from the child being hit by exhibiting outward indifference:

> In addition to failing to register any objections, others in the group can sustain the impression that the hitting has wider support through an outwardly indifferent demeanor....their outward indifference can help define the situation as one in which the child is surrounded by parents and other adults, as well as by siblings and other peers, who agree with what has taken place or who are insufficiently moved to object. (p. 14)

Carson (1986) in screening 1000 parents found only 21 who never hit their children. In fact, Carson (1986) notes that these parents continually felt that they had to defend their position of not hitting their children against the morally accepted cultural norm of spanking (Straus, 1994b, p.51).

This study suggests that childhood corporal punishment especially when witnesses are present is similar in a metaphorical sense to what Garfinkel (1956) has described as a "successful degradation ceremony" or ritual (p.420). Status degradation rituals were utilized in the ancient Mediterranean world to publicly humiliate and degrade the socially unacceptable individual or group of people (Malina and Neyrey, 1991c, p. 107). The early Christians underwent many so called "status-degradation rituals" which frequently were a combination of "verbal abuse" and "physical attacks" (deSilva, 1995, p. 158). Similarly, childhood corporal punishment is usually preceded by verbal threats followed by physical punishment (Davis and Kii, p. 13).

In a successful degradation ceremony the denouncer upholds the values of the community by his or her acts of public degradation of the individual in question. Furthermore, the witnesses show their support for these values by distancing themselves from the one being denounced (Garfinkel, 1956, p.423). The intent of a successful degradation ceremony according to Garfinkel (1956) is to induce shame and to alter a person's identity (p.420). Children who are frequently corporally punished acquire a new identity as a bad person who deserves to be hit. Part III will explore more in-depth the impact of childhood abuse on a person's concept of self, the world and their images of God (Doehring, 1993, Browning, 1991).

Corporal Punishment, Dissociation and the Cycle of Violence

Egeland and Susman-Stillman (1996) note that the earliest writings on child abuse emphasized its intergenerational nature, meaning that abusing parents were frequently victims of childhood abuse. This phenomena of observing that abusing parents often had histories of child abuse led "to the belief in a cycle of abuse across generations (Steele and Pollack, 1968)" (p. 1123). However, the question remains as to why there exists an intergenerational cycle of violence. Egeland and Susman-Stillman (1996) point out that most of the research in this area has focused on the intergenerational rate of transmission which is estimated to be about 30% (p. 1123). Thus the majority of parents do not repeat the cycle of abuse/violence. This section tries to ascertain why some parents who were physically punished as children repeat the cycle and others do not.

There is no doubt from the enormous literature on child maltreatment that child abuse can be harmful psychologically and physically (Ornduff, 1997; Kendall-Tackett, K.A., Williams, L. M., & Finkelhor, D. 1993; Malinosky-Rummell, R., & Hansen, D.J., 1993). Irwin (1996) in a study consisting of 239 Australian adults examined the association between the "perceived availability of emotional support in childhood" and adult dissociative tendencies. The study found that "perceived availability of emotional support in childhood" was a factor but that it "did not eliminate the relationship between childhood trauma and dissociation" (p. 701). Irwin (1996) used the Survey of Traumatic Childhood Events—STCE (Council and Edwards, 1987) to index childhood traumas. The STCE taps 11 types of childhood traumas:

> Interfamilial sexual abuse, extrafamilial sexual abuse, intrafamilial physical abuse, loss related to a friend, loss related to the family, isolation, personal illness or accident, parental divorce/separation and abortion/miscarriage, (extrafamilial) assault, loss of the home, and robbery. (Irwin, 1996, p. 703)

Pertinent to this study was the finding the intrafamilial childhood physical abuse was the highest predictor of dissociation in adulthood (hsr2=.061) even higher than intrafamilial childhood sexual abuse (hsr2=.042) (p. 704).

Physical child abuse and increased dissociative symptoms in adulthood may be a factor in the cycle of violence. A recent study (Pontius, 1997) has identified a new syndrome—Limbic Psychotic Trigger Reaction (LPTR). LPTR is a proposed new syndrome involving the limbic system of the brain. The limbic system from an evolutionary perspective is the historical site of aggression in all mammals involving the hypothalamus and the amygdala (p. 135). In human beings the frontal lobe system (FLS) is considered the evolved new brain which "mediates rule-governed behavior in an appropriate flexible way,"...(p. 135). Pontius (1997) suggests that LPTR patients have an overactive limbic system and an underfunctioning frontal lobe system (p. 127).

In Pontius's (1997) study of 14 homicidal white males it was demonstrated that at the time of the homicidal act they all experienced a "trigger stimuli" which revived past mild to moderate stresses (p. 125). Upon experiencing the "trigger stimuli" the homicidal men entered into a brief psychosis which is described as a partial limbic seizure. The partial limbic seizure was "'kindled' by highly individualized specific trigger stimuli" (p. 125). Other symptoms included flat affect, intact memory of unplanned motiveless homicidal acts, and autonomic arousal (p. 125).

Unclear is the extent to which these homicidal acts were totally without motive. Pontius (1997) highlights the lack of motive and strong emotion in these homicidal men:

> The typically bizarre acts of LPTR lack a motive and are committed with flat affect, in half of the cases against strangers, who unwittingly had provided the specific trigger stimuli (Table 1). For example, LPTR acts are not motivated by revenge, vigilantism, greed, rage, jealousy, envy, fame, or humiliation. (p. 136)

If the specific trigger which stimulated the brief psychosis is one of humiliation it is conceivable that these homicidal men were experiencing bypassed shame which by definition is affectless even though cognitively experienced (Lewis, 1971, Thompson, 1996).

But most pertinent to this study is the finding that "eight of the 14 cases of LPTR had a known history of brain injury" (p. 127). Pontius (1997) notes that head injuries and more specifically closed head injuries, (which was the case in her study) are frequently overlooked. She emphasizes that "...head injury is not necessary for 'seizure kindling' to occur, although it may well facilitate it" (p. 130). Unexplored is the association between childhood head injury caused by corporal punishment/physical abuse and later adult violence. Childhood head injuries may explain why a history of intrafamilial childhood physical abuse is more highly associated with dissociation than with any other form of childhood trauma (Irwin, 1996).

Learning to access coherently one's emotions is crucial to preventing intergenerational abuse (Fonagy et al., 1994). Still a troubling question is why some children repeat violence in adulthood and others do not? Egeland and Susman (1996) through their work with the University of Minnesota Mother-Child Project provide some insight into this age-old question (Jones, 1996, p. 1121). It was not the severity of childhood abuse that determined whether it would be repeated in adulthood. Rather, it was how the child maltreatment was recollected. Those mothers who repeated the cycle of abuse had accounts that "were disjointed and fragmented, sometimes forgetting whole chunks of their lives while at other times eulogizing parts of their childhood, inconsistently" (Jones, 1996, p. 1121). Those who cognitively and affectively remember their own childhood physical abuse may demonstrate greater empathy toward their own children. In other words those who are consciously aware of their own childhood pain may be less likely to inflict it upon their own children.

Studies have shown that parents who abuse their children display lower rates of empathy than non-abusing parents (Feshbach, 1989; Rosenstein, 1995; Marino, 1992; LeTourneau, 1981; Milner et al. 1995). In fact, Wiehe (1997) has suggested that "empathy training" should be a core aim of intergenerational violence prevention. It is a core assumption of this study that empathy is crucial to the prevention and mitigation of intergenerational violence. It an assumption of this study that the self-in-relationship therapeutic model with its emphasis on empathy is a step in that direction.

Summary

Social scientist Murray Straus (1994b) has made a major contribution by empirically documenting the detrimental impact of childhood corporal punishment upon individuals and upon society. Similarly to Greven (1990, 1992), Straus (1994b) believes that corporal punishment is one of the major factors in the cycle of violence in our world today. Straus refers to the family as the "cradle of violence," and his studies show that a childhood history of corporal punishment increases the likelihood that as an adult one will be in a violent relationship and be depressed. In recent studies Straus has shown that even small amounts of corporal punishment are harmful, increasing levels of aggression and may interfere with the internalized development of conscience (p. 144).

Since corporal punishment is often a public event, children can experience a double dose of shame: shame/humiliation because one is corporally punished and shame/humiliation because others witness the punishment. Likewise parents can feel a societal pressure to spank their children as a means of avoiding the public embarrassment/humiliation of being perceived as parents who are not in control of their own children.

Recent studies indicate a possible relationship between childhood physical abuse, dissociation and the cycle of violence or intergenerational violence. Irwin (1996) found that intrafamilial childhood physical abuse was the highest predictor of dissociation in adulthood. Egeland and Susman's (1996) work with the University of Minnesota Mothers-Child Project suggests that it is not the severity of childhood abuse that determines whether it is repeated in adulthood. But rather, those mothers who cognitively and affectively remembered their abuse were less likely to repeat the cycle of abuse.

Building on the works of Helen Block Lewis (1971), Alice Miller (1983, 1984) and Philip Greven (1990, 1992), this study suggests a new term: bypassed child abuse which is a form of dissociation. "Bypassed child abuse" is child abuse that was affectively and /or cognitively repressed in childhood and is overtly expressed emotionally and physically in the behavior of adults against their own children.

Finally, it is a core assumption that empathy is crucial to the prevention and mitigation of intergenerational violence. It is an assumption of this study that the self-in-relationship therapeutic model with its emphasis on empathy provides a model for understanding the role of empathy in childhood.

Part III will examine the religious and theological literature related to shame, images of God and violence.

Part III: Religious and Theological Literature

1. Pastoral Theological Perspectives on Shame

Introduction

Shame has not been considered by theologians during the twentieth century with the exception of Dietrich Bonhoeffer (Patton, 1985) and Rita Nakashima Brock (Fowler, 1993). Many of the pastoral theologians who have written on shame (Capps, 1983, 1995; Patton, 1985; Thompson, 1996; You, 1997) have used almost solely contemporary psychoanalytic and self-psychological definitions of shame, which have tended to be a-contextual. In recent writings, Fowler (1996) has expanded the pastoral theological understanding of shame by emphasizing that shame can also be the consequence of social discrimination. But practically no pastoral theologian has examined the shame/honor system of the first century eastern Mediterranean world and its relationship, if any, to contemporary understandings of shame.

Part III is divided into three sections. The first section examines the contribution of key pastoral theologians to the shame literature. The second section reviews the literature on images of God as it relates specifically to trauma and violence. And the third section enters into conversation with contemporary biblical literature on the shame/honor system of the ancient Mediterranean. The purpose of this section is to gain deeper insight into shame, images of God and its relationship to the intergenerational cycle of violence in contemporary life by examining and dialoguing with these ancient and sacred texts.

James Fowler's Shame Continuum—Healthy Shame to Shamelessness

James Fowler (1993, 1996) has not only built on the works of Carl Schneider (1977), but he has also highlighted the importance of shame in the development of faith (1993, 1996). Fowler asserts that shame is one of the most neglected emotions of the twentieth-century (Fowler, 1996, p. 12). He challenges anthropologist Ruth Benedict's largely unquestioned notion spelled out in her classic study The Chrysanthemum and the Sword (1946) that there are shame cultures, meaning Eastern societies (Japan, China, and Korea) and guilt-oriented societies (meaning Europe and North America). Furthermore, he contends that shame is not only a neglected emotion, it is also a denied emotion, which pervades western society. But most critical for this study is his assertion that it is the denied, invisible aspects of shame, or what Helen Block Lewis (1971) calls "bypassed shame" or what Scheff and Retzinger (1991) call "shame that has gone underground" that becomes a major factor in interpersonal and societal violence:

...Though shame has been more invisible in Western societies in this century, especially in the United States, it pervades our personal and collective lives in ways that underlie a great deal of the self-destructive and violent patterns of our society. (Fowler, 1996, p. 12)

Much of Fowler's understanding of shame is built on the works of Helen Block Lewis (1971), Donald Nathanson (1987, 1992), Silvan Tomkins (1987) as translated by Nathanson, and Carl Schneider (1977). Fowler's definition of shame and differentiation of shame from guilt is based on the works of Helen Block Lewis:

> While guilt is about something one does, shame is about something one is. While guilt brings the judgement of an inner voice for something one has done, shame involves the sense of being seen and exposed as defective or flawed. (p. 12)[11]

Fowler expresses the opinion that shame is more global than guilt, having a greater global impact on our feelings about ourselves than guilt (Fowler, 1996, p. 92). As previously stated David W. Harder (1995) disagrees that shame necessarily affects the self in a more global way than guilt (p. 382). Similarly to Helen Block Lewis's differentiation of shame from guilt, Fowler believes that guilt does not affect a person's deep sense of self worth: "I can do wrong things and still think of myself as a good or worthy person" (p. 92), but when one experiences shame it has a much more global affect upon one's sense of character:

> With shame, however, the negative self-evaluation is more holistic: It is the self I am that I now must perceive as flawed or unworthy.... Shame is the awareness of the self as disclosed to others, or to the self, as being defective, lacking, or inadequate. Shame involves a painful self-consciousness in which we feel exposed to others and to ourselves as deficient, weak, or helpless—and, at worst, contemptible. (p. 92)

Core to Fowler's research is the expansion of Carl Schneider's (1977) seminal theological work on shame. Continuing to develop Schneider's shame categories, Fowler locates shame along a five-step continuum from healthy to unhealthy shame: 1) healthy shame, 2) perfectionist shame, 3) shame due to enforced minority status, 4) toxic shame, 5) and shamelessness. For purposes of this study I will focus on Fowler's understanding of healthy shame as it relates to guilt and conscience, and toxic shame, enforced minority status and shamelessness as it relates to violence.

Building on the work of Carl Schneider (1977), Fowler acknowledges two crucial aspects of healthy shame: discretionary shame and disgrace shame. For Fowler discretionary and disgrace shame serve different functions. Disgrace shame serves as a "custodian of personal worthiness," (p. 111) whereas discretionary

---

[11] Throughout this study I will suggest the analogy: guilt is to sin as shame is to image. Guilt has to do with rules and regulations. Shame has to do with one's core identity, one's image as reflected by God and one's "community of opinion."

shame protects a person's so called membership in valued communities. Disgrace shame helps to protect our sense of worth by refusing to participate in acts that make us feel terrible about ourselves, and discretionary shame helps us to be sensitive to the opinion of valued others (p. 107). For Fowler discretionary shame serves "an indispensable role in the formation of conscience" (p. 13), serving as an inner voice, an instinctive knowing of right from wrong (p. 92):

> Discretionary shame gives us an almost instinctual 'early warning system' that something we are feeling or thinking of doing could lead to the diminishment of self respect, and if known to others, a decrease in their confidence and care in our direction. (p. 114)

Furthermore, Fowler highlights the relational aspect of discretionary shame. Discretionary shame helps to strengthen and maintain the bonds between people and their communities by creating a heightened instinctual sensitivity to the evaluation of others (p. 105):

> This variant of shame includes tact, sensitivity, respect for others, and respect for the values that the self shares with those to whom he or she prizes connection. (p. 104)

The anticipatory aspect of discretionary shame is maintained by what Fowler calls "moral imagination," one's ability to imagine what the evaluative response of others might be given certain actions or non-actions (p. 105).

For Fowler disgrace shame cuts to the core of one's identity, one's character, and one's personhood:

> Disgrace shame, on the other hand, is the pervasive sense of self-disapproval we feel when we have inadvertently or by design done something that reveals us to others— and to ourselves—as unworthy or less than we want to be. Healthy shame in both of these modes constitutes an indispensable foundation for conscience. (p. 114)

Third on Fowler's "continuum of shame experiences" is "Shame Due to Enforced Minority Status," (pp. 118-121) shame that becomes internalized based on social discrimination or what Fowler calls "ascribed"[12] shame. Fowler contends that there is a link between shame and the increase of violence in this country related to interethnic conflict, tensions related to religious authority, gender constructions, sexual orientation and attitudes toward the poor:

---

[12] For Fowler "ascribed" shame has "to do with the social environment's dis-valuing of some qualities over which they have little or no control" (p. 119) such as race, gender, ethnic background, social-economic status etc.

The upsurge of violence and interethnic conflict in this nation and the world can be illumined more broadly by attention to shame in interpersonal and intergroup relations. (p. 94)

Fowler contends that "shame due to enforced minority status has largely been neglected by the popular discussion of shame," (p. 121), and that this kind of shame actually cuts across the entire shame continuum:

> In this respect, it makes sense to view shame due to enforced minority status not so much as a particular form of shame placed on the continuum...but rather as a factor that can be present in accompaniment with any types of shame from 'healthy' to 'perfectionist' to 'toxic' shame, and to 'shamelessness.' As Maya Angelou puts it so graphically, this form of shame, in accompaniment with any of the other forms, 'is the rust on the razor that threatens the throat.' (p. 121)

Fowler reminds us that shame is not necessarily healed by a sole focus on the inner self if shame is a form of social discrimination due to enforced minority status:

> This variant of shame cannot be healed without attention to issues of economic and political justice, equality, and the effective affirmation of inclusiveness in society. (p. 121)

Fourth on Fowler's "continuum of shame experiences" is toxic shame (pp. 122-126). It is under the category of toxic shame that Fowler sees a link between "physical, emotional, and possibly sexual abuse" and shame. Toxic shame, a popular term coined popular by John Bradshaw, is a shame that Fowler feels can break the heart—the core self—"the deepest felt truth of an authentic self" (p. 122).

For Fowler toxic shame can be the result of childhood physical abuse and can contribute to an intergenerational cycle of violence:

> ...As parents themselves they may recycle the violence and abuse of their own childhood due to unconscious identification with the parental aggressors of their own experience and the unrecognized and unaddressed pool of anger carried deep in the memory cells of their bodies. (p. 125)

On the far end of Fowler's shame continuum is what he calls shamelessness—the most destructive form of shame—whose roots Fowler believes lie "in severe disruptions of childhood relations of intimacy and reciprocal love with parents or caregivers" (p. 126). These people are really without conscience:

> In its hardened and extreme forms we are speaking here of the sociopath personality. This is the person who so lacks empathy and compassion, who has such measureless rage that he [sic] can injure or destroy others with little or no feelings of remorse, guilt, or shame. (p.127)

This study takes issue with Fowler's last step in his continuum: shamelessness. Using the example of Charles Manson, Fowler argues that violent offenders are shameless. Manson who was "regularly beaten" during his institutionalized childhood described himself as dead: "I'm already dead, have been dead all my life"...(p. 130). Gilligan (1996) maintains that such violent offenders exhibit such high levels of shame that they have experienced a "death of the self" which denies them access to conscious feelings which are critical to the development of an internalized conscience.

Fowler says that a lack of "affective attunement" (p. 126) by parents "combined with abuse, neglect, and disvaluing treatment" can cripple a person's capacity for "empathic feeling and knowing with others" which Fowler calls conscience[13]. Corporal punishment, which Fowler does not specifically consider, is an example of this lack of "affective attunement."

This study argues that what Fowler is describing is not shamelessness but rather guiltlessness. Both Gilligan (1996) and Tangney (1995a) can be used to critique Fowler by suggesting that violent offenders are not shameless but rather guiltless. As previously noted, empirically Tangney et al. in a series of studies (Tangney, 1995b; Tangney, Wagner, Barlow, Marschall, & Gramzow, 1994; Tangney, Wagner, Fletcher, & Gramzow, 1992) and theoretically Gilligan (1996) have found a correlation between high shame and outwardly "directed anger and hostility" (Tangney et al. 1992, 1994, 1995) and guiltlessness—which is associated with one's inability to manage hostility and anger in a constructive manner.

Fowler, an authority on the works of Erik Erikson, emphasizes that Erikson's first two psychosocial stages "are of enduring importance for understanding the forming of shame in the development of the self" (p. 107). Furthermore, he writes in detail about Erikson's stage two: "autonomy versus shame and doubt," describing it as a time which coincides "with the maturation of the sphincter muscles and with the cultural expectations that children will learn to control the release of bladder and bowels" (p. 109). He further notes that at the same time that this maturation process is going on in the life of the child, parental figures "are trying to establish limits and curb their children's angry outburst"...(p. 109). Fowler does not refer to childhood corporal punishment in relationship to shame. Fowler does acknowledge the link between toxic shame and early childhood "emotional, physical, or sexual abuse" (p. 113).

John Patton—Shame Blocks Guilt

John Patton (1985) has written primarily on shame in the context of forgiveness. Nonetheless, Patton's insight that shame can stand in the way of our

---

[13]What Fowler describes as conscience—a form of "empathic feeling and knowing with others"—Tangney describes as guilt.

ability to acknowledge our guilt is critical in trying to understand why some violent offenders seem to have high levels of shame and low levels of guilt.

> Forgive us our sins—for we acknowledge our shame that we may recognize our guilt. (p. 39)

Like other theorists (Jordan, 1989; Lewis, 1971, 1976, 1987a) Patton views shame as relational and personal and can only be acknowledged in the midst of an empathic relationship.

Patton recognizes Dietrich Bonhoeffer's unique twentieth century theological contribution to the understanding of shame. Reflecting on the Fall in Genesis 3, Bonhoeffer (1955) interprets shame in the context of the human beings' sense of being disconnected from God, being in a state of disunion (p. 43). Patton interprets Bonhoeffer's view of shame essentially as "humankind's grief over its estrangement from God" (p. 43). For Bonhoeffer shame is healed as one regains a sense of connection in relationship to God and others (p.44).

Donald Capps—Theology of Shame

Donald Capps (1993) argues that shame, which he defines as a sense of inner "wrongfulness," is the pastoral theological issue of contemporary society:

> In our times we are much more likely to experience this 'wrongfulness' according to shame, rather than guilt, dynamics. (p. 3)

Shame cuts to the core of a person's sense of self and according to Capps is a major issue in contemporary society although frequently denied as such (p. 96). Capps (1993) focuses on narcissism as a way of demonstrating the negative impact of shame. Narcissism according to Capps is a highly shame-prone personality disorder. He reminds the reader that psychoanalytic theory suggests that narcissism is rooted in pre-Oedipal experience, i.e., before the age of three, and it is related to issues of separation and individuation. This so-called pre-Oedipal age frame corresponds to Erikson's second developmental stage "autonomy vs. shame and doubt" (p. 28). Capps, relying heavily on the theory of Heinz Kohut, traces what he feels happens developmentally during this period of childhood to produce narcissistic adults. Capps traces the etiology of the narcissistic self to inadequate mirroring on behalf of a parent (usually the mother). Inadequate mirroring in essence is a lack of parental warmth and empathy on behalf of the parent toward the child. This faulty parenting produces in the child what Kohut calls the Tragic Self:

> The Tragic Self knows very little guilt, but is well acquainted with feelings of deep shame, which are immobilizing and debilitating. (p.33)

Capps (1993) does not acknowledge a possible relationship between adult shame in narcissistic adults and early childhood corporal punishment. By not questioning Eriksonian and Kohutian assumptions that shame-prone adults were simply deprived of parental warmth and empathy, Capps lost an opportunity of helping others expand their visions of the etiology of adult shame and the impact of childhood corporal punishment on adult functioning. Capps (1983, 1992, 1993, 1995) who has written extensively on shame and child abuse from a theological/biblical perspective has served as an impetus for this study's attempt to examine the relationship between shame and childhood corporal punishment.

Capps (1993) argues that in order for contemporary theology to be relevant it needs to develop a theology of shame. He calls shame the deadliest sin of our time since it instills in people "a deep inner sense of wrongness" (p. 41). People who suffer from narcissistic disorders have frequently been condemned in the church as selfish people rather than being understood as people filled deep down with an inner sense of shame—wrongness—and self-contempt (p. 35).

Capps (1993) correlates shame and our image of self: "shame is a reaction to the failure to live up to one's own self-ideals" (p. 72). Referring to Helen Lynd (1958), Capps argues that shame involves the entire self and unlike guilt cannot be externalized: "We _perform_ guilty actions, but we _are_ our shame" (p. 74). Shame cuts to the core of oneself, "is deeply visceral and gut wrenching; it is usually felt in the pit of the stomach" (p. 75). Capps acknowledges a relationship between shame and violence in stating that the experience of feeling critically exposed by others or humiliated can evoke rage (p. 76). But he goes one step beyond seeing solely a relationship between shame and violence. Quoting Richard Sennett (1980) he concurs that inducing shame can be a form of violence: "Shame has taken the place of violence as a routine form of punishment in Western societies" (Capps, 1993, p. 138).

Theologically Capps (1993) views the shame experience as an experience of isolation and disconnection. Capps reminds the reader that according to Tillich "sin is separation, estrangement from one's essential being" (p. 45). He refers to shame as tragic estrangement. To illustrate his point he quotes from Elie Wiesel's _Night_ in which Wiesel, a teenager in a Nazi concentration camp wishes for the death of his father:

> It was daytime when I awoke. And then I remembered that I had a father. Since the alert, I had followed the crowd without troubling about him. I had known that he was at the end, on the brink of death, and yet I had abandoned him. I went to look for him. But at the same moment this thought came into my mind: 'Don't let me find him! If only I could get rid of this dead weight, so that I could use all my strength to struggle for my own survival, and only worry about myself.' Immediately I felt ashamed of myself forever. (Capps, 1993, p. 81)

He makes an excellent point, noting that whereas it might be helpful in a cathartic sense to talk about a guilty experience, this is not necessarily true of shame (p. 81). Thus we tend to want to hide our experiences of shame for fear of feeling even more shameful or inwardly wrong or defective: "The assumption that self-disclosure makes a person feel better does not always apply to experiences of shame"(p. 82).

Summary

James Fowler, building on Helen Block Lewis's (1971) notion of "bypassed shame," and Scheff and Retzinger's (1991) notion of "shame that has gone underground," believes that it is the denied, unconscious, invisible aspects of shame that become a major factor in interpersonal and societal violence.

Developing Carl Schneider's understanding of disgrace and discretionary shame, Fowler has created a five-step shame continuum from healthy to unhealthy shame (shamelessness). Fowler makes a major contribution to the literature by focusing on shame based on internalized social discrimination, which he refers to as "shame due to enforced minority status." He argues that such shame based on societal discrimination has been basically ignored in the shame literature.

Similarly to other theorists, Fowler acknowledges that shame as the result of childhood physical abuse can contribute to an intergenerational cycle of violence especially if the pain of one's childhood is not recognized or remembered.

This study takes issue with Fowler's last step in his continuum: shamelessness. Fowler argues that violent offenders are shameless. Both Gilligan (1996) and Tangney (1995) can be used to critique Fowler by suggesting that violent offenders are not shameless but rather guiltless.

Finally, Fowler who is both a developmentalist and an authority on Erik Erikson, does not mention childhood corporal punishment in relationship to shame. Fowler does acknowledge the link between toxic shame and early childhood "emotional, physical, or sexual abuse" (p. 113).

John Patton's major contribution is his acknowledgement that shame can stand in the way of acknowledging guilt. This is consistent with others (Gilligan, 1996) who argue, for instance, that violent offenders have high levels of shame and low levels of guilt. Similarly to others, Patton stresses that shame is healed in the midst of empathic relationships.

Donald Capps views shame as an experience of isolation, disconnection and inner "wrongfulness." He calls for a theology of shame to address these issues. Relying on Kohutian and Eriksonian theory, Capps argues that shame has its etiology in "faulty mirroring," a lack of parental warmth and empathy on behalf of the parent toward the child before the age of three. Critical to this study is Capps's acknowledgement of a relationship between shame and violence and his awareness that Western societies routinely use shame tactics as a form of punishment (Capps, 1993, p. 138).

2. Images of God and Violence

Object Relations and Images of God and Violence

By reviewing the works of Miller (1983, 1984), Greven (1977; 1990, 1992), Capps (1992, 1995), Straus (1994b) and Ellison and Sherkat (1993), I have discussed to what extent corporal punishment still has religious meaning. Viewing childhood corporal punishment from an object relations perspective suggests that a child's internal representations of self and others are formed within one's early interpersonal environment and "influence the creation and projection of God image in later life" (Brokaw and Edwards, 1994). Doehring (1993) sees a correlation between childhood abuse and God representations or God images (p. 9). Citing Greven (1990, 1992), Doehring notes how frequently the autobiographical literature of Protestant evangelicals who experienced childhood physical abuse affirmed "both loving and wrathful representations of a God who uses fear and the threat of punishment to obtain obedience" (p. 9).

Doehring (1993) and Browning (1991) argue that deeply embedded within human beings are core metaphors and narratives that orient and inform peoples' world view, concepts of self, and images of God. For instance, traumatization (such as severe corporal punishment) can impact a person's core images of who they are as a person made in God's image (p. 45). Instead of a benevolent image of God, a trusting image of creation endowed with goodness (Niebuhr, R.,1941), and a loving self concept, a severely traumatized person might develop an image of creation as dangerous, terrifying, malevolent and untrustworthy, a self concept of an innately bad person, and a wrathful image of God.

Thus it is a hypothesis of this study that there are relationships among shame, images of God, and the cycle of violence in adults who experienced childhood corporal punishment. By understanding some of the correlations among shame, guilt and images of God, I may be able to differentiate those adults who are more likely to break the cycle of violence.

Spero (1992) and Doehring (1993) as well as other object relations theorists (Rizzuto, 1979; Meissner, 1977, 1978, 1984, 1987; McDargh, 1983) have acknowledged that images of God or God representations are frequently formed in early childhood and are correlated with a child's parental image(s). These God images "may remain static and/or repressed" (Doehring, 1993, p. 6) throughout a person's developmental life. The empirical research on images of God (Lambert, Triandis, and Wolf, 1959; Gorsuch, 1968; Wootton, 1990; Doehring, 1993) will be discussed examining how this literature supports an inter-relationship between violence and God images.

Empirical Research and Images of God and Violence

An important early empirical study on images of God was Lambert, Triandis, and Wolf's (1959) classic cross-societal study in which they hypothesized "that beliefs in the malevolence of the supernatural world reflect punitive practices in infant and child rearing, while beliefs in the benevolence of the supernatural world reflect nurturing practices in infant and child training" (p. 162). Lambert et al. studied nonliterate societies and according to Straus (1994b) they "found that societies that rely on corporal punishment also tend to have a religious system in which deities are punitive" (p. 191). Investigating the "antecedents of aggression" by both direct field study and "from ethnographic reports of 62 societies," (p. 162) the researchers found that there was a significant correlation (p=.05) between the absence of pain inflicted by a careprovider and the image of a non pain inflicting deity (p. 164). There also was a correlation between "high pain in the treatment of infants"[14] and gods who have properties of being capricious—erratic and emotionally impulsive:

> Societies with predominantly aggressive deities and with high pain in the treatment of infants have capricious gods and spirits in six out of seven cases, and the societies with predominantly benevolent deities and with low pain in infant treatment lack capricious gods and spirits in seven out of seven cases (p=<. 004). (p. 167)

They also found that "children in societies with aggressive deities are more self-reliant, more independent, and less nurturing than those in societies with benevolent deities" (p. 166). Even though the Lambert et al.'s (1959) study is a groundbreaking study illustrating the relationship between images of God (God representations) and parental behavior, it is difficult to envision this study as being representative of contemporary cultures.

Spilka, Armatas, and Nussbaum (1964) were the next significant empirical researchers to note "the possible relationship between religious conceptualization and behavior" (Gorsuch, 1968, p. 56). Gorsuch (1968) built specifically on the works of Osgood, Suci, and Tannenbaum (1957) and Spilka et al. (1964). Gorsuch's (1968) study sought to include a sample of both religious[15] and non-religious people given his conviction that there may be a systematically different concept of God held by religious people than by non-religious people.

Gorsuch (1968) identified four major factors involved in the concept of God:
I. Traditional Christian, which consists of two sub-factors—God as

---

[14] In the Lambert et al. (1959) study, "pain inflicted by nurturant agent included such things as cold baths, depilation, and so on, as well as physical punishment" (p. 163).
[15] While Gorsuch doesn't indicate how he distinguished between religious and non-religious people it can be inferred that he is talking about religious practice.

Companionable and God as Benevolent Diety, II. Wrathfulness, III. Omni-ness, and IV. Potently Passive.

The Traditional Christian which Gorsuch considers a "third Order factor" describes a God who is actively engaged with and concerned for humankind (p. 60). According to Gorsuch (1968) this active concern for and involvement with humankind is "reflected in its use of such adjectives as all-wise, divine, firm, glorious, just, kingly, majestic, omnipotent, powerful, real, righteous, sovereign, and strong" (p. 60). Furthermore, the Traditional Christian also embodies a positive image of a Deity who is in essence favorably oriented toward human beings (p. 61). Gorsuch (1968) states that this favorable orientation toward humankind is reflected in the use of such adjectives as "charitable, fair, faithful, fatherly, forgiving, gentle, guiding, helpful, kind, loving, merciful, supporting, and warm" (p. 61).

Lawrence (1991) has criticized Gorsuch's (1988) use of adjectives rather than sentences, arguing that subjects are more likely to respond to "their God concept rather than to their God image" (p. 12). Lawrence refers to the distinction that Rizzuto made in 1970 between God concept and God image at the annual meeting of the Society for the Scientific Study of Religion. Gorsuch had presented his works before this same body a year earlier (p. 12).

Second order factors consist of God as Benevolent Deity and God as Companionable. God as Benevolent Deity embodies simultaneously both a sense of transcendence and immanence. The immanent benevolent deity is described by "such variables as comforting, not distant, forgiving, not impersonal, not inaccessible, loving, merciful, not passive, protective and redeeming" (p. 61). The benevolent deity is similar to the companionable deity except that the companionable deity lacks a sense of transcendence. Gorsuch suggests that there is not only a relationship between the image of a companionable deity and "more liberal and humanistic Christian bodies" but also a relationship between the image of a benevolent deity and religious bodies that hold a more transcendent view of God (e.g., Barthian) (p.64).

The empirical dimension of this study in its investigation of the roots of violence and shame will closely examine the image of God perceived as a benevolent and loving deity. It is an hypothesis of this study that there is a negative association between benevolent images of God and adult partner violence and adult shame, meaning those who display higher levels of benevolent images of God will also display lower levels of adult partner violence and adult shame.

While Gorsuch's (1968) study further identified eight primary factors: kindliness, wrathfulness, deisticness, omni-ness, evaluation, irrelevancy, eternality and potently passive, this study will examine primarily Gorsuch's God concept of benevolent deity and his second major factor of Wrathfulness. According to Gorsuch the concept or image of God as wrathful reflects judgmental, punishing and religiously fundamentalist aspects of God:

One suspects that this factor [the wrathful image of God] would differentiate between those people who are members of the movements which warn mankind [sic] that he [sic] must be careful lest he [sic] be damned to eternal hell and punishment by offending God. For this reason, it would probably differentiate between those with a fundamentalist approach to religion and those who are generally regarded as liberals or humanistic. (p. 61)

Gorsuch's adjectives used to describe a wrathful God are "avenging, blunt, critical, cruel, damning, hard, jealous, punishing, severe, sharp, stern, tough, wrathful" (p. 59). Gorsuch (1968) found that wrathfulness was not related to any other of the primary factors and that it had a reliability of .83 (pp. 61-62).

It is an hypothesis of this study that a wrathful image of God will be positively associated with adult shame and adult violence, meaning those individuals who display higher levels of wrathful images of God will also display higher levels of adult partner violence and adult shame.

Of potential interest to this study on violence are Gorsuch's factors six "Deisticness" and nine "Irrelevancy." It will be interesting to note in this study whether subjects who had experienced physical abuse as children hold an image of God as Deistic as shown in the adjectives "distant, impersonal, inaccessible and passive" and Irrelevant, as shown by the adjectives "feeble and weak"(p. 62). Though not a hypothesis, this study will note whether subjects who had experienced physical abuse as children hold an image of God as not being protective. In other words do adults who were corporally punished/physically-abused hold an image of God of simply not being there to protect them?

Gorsuch (1968) compared his results with those of Spilka, Armatas and Nussbuam (1964) and was able to designate three factors as "firmly established" (p. 62). Two of these factors are factor four Deisticness and Factor five Wrathfulness.

Gorsuch (1968) suggests the need of more "cross-cultural conceptualization of God" given the fact that the general concept used in this study was that of a traditional Christian deity (p. 64).

Unfortunately, nearly twenty years after Gorsuch's (1968) initial conceptualization of a God concept, he still uses unreflectively the adjective "fatherly" to describe God. There seems to be no reflection by Gorsuch (1968; Schaefer and Gorsuch, 1992) of the extent to which God images are typically male dominated in our culture (Foster and Keating, 1992) (Hood, Spilka, Hunsberger, & Gorsuch, 1996). Furthermore, for many women such a fatherly image is related to the continuation of patriarchy, power differentials, abuse and the perpetuation of violence (Brown, J. and Bohn, C., 1989; Daly, M. 1973). Recent research Vergote and Tamayo (1981) has questioned the relationship between "fatherly" and image of God, arguing that there may be even a greater association between a person's image of God and mother.

Also research has suggested that warm and loving relationships with one's parents are positively associated with warm and loving images of God (Godin and Hallez 1964; Potvin 1977) (Hood et al., 1996). This research supports the hypothesis of this study that the behavior of one's parents is related not only to one's images of God but also ultimately to the intergenerational cycle of violence (Mihalie and Elliott, 1997).

According to Doehring (1993), Wootton (1990) building on the works of Hammersela et al. (1986), Spilka et al. (1964) and Gorsuch (1968) "began with four characterizations of God: omni-ness, deisticness, wrathfulness and traditional Christian" (p. 42). Wooton adapted these four dimensions of God and came up with four images of God with the following characterizations: benevolent, malevolent, active or passive:

Loving God—benevolent and active
Observing God—benevolent and passive
Absent God—malevolent and passive
Wrathful God—malevolent and active (Doehring, 1993, p. 42).

In his study Wootton (1990) administered three scales: Adjective Characterization of God Task (ACGT), Wootton Metaphor Characterization of God Task (WMCGT), and Wootton Adjusted Ranking Characterization God Task (WARCGT) to a sample of 101 undergraduates (Doehring, 1993, p. 43).

The results of his study were that the loving and wrathful scales were supported as valid categories and the observing and absent scales were not (Doehring, 1993, p. 43). Perhaps of most value to this study is the fact that "Wootton's three measures of God representation have scales for loving and wrathful God representations that have been shown to be valid" (Doehring, 1993, p. 45) even though there still appears to be as Doehring (1993) states "no standardized or even widely used instruments for measuring God representations" (p. 45).

Building specifically on Wootton (1990), Doehring's (1993) psychodynamic study examined the "inter-relationship between experiences of childhood and adolescent abuse, and the way women as adults consciously describe God" (p. 1). Her sample consisted of 47 women who volunteered for this study. They ranged in age from 21 to 58 years (Doehring, 1992, p.v).

In this study Doehring used the term God representations to describe her subjects' "conscious and unconscious images of God" (p.5):

A God representation is a type of object representation. The term, object representation, is used by psychodynamic psychologists to describe the way people psychically, or internally, represent someone (the external object) with whom they are in relation. (p. 5)

Doehring (1993) further builds explicitly on the works of Gorsuch (1968) and Wootton (1990) by using their categories to describe peoples' conscious images of God or God representations. Furthermore, her study specifically employed Wootton's (1990) "four basic types of God representations" to describe God: the loving God, the observing God, the absent God, and the wrathful God (Doehring, 1993, p. 8).

Doehring (1993) hypothesized a positive relationship between wrathful God and absent God representations and traumatization. In essence, those subjects who experienced higher levels of childhood and adolescent abuse would display higher levels of wrathful God and absent God representations or images of God. Likewise she hypothesized a negative relationship between loving God representations and observing God representations. In essence, those subjects who experienced higher levels of childhood and adolescent abuse would display lower levels of loving and observing God representations or images of God.

Results of her study found that childhood and adolescent traumatization— whether it be sexual abuse, the witnessing of domestic violence and/or physical abuse (Doehring, 1992, p. 1)—is only related to God representations or images of God when it is severe (p. vi). Doehring (1992) interpreted these findings in two ways:

> A simple interpretation of these findings was that traumatization is not inter-related with God representations until it is severe. A more complex interpretation is that traumatization is inter-related with God representations and this inter-relationship is repressed, until traumatization is severe. (p. vi-vii)

One possible critique of Doehring's (1993) study on childhood and adolescent traumatization and representations of God is a very subtle tendency in her theory to assume that the child who has been traumatized in some ways bears some responsibility because of innate personality factors (p. 3), lower levels of psychological functioning and or poorly developed coping skills (p. 12). For instance, Doehring explains what can appear as a hierarchical view of human development:

> The assumption I am working with is that rigid, limited God representations represent a lower or frozen level of development, while flexible, complex God representations correspond to a higher level of development. (p. 51)

However, to her credit Doehring cites leading trauma specialists: (van der Kolk, 1987 and Herman, 1992) to support her claim that, indeed, preexisting personality factors and internal dispositions may be related to a person's ability to cope with trauma. Furthermore, early childhood trauma may have a constricting impact on adult functioning (Herman, 1992). Upon an initial reading of Doehring (1993) one might conclude that her psychodynamic orientation unknowingly pathologizes even the victims of childhood and adolescent trauma (Stone Center) by subtly suggesting that "limited God representations" represent a lower level of human development because of a person's "constitutional endowment" (p.3). Yet Doehring (1995) makes it crystal clear that we must not judge people's "God images and the relationships they depict" (p. 114) because these God images may be a necessary coping mechanism:

> Individuals who cope with traumatization through rigid God representations may find some sort of relief in preserving their parental and God representations as good, and in creating a world where strict punitive laws order life...Such religious systems may serve as a protection against the primitive imagery and may create an external structure for the self. (p. 115)

However, a word of caution must be noted. Adults who experienced childhood trauma may experience some relief in "preserving their parental and God representations as good" (p. 115). Nonetheless the University of Minnesota Mother—Child Project found that mothers who had experienced childhood abuse and who inconsistently "eulogized parts of their childhood" were at greater risk of abusing their own children (Jones, 1996, p. 1121).Finally, Gorsuch (1988) and Kirkpatrick (1986) have been critical of psychodynamically oriented research of "representations of God or images of God" arguing that this research is flawed:

> ...These psychodynamic approaches tend to focus on the underlying psychoanalytic explanation of the origin of God concepts, and the relevant psychodynamic research has been criticized for serious methodological and conceptual problems, as well as an inadequate theoretical basis. (Hood, Spilka, Hunsberger, and Gorsuch, 1996, p. 55)

A multi-method research approach may be able to address such concerns without resorting to the blanket dismissal of any one theory and/or methodology as being inherently flawed.

Summary

As the review of the literature demonstrates, there is a relationship between childhood abuse and images of God. In fact, a severely traumatized child is likely to develop not only a self-concept as an innately bad person, but also an image of God as wrathful and/or punitive.

Lambert, Triandis and Wolf's (1959) classic cross-societal study found a relationship between the reliance upon corporal punishment of children and the image of punitive deities. Other researchers—Spilka, Armatas, and Nussbaum (1964) have noted a relationship between religious conceptualization and behavior.

This present study specifically examines Gorsuch's (1968) concept of a benevolent deity. It is an hypothesis of this study that there is a negative association between benevolent images of God and adult partner violence and shame, meaning those who display higher levels of benevolent images of God will also display lower levels of adult partner violence and adult shame.

This present study also specifically examines Gorsuch's (1968) concept of a wrathful deity. Gorsuch's image of God as wrathful reflects judgmental, punishing and religiously fundamentalist aspects of God. Furthermore, it is an hypothesis of this study that a wrathful/punitive image of God will be positively associated with adult shame and adult violence, meaning those individuals who display higher levels of wrathful/punitive images of God will also display higher levels of adult partner violence and adult shame.

Though not a hypothesis, this study will note whether subjects who had experienced physical abuse as children hold an image of God as not being protective. In other words do adults who were corporally punished/physically-abused hold an image of God as simply not being there to protect them?

Current research supports the hypothesis of this study that the behavior of one's parents is related not only to one's images of God but also ultimately to the intergenerational cycle of violence (Mihalie & Elliott, 1997).

3. Biblical/Theological Perspectives on Shame, Images of God and The Cycle of Violence

Introduction

This final section explores biblical material in the area of shame, violence and images of God. As noted earlier, the bible has been used by some Christians, especially evangelical and fundamentalist Christians to support the use of corporal punishment. Thus it is important to acknowledge that biblical literature has been given a role in the formation of a culture which engages in and justifies the use of corporal punishment. It would be negligent not to explore the use of the bible when the topic is corporal punishment and its relationship to shame, violence and images of God. The intent of this section is not to counter those Christians who use the bible to justify childhood corporal punishment by giving an alternative interpretation of the texts they use or finding other texts that would be the opposite of the texts they use. Nor is the intent of this section one of exploring primary sources or providing an exegetical component. Rather, this section reviews biblical material in the area of shame and violence and images of God by a group of highly regarded scholars who approach the texts sociologically, politically, theologically and simply in terms of Christian community life.

This section reviews perspectives on scripture, perspectives that are primarily descriptive rather than prescriptive. That is, those who support corporal punishment by using certain texts do so in a prescriptive way. The biblical literature that is reviewed in this section is descriptive, describing what the biblical literature was about in the world of that day. Thus this section offers an alternative way of approaching biblical material from that of evangelical/fundamentalist Christians who use a prescriptive approach. Whereas biblical texts in the hands of some Christians justify corporal punishment by their prescriptive perspective, the descriptive perspective that is offered in this section provides an alternative approach to the problem of the cycle of violence. The descriptive approach shows that the bible can provide insight into violence prevention. By examining the early Christian community as presented by deSilva (1995) one is presented an alternative perspective on how to break the cycle of corporal punishment and angry paternal images of God by urging "communities of encouragement" that counter cultural structures of shame and shaming.

The problem of the relationship of shame, images of God and the cycle of violence is as old as the Greco-Roman society, a society that is reflected directly and indirectly in biblical material. Because a scriptural understanding of human nature informs our entire Judeo-Christian heritage, this section explores the meaning of shame/violence in light of the certain values of the Mediterranean world (Pitt-Rivers, 1966, 1974; Baroja, 1966), and more specifically in light of current biblical research (Huber, 1983; deSilva 1995; Malina and Neyrey 1991a, 1991b, 1991c; Crossan, 1992).

According to contemporary biblical scholars (deSilva 1995; Malina and Neyrey 1991a, 1991b, 1991c; Crossan, 1992) shame played a significant role in the culture of the Greco-Roman Mediterranean world. For instance, the early Christian community was hated, shamed, persecuted, degraded and physically abused (deSilva, p. 152) for not conforming to the value system and God images of the dominant Greco-Roman culture. DeSilva presents the thesis that in order to survive shame and persecution, the early Christian community as depicted in the Epistle to the Hebrews maintained an alternative view of God.

In essence, the early Christian community provided an alternative image of God that offered them another way of looking at the status based shame/honor system of the dominant Greco-Roman culture. New Testament scholar David deSilva (1995) argues that by refusing to have their identity defined by the approval or disapproval of the Greco-Roman culture, the early Christian community as depicted in the Epistle to the Hebrews reversed the dominant shame/honor system. Thus these early Christians became proud of being a part of what the culture regarded as shameful and taught each other how to "despise shame" (Hebrews 12:2).

According to deSilva (1995) these early Christians as depicted in the Epistle to the Hebrews were able to resist the degrading and abusive value judgements of them by the dominant Greco-Roman society by having their identity redefined by what they viewed as God's "court of opinion" or "court of reputation." According to deSilva (1995) the first century Mediterranean world was a shame sensitive culture (p. 5). Shame/honor was a major dynamic not only in the lives of biblical people, but also in the cultural discourse of antiquity (Johnson, 1986). Malina and Rohrbaugh (1992) have emphasized that Mediterranean people were "'other oriented' people" who depended "on others to provide them a sense of who they were" (p.21).

Shame was reputation related and other focused (deSilva, 1995; Huber, 1983). The opinion of valued others was highly significant in this world (Malina and Rohrbaugh, 1992). Cultural-anthropologist Julian Pitt-Rivers (1966, 1974) develops this theme by depicting a Mediterranean person whose self is valued only in relationship with certain social groups. Pitt-Rivers describes the opinion of significant others as one's "court of reputation" (p. 27), "that body of significant others to whom one looks for approval (honor) or disapproval (shame)" (deSilva, p. 25).

The following review is divided into four sections. The first section reviews the seminal work of Lyn Betchel Huber (1983). The second section reviews aspects of the work of Pitt-Rivers (1966, 1974) because he has provided a model used by certain New Testament scholars (Malina and Neyrey, 1991a, 1991b, 1991c) who are currently writing about shame and honor. Section three reviews the works of Malina and Neyrey (1991a, 1991b, 1991c). Section four reviews the work of deSilva (1995) who serves as a violence prevention model for this book. In the summary I will discuss how the work of deSilva (1995) brought into dialogue with that of Donald Klein can serve as a violence prevention model.

Lyn Bechtel Huber –The Biblical Experience of Shame/Shaming

Lyn Bechtel Huber's (1983) dissertation provides some of the earlier research on shame in the Hebrew scriptures. Huber found a sparsity of biblical research on shame and attributed the apparent lack of research to western society's guilt orientation (Patton, 1985, p. 42). Her study served as a source for pastoral theologian John Patton's (1985) early work on shame. Huber's study addresses two important questions: the importance of shame in ancient Israel as a part of the social and religious experience, and the functional role of shame/shaming within that society (p. 3). It is the functional role of shame/shaming that is most critical to this study.

Methodologically Huber (1983) employs both a psychoanalytic and social anthropological understanding of shame. Critical to this study is her differentiation between shame and shaming. The psychoanalytic perspective focuses on the individual experience of the emotion shame, while the social anthropological perspective demonstrates "how the 'sanction of shaming' functions within the social structure of various societies" (p. 7).

For Huber (1983) shame is an emotional response while shaming is "the stimulus/sanction/action" (p. 5). In other words "shaming" is the act of trying to inflict shame on another person or group of people. Huber's study emphasizes that "shaming" in biblical society served the function of punishment; in essence, to shame is to punish. Shaming is more subtle than other forms of punishment (e.g. physical), but not necessarily less destructive.

Huber's (1983) study of biblical shame is not exhaustive. But it does present a critical analysis of the strengths and weaknesses of the arguments of a variety of seminal scholars interested in the topic of how shame is represented in the bible (p. 11). Huber begins her study by reviewing the work of Johannes

Pedersen (1926) and David Daube (1969) referring to their works as the "cultural approach." She then reviews the works of Klofenstein (1972) and Seebass (1970) which she refers to as the "philological approach." Finally, her appendix focuses on a contemporary understanding of "the social experience of shame/shaming" which highlights psychoanalytic thinkers.

Core to Pedersen's (1926) argument is his insight that shame in biblical Israel is interrelated with honor. For Pedersen both shame and honor are conditions of the soul (p. 12). Shame empties the soul whereas honor fills it (p. 12). Honor implies a certain superiority whereas shame implies inferiority (p. 16).

David Daube (1969) noted the interconnectedness between shame and reputation in the Deuteronomic Code. Daube points out that the opinions of others, "'what other people think'" (p. 19) were strong motivators to avoid "shameful appearances in the eyes of others (Deut 17:2; 21:1, 22:22; 23:13-15),"(p. 19). Huber (1983) criticizes both Pedersen (1926) and Daube (1969) for not having a working definition of shame. But one could also criticize Huber for importing a contemporary working definition of shame—a psychoanalytic one—into these ancient texts. Probably Daube's (1969) greatest contribution was his insight that shame especially in the Deuteronomic Code is related to one's public image in the eyes of others and in the eyes of God. This insight becomes a core theme through much of recent New Testament literature, which sees shame as a pivotal ancient Mediterranean value.

In reviewing the works of Klopfenstein (1972) and Seebass (1970), Huber (1983) makes her case that shame and guilt are separate emotional reactions in the biblical literature. Huber emphatically states that there is no linguistic "connection in Hebrew between shame and guilt" (p. 55). Unlike Seebass (1970), Klofenstein (1972) understands shame as a manifestation of guilt: "God shames to prove guilt, to punish, or to make people conscious of the guilt" (p. 27). Again the act of shaming is intimately tied to punishment.

Critical to this study is Seebass's notion that shame/shaming "can lower a person's social status" (Huber, 1993, p. 37). Huber argues that it is this aspect of being "brought low or down" that is critical to her analysis of "the function of shame/shaming in Israelite society" (p. 50) as a form of social control (p. 56).

In the ancient Mediterranean world defeating a person or group in diplomacy or war was frequently used as a shaming tactic (pp. 64-66). Shaming actions tend to have an inhibiting, distancing and silencing effect (pp.58 ff.). Huber (1983) points out that shame in biblical Israel frequently involved power differentials, meaning the defeated or shamed person is powerless and inferior while the shamer is powerful and superior (p. 76). Huber (1983) argues that in ancient Israel shaming tactics were used to strip people of their human dignity by making them feel vulnerable, subjugated, defenseless, and inferior. Such an experience was a violation of pride, stripping people of their sense of self-worth and dignity (p. 92) and ultimately functioning as a form of social control and punishment.

Huber (1983) emphasizes the degree to which shame/honor in the ancient world was status-oriented and dependent on the opinion of others. Thus recognition, honor, respect in the eyes of others gives a person more status, a sense of superiority and dominance (p. 93). This heavy dependence on the opinion of others was also fraught with difficulty in the sense that one's reputation in the eyes of others—being shamed or honored—had to be continually sustained:

> One way of maintaining status is by lowering the status of other threatening people. (p. 93)

Huber (1983) refers to this need to shame others to maintain one's own status as the "see saw" effect of shame (p. 94):

> Humiliating others lowers them into an inferior position in the opinion of others, and consequently raises the shamer in status. (p. 94)

A shamed person may act aggressively in order to gain greater power and status. Thus in biblical Israel shaming can frequently be used for one's own advantage, heightening one's status by lowering the status of someone else (p. 115).

Core to Huber's (1983) understanding of the function of shame/shaming in biblical society is Daube's observation that in the legal policies of Deuteronomy there is a general concern for reputation and "what other people think" (p. 98). This intense focus on "opinion of others," makes people vulnerable to the function of shame/shaming as a form of social control.

The threat of being publicly shamed was three fold: the threat of emotional lack of support, the threat of rejection, and the threat of abandonment. This threat could entail both human and divine rejection and abandonment. To illustrate her point, Huber makes reference both to Job (p. 112) and Jeremiah as two major biblical figures who depended on their relationship with God and/or their "social group for identity, status, and esteem" (p. 119).

When Job perceived that God stripped him of his honor, he became more vulnerable to the shaming of his friends. In essence, he was no longer buoyed by the esteeming positive divine regard. In this ancient Mediterranean world, misfortune became a sign of God's disapproval "for which a person should feel shame" (p. 111). Job lost the support of his friends because they felt that he must have sinned given his obvious misfortune (p. 112).   Jeremiah illustrates the shame/violence spiral. Jeremiah's "reaction to his shaming is to take revenge or save face for having been shamed" (p. 119):

> Let my persecutors be shamed,
> but do not let me be shamed;
> let them be dismayed,
> but do not let me be dismayed;

> bring on them the day of disaster;
> destroy them with double destruction.(Jer. 17:18)![16]

Huber argues that Jeremiah's attempt to save face by having his adversaries shamed is the way that he attempts to regain his status and dominance (p. 120). Shaming serves the function of punishment with the intent of righting a wrong.

In her final chapter, Huber (1983) suggests that one of the ways people feel shamed by God is by holding an image of an abandoning God (p. 148):

> It is commonly believed in the ancient Near East that defeat and misfortune suffered at the hands of an enemy are the result of being abandoned by one's god (cf. 2 Kgs 18: 11-12, Jer 29: 15-19). (p. 148)

Thus it is shameful to feel either abandoned or rejected by God (p. 151).

Huber (1983) points out to what extent the Deuteronomistic theology was based on a reward and punishment principle—reward for good behavior and punishment for bad behavior:

> ...An aspect of the Deuteronomistic theology of reward and punishment is protection from shaming for the faithful as a reward for their faithfulness, and the putting to shame of the wicked, godless people as punishment for not honoring God and not upholding his [sic] teachings. (p. 156-157)

To build her case Huber (1983) cites Karen Horney (1950) acknowledging her important contribution in understanding a shame and violence cycle. [17] Horney explained the human impulse to take revenge on the shamer for his or her humiliation (p. 159). This face saving act of revenge is an attempt on the part of the humiliated person to restore his or her pride (p. 159).

Huber (1983) notes the correlation between anger and shame:

> And one of the reactions to being shamed is anger. This anger is expressed in the emphatic call for vengeance on those who have done the shaming. So in the call for vengeance there is an important venting of outrage. (p. 160)

The people of Israel had an image of God as the one who protects the righteous from undeserved shaming, and controls the behavior of the people by shaming/punishing the unrighteous (p. 166). In this ancient Mediterranean world everyone is perceived as being vulnerable to the effects of shame, even God. The behavior of the people of Israel can even be embarrassing for God:

---

[16] It is an assumption of this study that just as there is "an eye for an eye cycle of violence," there is also "a shame for a shaming" cycle of violence.

[17] Huber's tendency of using 20th century European concepts as a lens to look at Deuteronomistic theology is problematic because of the different cultural contexts.

...Israel is concerned about what her neighbors think, about how her neighbors perceive God. The possibility of a shameful reputation, instead of an honorable one, is held up before God as a motivation for him [sic] to protect and preserve them. (p. 170)

The point Huber (1983) attempts to make is that when one is concerned about one's reputation, one is more vulnerable to shame/shaming.

Huber (1983) concludes her seminal study by restating her thesis "that shame/shaming is a major social and religious concern within biblical society," (p. 203). In fact, drawing on Stendahl (1976), Huber argues that the strong emphasis on a "guilty conscience" is a Western society phenomenon which is simply not true of biblical society which was far more shame related with its concern for public approval or a "court of opinion" (p. 204). The people yearned for a "court of opinion" which would provide a sense of acceptance, honor, relatedness, belonging and significance. Huber (1983) insightfully notes that it was Israel's sense of "divine election" that provided such a esteeming "court of opinion":

> The doctrine of election means that no matter how insignificant, inferior, or shamed people may feel in relation to other people, they nevertheless belong and are accepted, supported, protected, and made to feel worthy by God. (p. 208)

In essence, the doctrine of divine election shielded the people of Israel from the shaming effects of the outer culture, thus enabling the people of Israel to be psychologically immune to its destructive and debilitating impact.

To her detriment, Huber (1983) methodologically employs contemporary definitions of shame and guilt from the psychoanalytic literature without critically reviewing them. For instance, she embraces the psychoanalytic developmental perspective that the origin of shame is a child's sexual curiosity (p. 34). Like most writers coming from a psychoanalytic perspective, there is no awareness on Huber's part that shame might also be developmentally linked, for example, to childhood corporal punishment. Thus like others in the psychoanalytic tradition (Freud, Erikson, Nathanson,) she wears "perceptual blinders" when it comes to perceiving that adult shame may have roots in childhood corporal punishment. To her credit Huber does note that "shame (the emotional experience or the emotional response) is often accompanied by the social sanction of shaming (the action that causes shame)" (p. 34). Yet her statements about biblical Israel and its shame/honor system tend to be global and seen through the lens of psychoanalytic thinking.

Furthermore, psychoanalytically oriented Huber (1983) never once mentions the seminal work of Pitt-Rivers (1966, 1968) whose understanding of the shame/honor system of the Mediterranean world has become the model for the New Testament scholarship of Malina & Neyrey (1991a, 1991b, 1991c) and deSilva (1995).

Pitt-Rivers—Shame—A Cultural-Anthropological Perspective

Pitt-Rivers, a cultural-anthropologist, has had an invaluable impact on current biblical thinking about the role of shame and honor in the patronage system of the ancient Mediterranean world. Using a global perspective, Pitt-Rivers examines "the notion of honour in the literature of Western Europe," and more contextually examines shame and honor through his intensive field work within Andalusian society (Peristiany, J. G., 1966, 1974, p. 12). Pitt-Rivers (1966, 1974) admits that his study gives an overview of shame and honor rather that considering "differences between countries and epochs" (p. 38). His broad-brush stroke approach is one of the major liabilities of his work especially as it is used and interpreted by others.

Pitt-Rivers (1966, 1974) emphasizes the dyadic and evaluatory nature of honor and how it is related to shame and status:

> Honor is the value of a person in his [sic] own eyes but also in the eyes of his [sic] society. (p. 21)

Shame is interrelated to honor with the notion that "to be put to shame is to be denied honor," (Pitt-Rivers, 1968, p. 504). Honor according to Pitt-Rivers is either ascribed or achieved, meaning one either inherits honor because of one's family of origin or one achieves honorable status because of one's own efforts. It is always about status and can be extremely competitive. Achieved honor frequently comes at the expense of others who are dishonored and/or humiliated (Pitt-Rivers;1966,1974, p.24). In fact, Pitt-Rivers (1968) argues that honor and dishonor (shaming) is actually how people compete for reputation (p. 504):

> Hence, honor is not only the internalization of the values of society in the individual but also the externalization of his [sic] self-image in the world. (p. 504)

However, in this Mediterranean patronage system, honor is never really achieved alone but rather because of one's connections. In fact, according to Pitt-Rivers (1966, 1974) the patronage system is held together by service and protection:

> In the struggle for life success depends in reality upon the ability, much less to defend one's rights against equals, than to attract the favor of the powerful. (p. 58)

Even though honor is a contest between equals, Pitt-Rivers (1966, 1974) clearly sees power dynamics in shame/honor societies (p. 57). For instance, commands from a superior are not necessarily humiliating. A superior who is dishonored or shamed by an inferior can choose to ignore the insult (p.31). It is exactly this ability to ignore shame or "despise shame" that David deSilva

(1995) argues is how the early Christian community as portrayed in the Epistle to the Hebrews survived the humiliating insults of the dominant culture.

Core to this work is Pitt-Rivers's notion of the intimate tie between honor and the physical body: "Any form of physical affront implies an affront to honor since the 'ideal sphere' surrounding a person's honor...is defiled" (p. 25). Thus Pitt-Rivers describes in broad-brush strokes the "Mediterranean person" of rural Andalusia as living by a spoken or unspoken "code of honor" which mandates that physical affronts need to be avenged or punished (p. 26). In this ancient Code of Honor a physical affront or an insult that is not avenged or punished can be seen as an act of cowardice and/or dishonor (pp. 26-28). Again Pitt-Rivers describes a generic and almost universal shame/honor system in which there is a belief that honor can be vindicated by physical violence (p. 29).

Not only is honor/shame intimately tied to the physical body, it is also intimately tied to public opinion or what Rivers (1966, 1974) calls "the court of reputation," a powerful tribunal whose negative pronouncements can kill: "For this reason it is said that public ridicule kills" (p. 27). For Pitt-Rivers shame is primarily concerned about reputation: "It is what makes a person sensitive to the pressure exerted by public opinion" (p. 42). Honor is about one's reputation in the eyes of others (Pitt-Rivers, 1968, p. 504). Pitt-Rivers (1966, 1974) emphasizes the sense of collective honor or shame:

> ...The dishonorable conduct of one reflects upon the honor of all, while a member shares in the honor of his group. 'I am who I am' subsumes 'whom I am associated with.' (p. 35)

Pitt-Rivers (1968) further argues that "the group defines a person's essential nature,":

> ...The family is the repository of personal honor, for honor is hereditary, not merely in its aspect as social status but also with regard to the moral qualities, which attach to it. Therefore, the dishonor cast on one member is felt by all. (p. 506)

Pitt-Rivers (1968) suggests that honor resides on the boundary between one's self image and one's perceived societal image of self. Finally honor according to Pitt-Rivers (1966, 1974) has a dual aspect—honor aspired to and honor as reflected back upon oneself by the society:

> To be dishonored is to be rejected from the role to which one aspired. 'I am who I am' is answered: 'You are not who you think you are.' (p. 72)

In such a shame/honor system the head of the group may symbolize honor for the entire group, and then it becomes the group responsibility to defend the honor of this particular person (p. 36).

The greatest flaw with Pitt-Rivers's (1966, 1968) works is not necessarily his original theory but rather how his theory has been interpreted and used. The greatest criticism perhaps should be leveled at those scholars who have used Pitt-Rivers as a model. It is questionable whether Pitt-Rivers's model of a Mediterranean person has any bearing on a person in the ancient Mediterranean world of 2000 years ago (deSilva, 1995, p. 22). There is also a concern that scholars who use Pitt-Rivers's model might describe a so-called "generic Mediterranean person" (deSilva, 1995, p. 18). It is important to emphasize that Pitt-Rivers (1966, 1974) acknowledged that what is perceived as honorable or dishonorable can differ from culture to culture:

> The individual's worth is not the same in the view of one group as in that of another, while the political authorities may view him [sic] in a different light again. (p. 22)

Nonetheless, he took a "transcultural" perspective in describing a generic shame/honor system and not describing specific cultures and epochs (Pitt-Rivers; 1966, 1974, p. 38).

Malina and Neyrey—Shame in the New Testament—A Social Scientific Approach

In 1986 Bruce Malina and Jerome Neyrey became part of a group of scholars whose intent was to utilize a social scientific approach to the interpretation of biblical texts (Neyrey, 1991, p. ix). The purpose was not to abandon the historical critical method but rather to expand it by utilizing the "social sciences in the task of understanding biblical texts in their full cultural context" (p. ix).

Pertinent to this study is Neyrey's (1991) awareness that methodologies are like lenses, which lend a certain perspective (p. xv). But no one model, methodology or perspective is all seeing:

> As a rule, people carry in their heads one or more models of 'society' and 'human being' which greatly influence what they look for in their experiences, what they actually see, and what they eventually do with their observations by way of fitting them along with other facts into a larger scheme of explanation. (Malina, 1991, p. 15)

Malina and Neyrey (1991a) building on the work of Pitt-Rivers claim that the pivotal values in the Mediterranean world are those of honor and shame. In essence, honor is self-worth confirmed by one's social group:

> Honor is the positive value of a person in his or her own eyes plus the positive appreciation of that person in the eyes of his or her social group. In this perspective honor is a claim to positive worth along with the social acknowledgment of that worth by others. Honor is linked with 'face' ('saving face') and 'respect.' At stake is how others see us, and so, how we see ourselves. (p. 26-27)

Building specifically on Pitt-Rivers, they argue that honor can only be understood in examining issues of power, gender, and precedence[18] (Malina and Neyrey, 1991a, p. 26, 41) within particular societal contexts:

> What is honorable is what people consider valuable and worthy.... Consequently, what might be deviant and shameful for one group in one locality may be worthy and honorable for another. (p. 26)

They further differentiate between ascribed honor and acquired honor: the former is inherited honor, such as wealth received, and the latter is earned honor, such as wealth obtained (p. 28). Finally, honor in the ancient Mediterranean world is a contest amongst equals for self-esteem and power (p. 30).

Pertinent to this study is Malina and Neyrey's (1991a) view of the intimate tie between honor and "one's physical person" (p. 35). Similarly to Pitt-Rivers (1966, 1968) they argue that an attack on a person's physical body is insulting and requires a response:

> A physical affront is a challenge to one's honor; unanswered it becomes a dishonor in the judgement of the people who witness the affront. A physical affront symbolizes the breaking of required social and personal boundaries, the entering of a person's bodily space without permission. (Malina and Neyrey, 1991a, p. 35)

Shame/honor societies evolve around the axis of public opinion: "public praise can give life and public ridicule can kill" (p. 36). Thus the witnesses to any kind of physical affront become critical in evaluating the degree to which one is dishonored or shamed by such an event (Malina and Neyrey, 1991a, p. 35). The cycle of violence is perpetuated by a belief within the Code of Honor system that when one is dishonored or shamed it is critical for that person to find a way to restore his or her honor (Malina and Neyrey, 1991a, p. 35). And because there is a collective sense of honor even "when God's agents the prophets are dishonored, God is dishonored" (Malina and Neyrey, 1991a, p. 60). Frequently the solution to insulting violence is insulting violence in return. And in the Code of Honor system especially a public insult to a family member or a god must be answered and dealt with.

Malina and Neyrey (1991a) clearly differentiate honor from shame. Honor "means a person's (or group's) feelings of self-worth and the public, social acknowledgment of that worth.... The basis of one's reputation, of one's social standing"... (p. 44). They argue that men are more honor conscious and women are more shame conscious:

---

[18] Precendence for Malina and Neyrey (1991a) means an internalized sense of worth that one has because of inherited status, being born into a certain family and/or holding a position of power. Thus the king of the nation (or the father of the family) simply cannot be dishonored within the group; he is above criticism. What he is guarantees the evaluation of his action. Any offense against him only stains the offender (p. 41).

(a) For males, shame is the loss of honor; shame, then, is a negative experience, as in being shamed; (b) for females, shame is the sensitivity to and defense of honor; female shame (having shame), then is a positive value in a woman; a woman branded as 'shameless' means for a female what being shamed means for a male. (p. 41-42)

In a sense they argue that for males shame or being shamed has a negative connotation in that it has to do with one's lack of self-worth and for women shame has a positive connotation since it is a form of conscience which continually sensitizes one to the opinion of others as in patriarchy (p. 44).

Is It Possible for Outsiders To See As The Natives See?

A critical review of the works of Malina and Neyrey (1991a, 1991b, 1991c) is offered by New Testament scholar David deSilva (1995). De Silva cautions against seeing shame/honor in every Mediterranean interaction at the risk of suppressing other important meanings and dynamics (pp. 11-12). De Silva (1995) reminds the reader that not all biblical scholars are convinced of the value of such a multi-method approach as employed by Malina and Neyrey:

They question the adequacy of modern social-scientific constructions for the interpretation of ancient texts. Frequently, they suggest that forcing everything in the ancient literature into the one axis of honor and shame results in the suppression of other equally important dimensions of language. (p. 11)

However, Malina and Neyrey (1991a, 1991b, 1991c) obviously believe that such a multi-method approach[19] will help the contemporary reader to have greater insight into the meaning of ancient texts.

Using a social psychological framework, Malina and Neyrey view honor and shame as the "pivotal values" through which the contemporary reader can understand life in the ancient Mediterranean world (Neyrey, 1991, p. xvii). Yet the contemporary reader might ask: "So what, why go back in time and try to see as the natives saw, value what they valued, understand what they understood" (paraphrase) (deSilva, 1995, p. 11). For Malina and Neyrey (1991a, 1991b, 1991c) in their study on shame and honor in Luke-Acts the reasoning is clear. They argue that by becoming sensitized "to another culture and its social structures, careful readers inevitably learn more about their own society by way of contrast" (Neyrey, 1991, p. xviii). The contrast is clear for Malina and Neyrey (1991a); the first-century Mediterranean person is dependent on others for his or her sense of self-worth while the self-actualized U.S. individual is not:

---

[19] Malina and Neyrey use a multi-method approach which includes the historical critical method, a social scientific and cultural-anthropological method.

Honor is ultimately the self-respect of dyadic persons who depend constantly on family and kin to affirm their self-worth....According to this dependency, honor conscious people contrast diametrically with U.S. individualism (see Geertz 1976; Malina 1986a). (p. 32)

On this point Malina and Neyrey (1991a) appear to participate in "selective inattention" (Straus, 1994b), failing to see to what extent women and other minority groups have had to be other directed—directed toward the dominant culture in order to survive.

Without any apparent awareness, Malina and Neyrey (1991b) seem to apply a male defined contemporary psychological perspective to their understanding of the first-century personality as a dyadic or group oriented personality:

For people of that time and place, the basic, most elementary unit of social analysis is not the individual person but the dyad, a person in relation with and connected to at least one other social unit, in particular, the family. People in this cultural area might be said to share 'an undifferentiated family ego mass' (Bowen, 1978). (p. 73)

Malina and Neyrey (1991b) seem to have no understanding of the self-in-relation theory of the Stone Center in its attempt to describe contemporary women's experience as being more relationship oriented than that of men (Jordan et al., 1991). Malina and Neyrey (1991b) claim that their methodology gives them a greater panoramic view and understanding of the ancient Mediterranean person as a way of learning more about our own society. Yet they grossly fail to see any relationship between the dyadic nature of the ancient Mediterranean person and contemporary women for whom shame and violence are such critical issues.

Failing to Bridge the Conversation

Thus, Malina and Neyrey (1991b) wear their own lenses of "selective inattention" by looking hundreds of years into the past to describe this first-century Mediterranean person without making any connection to contemporary life:

Dyadic persons are socialized to understand their role and status by the constant information fed to them by family, neighbors, clan, etc. (p. 84)

It is my assumption that scholars at the Stone Center would say, "that description sounds like the experience of many contemporary women and other minority groups who depend on the input of the dominant culture in order to survive." Malina and Neyrey (1991b) further describe the ancient Mediterranean society as one that is "embedded in relationships" (p. 94). They fail to acknowledge their own apparent value judgements as to what constitutes a healthy contemporary personality. Contemporary male psychology has emphasized separation and individuation as the hallmark of mental health, while women's connectedness and the focus on relationships have at times been pathologized (Jordan et al., 1991).

DeSilva—Resisting Cultural Shaming and the Cycle of Violence Through Community Maintenance

David Arthur deSilva (1995) examines one of the most violent and humiliating deaths known to humankind, the crucifixion of Jesus as reflected on by the Epistle to the Hebrews. By highlighting verse 12:2 "...who for the sake of the joy that was set before him endured a cross, having despised shame," deSilva (1995) notes that the focus of the author of the epistle is not on the excruciating physical pain of this violent execution, but rather on a greater pain—the humiliation of being killed in this culturally unacceptable way (p. 1).

In this first century Mediterranean world there was nothing more shameful than a shameful death (p. 167). And there was no death that was more shameful than crucifixion, death on a cross. Citing Hengel (1977) deSilva (1995) notes the inherent shame of crucifixion:

This form of execution was associated with 'the lower classes, i.e. slaves, violent criminals and the unruly elements in rebellious provinces.' (p. 167)

Thus the execution of Jesus by crucifixion was an act of total humiliation, a degradation ceremony that potentially stripped him not only of all societal status and honor, but also of all social memory (p. 168). DeSilva (1995) asks important questions:

But what does it mean for Jesus to have 'despised shame'? How are we to understand this description against the background of Greco-Roman culture? Moreover, what does it mean to present such an attitude as exemplary? (p. 2)

In essence, deSilva's study on the Epistle to the Hebrews tries to distinguish "between what the dominant culture evaluated as honorable and what the Christian minority group held up as honorable" (p. 18). In contemporary words, deSilva demonstrates how the early Christian community was able to "psychologically immunize" themselves by redefining their identity.

In the Greco-Roman world one's identity was heavily defined by the opinion of others, by one's "court of reputation" (Pitt-Rivers) or "court of opinion" (deSilva, p. 25). In this ancient world shame and honor are understood in the context of the evaluation of significant others (deSilva, 1995, p. 25). If a person or group of people experience affirmation by these significant others they are honored. Likewise if a person or group of people are devalued by these significant others, they are shamed. In essence, for deSilva one's court of reputation is "that body of significant others before whom one feels shame," (p. 64)...

DeSilva (1995) builds on Malina and Neyrey's (1991a) notion that shame is culturally specific, meaning: what might be deviant and shameful for one group in one locality may be worthy and honorable for another (p. 26). DeSilva (1995) argues that the early Christian community—a minority community—as depicted in the Epistle to the Hebrews was able to use the shame/honor system of the ancient Mediterranean world to their advantage, helping them "maintain their group cohesion and commitment" (p.27), and ultimately immunize themselves to the shaming effects of the culture around them. DeSilva (1995) further argues that minority groups in general survive by redefining "honor to serve the interests of the survival of the group and promotion of its culture over against a dominant society" (p. 65).

However, a major focus of deSilva's work is examining the source of a person's or group's approval or disapproval:

> From whom can one expect approval and honor for a particular action? From whom ought one to seek such approval and honor, and whose opinion ought one to disregard? What constitutes honor is group-specific; the definition of the body of 'significant others' will also define the constellation of attitudes, behaviors, and commitments which come together under the larger heading of 'honor.' (p. 42)

DeSilva (1995) points out that in the early church many people were persecuted for using the name Christian:

> ...for Pliny and Trajan, confession of the name of 'Christian' was enough to deserve execution.... (p. 152)

In fact, many people were dishonored and shamed by the dominant culture for the very use of the name (p. 152). Similarly to contemporary minority groups, the early Christians, according to deSilva, tried to live virtuous lives so that it was clear to the so-called "court of reputation" that the controversy was really in the name itself and not in the person or group (p. 152). But as this minority community refused to fully accommodate to "participation in Greco-Roman life," these early Christians were publicly humiliated (p. 157). The Greco-Roman world used dishonor as a "means of social control," a weapon to keep minority groups in line:

> The burning experience of disgrace, the stinging disapproval of society, was meant to lead the Christians back to a proper sense of shame, that is, to respect once more the values, relations, and traditions of the society. (deSilva, 1995, p. 158)

Humiliation came in the form of both physical and verbal abuse. There seemed to be almost a hierarchy of punishments: despiteful treatment, outrage, gross insult, assault and battery and the humiliation of crucifixion—the ultimate form of abuse (pp. 158-159). DeSilva emphasizes that these attempts at social control and public shaming have been termed "status-degradation rituals" (p. 159).

The point deSilva makes is that the early Christian community as depicted in the Epistle to the Hebrews resisted the dominant culture by learning how to "despise shame," refusing to allow shame to become a means of social control. The early Christians learned how to resist the debilitating effects of shaming by lifting up Jesus as a model to be emulated. DeSilva (1995) argues that Jesus was able to endure dishonor because he belonged to God's higher court of reputation and was not dependent on societal evaluations.

This minority culture was encouraged to overturn the dominant culture's honor rating system by no longer seeking its approval, but only God's approval. According to the author of the Epistle to the Hebrews, this conviction of total trust in God was shared by both Jews and Christians: "those who trust in God will not fall into disgrace, but rather come into honor beyond measure" (p. 207). Thus "despising shame" becomes a prerequisite to faith (p. 207). DeSilva (1995) argues that it is the intent of the author of the Epistle to the Hebrews to help his "addressees" to "despise shame," giving up societal honor and evaluation for that of God. Honoring God thus means that one is dishonored by the world.

In order to weather the dishonor of the world, the early Christian community as depicted in the Epistle to the Hebrews constructed what deSilva (1995) calls "an alternate court of reputation," the body of peoples whose opinions and evaluations are valued (p. 278). The author of the Epistle to the Hebrews, deSilva points out, continually points to Jesus and God as the ultimate evaluators of a person's worth. Again Jews and Christians shared this sense of God as the ultimate court of opinion:

> Their belief in a personal God who was involved in human affairs and would one day rise up in judgement of humankind allowed Jews and Christians alike to regard God as a significant other whose approval or disapproval could be earned and experienced. (p. 279)

Thus when a person knowingly does what is of value in the eyes of God that person's self-esteem and sense of self-worth is elevated in spite of societal opinions (p. 279).

For the author of the Epistle to the Hebrews the early Christian community became "the earthly counterpart to the divine court of reputation" (p. 284). To this end, the early Christians sought to reinforce each other in maintaining the faith community's unique values while at the same time building up each other's sense of self-worth. This mutual reinforcement decreased the temptation that members would seek approval "from other groups, whether the Jewish communities or the Greco-Roman culture" (p. 285).

Thus the early Christian community as depicted in the Epistle to the Hebrews became a powerful court of reputation for its believers through community maintenance. This community maintenance reinforced and affirmed the member's unique values, beliefs and hopes (p. 286), values often opposed to the dominant culture:

> The society may honor the wealthy and place the poor below the rich in its estimation, but such worldly norms are not to pass into the Christian community (cf. Jas 2:1-7; 1 Cor 11:22). (p. 286)

Furthermore, community maintenance was sustained by "the enterprise of mutual encouragement" (p. 287). The early Christian community not only became a significant court of opinion for its members but it also stressed the inherent value and worth of each person as a child of God (p. 296, 290). Because of the affirmation of valued others, the members were equipped with the necessary inner resources to resist the shaming tactics of the dominant culture. In essence, the faith community was maintained by its relational connectedness:

> The members of the community are collectively to take responsibility for the encouragement of each individual, to be accountable to and for one another, in order that no individual should begin to become detached from the group, that is, cease to regard the community as the body of his or her significant others, whose approval means life and self-respect. (deSilva, 1995, p. 287)

Thus the faith community was maintained by an image of a God who accepted each member as a child of God (p. 290) and was not ashamed to associate with them (p. 293). This affiliation as an adopted child of God not only honored each member but also built up their sense of self-respect in the face of a condemning, shaming and devaluing dominant culture. The author of the Epistle to the Hebrews seeks to reframe the negative evaluation of the Greco-Roman society. Suffering, loss of status and property now become signs "of their adoption into the family of God" (p. 295). Disgraceful rejection by the dominant culture means grace filled acceptance by God.

Quoting Aristotle, deSilva (1995) notes a spiral of escalating anger stemming from the experience of being slighted or devalued by significant others (p. 42):

> Men [sic] are angry at slights from those by whom they think that they have a right to expect to be well treated;...(p. 43).

Likewise, deSilva (1995) argues that people are angry when slighted by those people who most matter. Furthermore, anger related to being devalued by significant others can be an attempt to assert self esteem by "inflicting some injury or penalty on the offending party" (deSilva, 1996, p. 43).

Shame is not seen in a purely negative light. In fact, deSilva reminds the reader that for Aristotle shame is a form of conscience:

> One who fears disgrace is an honorable man [sic], with a due sense of shame; one who does not fear it is shameless. (p. 64)

But Aristotle goes on to argue that the fear of disgrace is not enough to curtail the behavior of the majority of people. Many people are motivated by the fear of punishment and because of this they need to have placed before them the threat of penalties:

> For it is the nature of the many to be amenable to fear but not to a sense of honor, and to abstain from evil not because of its baseness but because of the penalties it entails. (p. 64)

DeSilva emphasizes that the author of the <u>Epistle to the Hebrews</u> underscores the importance of resisting the shaming and potentially debilitating effects of the dominant culture. In modeling Jesus, the early Christian community learned how to "despise shame," or to become immune to the shaming tactics of the Greco-Roman culture. In spite of being immune or shameless to the evaluation of the dominant culture, (p. 304) the members of the early Christian community were encouraged to display "proper shame" within their own faith community:

> —that is, sensitivity to one's honor rating—within the Christian group, and thus to be held accountable to the group's values and commitments. (p. 304)

One's true honor and self-esteem resides in being faithful to the divine court of opinion, thus maintaining the image of one who is a child of God (p. 312).

DeSilva (1995) critically reviews current New Testament research especially the works of Bruce Malina (1981) and John Neyrey (1994) which tend to view the ancient Mediterranean culture almost solely through the lens or axis of shame and honor (p. 11). Citing John Neyrey, deSilva (1995) argues that these proponents of cultural-anthropological insights claim that by paying attention to the dynamics of honor and shame in these ancient texts, one can "see as the natives see,...value what they value;...understand how and why they act the way they do" (p. 11). DeSilva points out that opponents have questioned the wisdom of such a single minded focus on shame and honor in the ancient texts suggesting that such a focus is, in fact, reductionistic.

Malina (1997) is highly critical of deSilva's (1995) attempt "to guard against the pitfalls of applying modern social scientific constructs to an ancient text" (p. 378) by relying instead on chosen ancient texts—primarily the rhetorical handbooks. Malina argues that the ancient texts that deSilva has chosen can not be adequately understood without understanding their context. Such a contextual awareness could be enlightened by a social-scientific interpretation of the bible, which Malina believes, deSilva grossly lacks (p. 379).

> The naïve belief that a collection of passages intuitively chosen as parallel to some NT passage thereby explains and clarifies that passage remains what it is –a naïve belief. The fact is that meanings come from social systems, including meanings in the past. And without some insight into the social systems of antiquity, the meanings are more those of the interpreter than of past authors.

Moreover, the belief that a citation of a passage from the ancient world is self-explanatory is a delusion as long as the social system within which the passage makes sense is not available to the modern scholar (reader). (p. 378)

It is, indeed, questionable that a contemporary person can ever totally see, value and understand life in the ancient world. However, it is an assumption of this study that deeper insight into the biblical shame/honor system can give the contemporary reader "a new way of looking at things" (Ricoeur, 1971).

Summary

Lyn Bechtel Huber (1983) provided some of the earliest research on shame in the Hebrew scriptures. Critical to this study is Huber's notion of the functional role of shame/shaming as a form of social control and punishment within Israel. Huber emphasizes the extent to which people in the ancient Mediterranean world were concerned about reputation in the eyes of others. This intense focus on the "opinion of others," or on one's "court of reputation" made the Hebrew people especially vulnerable to the function of shame/shaming as a form of social control and/ or punishment. Huber argues that it was the doctrine of divine election that shielded the people of Israel from the shaming effects of the outer culture, thus enabling the people of Israel to be psychologically immune to its destructive and debilitating impact. To her detriment, Huber (1983) methodologically employs contemporary definitions of shame and guilt from the psychoanalytic literature without critically reviewing them and/ or questioning their relevance to a culture that existed 2000 years ago.

Pitt-Rivers (1966, 1968), a cultural-anthropologist, has had an invaluable impact on current biblical thinking about the role of shame and honor in the patronage system of the ancient Mediterranean world. In fact, his theory has served as a model for certain New Testament scholars. Rivers argues that shame/honor is intimately tied to public opinion or what he calls "the court of reputation" (p. 27).

Pitt-Rivers stresses that according to the ancient Code of Honor, "valued others" serve as one's court of reputation or of opinion. The Code of Honor mandates that physical affronts or insults against one's person or against one's valued "court of reputation" need to be avenged by punishing others. The greatest flaw in Pitt-Rivers's (1966, 1968) work is not the theory as much as contemporary applications of his model. It is questionable whether Pitt-Rivers's model has any bearing on a person in the ancient Mediterranean world of 2000 year ago.

Malina and Neyrey are part of a group of scholars whose intent is to utilize a social scientific approach to the interpretation of biblical tests. Building on the theory of Pitt-Rivers they claim that pivotal values in the Mediterranean world are those of honor and shame. Honor is linked with "saving face" and "respect." They argue that shame/honor societies evolve around the axis of public opinion. The cycle of violence is perpetuated by a belief within the Code of Honor system that when one is dishonored or shamed it is necessary for a person to find a way to restore his or her honor even if it means resorting to violence. Frequently the solution to insulting violence is insulting violence in return.

Malina and Neyrey are convinced that their multi-method approach with its emphasis on shame/honor as the pivotal values will give greater insight into the meaning of ancient texts. Even though they argue that it is, indeed possible, "to see as the natives see," Malina and Neyrey wear their own lenses of "selective inattention," failing to see to what extent contemporary life (especially for women and other non-dominant groups) is dyadic and group oriented.

In his study on the Epistle to the Hebrews, David Arthur deSilva (1995) examines one of the most violent and humiliating deaths known to humankind, the crucifixion of Jesus. DeSilva points out that the crucifixion of Jesus was an act of total humiliation, a degradation ceremony that potentially stripped him of all societal status and honor. In contemporary words, deSilva demonstrates how the early Christian community was able to "psychologically immunize" themselves by redefining their identity. They redefined their identity by the construction of an alternate "court of reputation." DeSilva stresses that the author of the Epistle to the Hebrews continually points to Jesus and God as the ultimate evaluators of a person's worth and self-esteem in spite of societal shaming; thus the earthly Christian community became "the earthly counter part to the divine court of reputation" (p. 284).

DeSilva (1995) argues that the early Christian community—a minority community—in refusing to fully accommodate to "participation in Greco-Roman life," was publicly humiliated. He emphasizes that this early Christian community resisted the dominant culture by learning how to "despise shame," refusing to allow shame to become a means of social control. Furthermore, the early Christian community as described by deSilva resisted shame through community maintenance which was sustained by "the enterprise of mutual encouragement."

Closing

If it is, indeed, questionable that a contemporary person can ever totally see, value and understand life in the ancient world. One wonders about the value of a social scientific study entering into conversation with ancient texts. The task at hand is not to transport the present into the past or to import the past into the present. But rather the task at hand is to examine the most significant aspects of the shame/honor system of the ancient Mediterranean world to see if there are clues as to how one might proceed today in mitigating and preventing violence.

Shame and violence are dyadic experiences, which can be mitigated and prevented within connected relationships and/or communities, which become esteeming environments of encouragement and respect. This study suggests that the community models of the future, models which can best heal the destructive impact of shame and violence are those which are not only encouraging and validating but also based on empathy (Jordan, 1984, 1989, 1997; Tangney, 1995a). Such communities not only affirm a person's intrinsic worth, but they also help people experience a sense of being known and understood (Wiehe, 1997, p. 1192). This study underscores that current research has found that empathy is intimately related to the mitigation and prevention of violence and the diminishment of childhood abuse (Wiehe, p. 1191). Thus it is a belief of this study that the creation of such affirming and empathic communities will not only decrease violence and the destructive aspects of shame, but will also curtail the cycle of intergenerational violence.

CHAPTER 3

Methodology

Introduction

The purpose of this chapter is to describe the methodology used in this study. The chapter is divided into five sections. The first section states the hypotheses that were developed and tested in this research project. The second section describes the data collection procedures. The third section describes the demographics of the sample. The fourth section describes the five instruments that were used in the study in terms of their psychometric properties and usefulness as research instruments. The fifth section of this chapter describes the data analysis, which is presented in more detail in Chapter Four.

As was stated in Chapter One an interdisciplinary research methodology consisting of three steps is employed in this study. In the first step, a revised correlational method is used to understand how various literatures on shame, violence, corporal punishment, and images of God (i.e., pastoral theological perspectives on shame; biblical/theological perspectives on shame, honor and images of God; social scientific perspectives on shame, violence, images of God) are related to each other.

In the second step, an empirical research design is employed to test the statistical significance of correlations of measures among shame, guilt, violence and images of God. In the third step, these empirical findings are brought into dialogue with the cross-disciplinary review of literature undertaken in the first step, in order to elaborate the meaning of the findings. These elaborated meanings will ultimately be related to practice (i.e., clinical and pastoral practice).

This interdisciplinary and multi-method research model consists of three steps or "moments." The first moment consists of comprehensive interdisciplinary research, employing a "revised correlational methodology" (Browning, 1991;

Tracy, 1983; Tillich, 1951) which coordinates the questions and findings of diverse areas of inquiry: religious, theological and psychological resources (both theoretical and empirical). Chapter Two is an example of such a revised correlational method.

The second moment consists of an empirical study, which draws upon a more limited literature and only indirectly builds upon and extends the diverse and comprehensive literature of the first moment. This second moment is "mono-method," employing only one methodology: the empirical method. It is this empirical method that is primarily discussed in this Chapters Three and Four.

The third moment of research is once again not only interdisciplinary and comprehensive but also pragmatic and practical (Chopp, 1995; Browning, 1991). This third moment is the final moment in what Browning calls a "practice-theory-practice" model meaning that the findings of the second moment (empirical research) address and influence the questions, issues and concerns formulated in the first moment. The revision progresses from step to step. Furthermore, this third moment involves a practical "emancipatory praxis,"(Chopp, 1995) which envisions a present and future world in which the expression of violence in adults is minimized. The third moment will be best-expressed in Chapter Five.

As the review of the literature has demonstrated, the cycle of violence in adults who have experienced childhood corporal punishment is multifaceted. In an attempt to investigate why some adults who were corporally punished as children continue the cycle of violence and others do not, I have also designed a cross-disciplinary quantitative study to explore relationships between shame, images of God and violence. The following hypotheses were tested:

Research Hypotheses

Hypotheses Concerning Relationships Among Childhood Corporal Punishment, Adult Partner Violence, Shame and Images of God

1)   There will be a positive relationship between childhood corporal punishment and adult partner violence: those who experienced higher levels of childhood corporal punishment will tend to display higher levels of adult partner violence.

2)   There will be a positive relationship between childhood corporal punishment and adult shame: those who experienced higher levels of corporal punishment will tend to display higher levels of adult shame.

3)   There will be a relationship between childhood corporal punishment and images of God. (a) There will be a negative relationship between childhood corporal punishment and benevolent/loving images of God: those who experienced higher levels of childhood corporal punishment will also tend to display lower levels of benevolent/loving images of God.

(b) There will be a positive relationship between childhood corporal punishment and wrathful/punitive images of God: those who experienced higher levels of childhood corporal punishment will also tend to display higher levels of wrathful/punitive images of God.

Hypotheses Concerning Relationships Among Adult Partner Violence, Shame, and Images of God

4) There will be a positive relationship between adult partner violence and shame: those who display higher levels of adult partner violence will tend to display higher levels of shame.

5) There will be a relationship between adult partner violence and images of God. (a) There will be a negative relationship between adult partner violence and images of God: those who display higher levels of adult partner violence will tend to display lower levels of benevolent/loving images of God. (b) There will be a positive relationship between adult partner violence and wrathful/punitive images of God: those who experienced higher levels of adult partner violence will also tend to display higher levels of wrathful/punitive images of God.

6) There will be a relationship between adult shame and images of God. (a) There will be a negative relationship between shame and images of God: those who display higher levels of shame will tend to display lower levels of benevolent/loving images of God. (b) There will be a positive relationship between shame and wrathful/punitive images of God: those who experienced higher levels of shame will also tend to display higher levels of wrathful/punitive images of God.

Additional Questions:

The following additional questions will be explored:

Relationships Concerning Corporal Punishment, Religion, Parental Warmth, Attitudes Toward Spanking Children, Adult Suicidality and Depression and Adult Detachment

1) Is there a relationship between degree of corporal punishment experienced as a child and the role of religion in current life?

2) Is there a relationship between childhood corporal punishment and image of parent as cold and uncaring?

3) Is there a relationship between adult partner violence and image of parent as cold and uncaring in adults who experienced childhood corporal punishment?

4) Is there a relationship between whether or not respondent was corporally punished as a child and attitudes toward spanking children?

5) Is there a relationship between being corporally punished as a child and adult suicidality and/or depression?

6) Is there a relationship between adult detachment and childhood corporal punishment?

7) Is there a relationship between shame in adults who experienced childhood corporal punishment and image of parent as cold and uncaring?[20]

Relationships Concerning Partner Violence, Gender and Beliefs About Human Nature

8) Is there a relationship between gender and violence?

9) Is there a relationship between a person's beliefs about human nature and violence (i.e. human nature is basically good versus human nature is basically corrupt and perverse)?

C. Further Questions

10) Did mother or father do the most hitting?

11) Is there a relationship between the number of times hit and being hit with an object?

12) Is there a relationship between age respondent was corporally punished by parent and adult suicidality and depression.

13) Is there a relationship between adult partner violence and adult guilt?

---

[20] Questions 2 and 3 are critical because of the possibility that the effect of frequent corporal punishment is the result of the lack of parental warmth and nurturance (Straus and Hill, 1997, p. 4).

Most of these questions examine the relationship between demographics, early childhood experiences including the degree of corporal punishment, parental discipline and religious beliefs.

Data Collection Procedures

Participants in this study were 277 men and women who were either college, university or seminary students or members of primarily mainline Protestant churches in New England.

The sample was obtained by contacting either church clergy or professors. Clergy and university, college and/or seminary faculty were contacted either through email, an initial letter, and phone calls. If contact was initially made via the phone, the clergyperson or faculty member also received a letter explaining the study as well as a copy of the Informed Consent Form. Once a professor agreed to have his or her class participate in the study, this researcher made a presentation explaining the study in all the classes (except two) either at the beginning of a class or at the end and then asked for volunteers. At that point the potential volunteers were handed an Informed Consent Form which they were asked to read and sign. Once these were signed they were handed a Research Packet which they were encouraged to complete within the next few days and return to class within a week. Usually this researcher returned to the classes to pick up the completed Research Packets, or retrieved them from a designated box in or near the Professor's office. In two seminary classes the seminarians returned the Research Packets in a self-addressed stamped envelope. The completed Informed Consent Forms were collected prior to distributing the Research Packets in order protect confidentiality and anonymity.

In the churches the Pastors identified groups who could be asked to participate. Some of these groups were men's groups, choirs, deacons, women's groups, Lenten study groups, boards of Christian Education, church school teachers and Bible study groups. The Pastor would estimate how many people would most likely participate. From this number Research Packets, Informed Consents, Letters of Invitations, and Instructions were sent to each church Pastor. She or he would first distribute and collect the Informed Consents before distributing the Research Packets in order to insure anonymity and confidentiality. The Pastors collected the Research Packets and returned them along with the Informed Consents in the already provided self-addressed stamped priority mailbox.

Thirteen churches in New England participated in this study. Twelve of these churches are affiliated with the United Church of Christ, one with the United Methodist Church. One large Evangelical Church in a major urban area was invited to participate. However, after a month of negotiations the associate pastor claimed that he could not interest anyone in participating. Five seminary classes from three different seminaries in a large northeastern city participated in this study. And six classes of mostly freshman and sophomores from a major Northeastern university participated in this study. These students were from three sociology classes and three elementary education classes. Some students and young adults were recruited through Intervarsity Christian Fellowship. Also students from a master's social work program at a Catholic College in the Northeast participated in this study.

A total of 396 Research Packets were distributed to participants of which 277 were returned, for a return rate of 69.9%. Upon completing the Informed Consent Form each potential participant was handed a Research Packet which included a list of instructions as well as an Invitation to Participate in Research form. The Research Packet was in booklet form and included a detailed Demographics Questionnaire which focused on questions about childhood discipline, the Cook Internalized Shame Scale (ISS), the God Adjective Checklist (GAC), the Revised Conflict Tactics Scales (CTS2), and the Test of Self-Conscious Affect (TOSCA) in this order

A letter of Invitation to Participate in Research was enclosed in each Research Packet. The letter explained the purpose of the study, the requirements for participation, and the procedures involved in completing the study. The purpose of the study was stated as one that "considers the relationships among shame, images of God, and conflict negotiation in adults who were corporally punished as children." No further information was given in order to prevent biased responses to the instruments.

Included, as well in the Invitation to Participate in Research was an explanation of the possible risks and benefits to the participants. It was explained that painful memories of physical or others forms of past abuse may surface and the participants were encouraged to call the researcher to ask questions or discuss these feelings. Confidentiality was assured by stating that the researcher was the only person who had access to the collected data from the self-report instruments and that they would be stored in her home office, in a locked file cabinet. The participants were informed that the research packets were numerically coded in order to keep track of the return rates, but that their identity would not be known. The instruments were coded before they were distributed.

They were informed that their name would not be written on the instruments and that the Informed Consent Forms would be kept separate from the research packets thus insuring anonymity. They were also assured that under no circumstances would their identity be revealed in reports of the research. Because the Research Packet was in booklet form, the order in which the instruments were to be completed was assured. It was estimated that it would take forty-five minutes to one hour to complete the 27 page Research Packet. The Instruction Sheet not only gave information regarding the collection of the Research Packets but also requested participants not to write their names on the materials.

Instruments

Participants were asked to complete the Research Packet, which included a detailed demographic questionnaire and four-self report instruments. The following section will describe the instruments used in this research as well as the demographic questionnaire.

The Demographics Questionnaire

The 14 page Demographics Questionnaire was composed of questions from the Traumatic Antecedents Questionnaire developed by Herman and van der Kolk (1990), a Demographics Questionnaire, designed by Heather P. Wilson for her 1994 dissertation Forgiveness and Survivors of Sexual Abuse, and the Straus and Donnelly (1992) CPS.QS\SPS1 Questionnaire, Family Research Laboratory, University of New Hampshire. Parts B-G are drawn directly from the Straus and Donnelly (1992) questionnaire. The Demographics Questionnaire focused on background information, questions about childhood discipline, childhood physical punishment, and the child-parents relationship of the subjects in the study.

The Cook Internalized Shame Scale (ISS)

The Cook Internalized Shame Scale (ISS) was first developed starting in 1984. It was originally designed to measure "the extent (based on a frequency scale) to which respondents have internalized shame feelings" (Cook, 1994, p. 1). Over the years the conceptual framework for the ISS has come to be based on Silvan Tomkins's Affect theory and the subsequent theoretical work of Donald Nathanson (Cook, p. 13). However, initially Cook developed his shame theory based upon the works of psychologist Gershen Kaufman (1992) and psychoanalysts Helen Block Lewis (1971) and Leon Wurmser (1981). Cook (1994) relied on case material from their clinical practices (p. 4) focusing on phenomenological descriptions of shame feelings:

> Using affect theory as an overall description of human emotion, Kaufman had introduced the idea that the degree of psychopathology was roughly proportional to the degree to which shame affect had become internalized within the personality. Thus, Cook called his new test 'The Internalized Shame Scale.' (Cook, 1996, p. 133)

The ISS consists of 30 items. There are two scales: a shame scale and a self-esteem scale. The shame score on the ISS is derived from the 24 negatively worded items. The self-esteem score is derived from the six positively worded items. The self-esteem items actually come from the Rosenberg Self-Esteem Scale (Rosenberg, 1965) (Cook, 1994, p. 3). Responses are given on a five-point scale from: never, seldom, sometimes, often and almost always. Responses for the items are assigned a numerical value of zero to four, with the higher numbers indicating a higher levels of internalized shame or specifically "high scorer is reporting frequent feelings of shame as represented by the items" (Cook, 1994, p. 2). However, a low shame score does not mean that a person has a positive self-esteem or little internalized shame. Cook (1994) rightly remarks: "Some persons can be so well defended against the recognition of shame feelings that they will not report their presence when responding to this scale" (p. 2). Scores can range from 0-96 and the range for the self-esteem score is from 0-24.

In the area of empirical shame research, the ISS is the most widely used psychometric instrument (p. 1) and has consistently shown high reliability throughout its development (p. 4). Furthermore, the ISS measures with a high degree of consistency, whether measuring a clinical or non-clinical sample (p. 12). The recent studies of Rybak (1991) and McFarland (1992) reported reliability coefficients in a range from .94 to .97 (Cook, 1994, p. 12). From Cook's own studies he reports a reliability coefficient of .95 and .96, thus indicating very "high internal consistency" (p. 9).

Not only was the ISS developed with the intent that it could be used with clinical populations, it is, in fact, the only shame scale that has been used extensively with clinical populations (Cook, 1996, p.133). It is also important to note—especially when interpreting the shame scores—that the sample for this study was not drawn from a clinical population.

Pertinent to this study is the differentiation between guilt and shame as well as the difference between trait versus situational shame. Cook (1996) argues that it is very difficult to differentiate shame from guilt and argues that guilt is, in essence, a variant of shame (p. 134). He consistently argues that shame is more related to psychopathology than guilt (p. 152). Following Tomkins's and Nathanson's thinking, Cook (1996) argues that shame does not require cognitive ability whereas guilt does, and guilt is more related to issues of "conscience, social control and morality" (p. 147).

The ISS measures trait shame, that is to say internalized shame. However, a trait approach to the measurement of both shame and guilt can lead to a great deal of confounding as is noted especially in Harder et al.'s (1992) Personal Feelings Questionnaire—2 (PFQ2).

This study uses the ISS, which measures trait shame, and the TOSCA, which measures situational guilt to address the issues of confounding. McFarland (1992) found no correlation between the situational guilt scale (TOSCA/SCAAI) and the ISS (Cook, 1996, p. 150).

Cook (1996) is of the opinion that "shame references the entire self while guilt is triggered by specific acts" (p.154). Furthermore, the ISS reflects Nathanson's understanding that shame is about the self, whereas guilt as a variant of shame is "the coassembly of shame with fear of reprisal or punishment" (p. 135). The shame aspect of this coassembly makes one want "to hide the misdeed" whereas the guilt aspect causes one to experience fear that one will be punished for the transgression (p. 139).

Cook (1996) argues that the ISS is a much more sensitive measure of the internalization of shame than adjective-based scales such as those used by Harder and situation-based scales as used by Tangney.

Tangney (1996) offers an important critique of the Cook ISS Internalized

Shame Scale. She points out that the ISS presents problems in terms of discriminant validity meaning that it is difficult to distinguish self-esteem from shame. She points out that Cook (1988) defines "internalized shame" as an "'enduring, chronic shame that has become internalized as part of one's identity and which can be most succintly characterized as a deep sense of inferiority, inadequacy, or deficiency'"(Tangney, 1996, p. 745). But the problem remains that Cook's attempt, according to Tangney, to differentiate shame from self-esteem is weak at best. Cook basically refers to self-esteem as a "less dynamic" concept than shame, meaning that poor self-esteem is less emotionally intense and painful than shame. But Cook's distinctions are vague given the fact that many of the shame items in the ISS according to Tangney "clearly tap self-esteem issues" (p. 745). Moreover, the ISS is highly correlated with measures of self-esteem (p. 745).

The God Adjective Checklist (GAC)

The God Adjective Checklist (1968) was first developed as a research instrument to measure one's concepts of God. Gorsuch (1968) originally classified God concept according to nine factors: Evaluation, Benevolency, Wrathfulness, Deisticness, Eternality, Omni-ness, Irrelevancy, Sovereignty, and Potency. Similarly to Brokaw and Edwards (1994) it was my intent to use the GAC to test hypotheses regarding benevolent/loving God images as well as wrathful/punitive God images. Originally Gorsuch (1968) found reliability coefficients of .71 for Deisticness, .49 for Irrelevance, .89 for Omniness, and .83 for Wrathfulness. Hall, Tisdale, and Brokaw (1994) report "that several studies have supported the validity of the GAC" (p. 404).

The Adjective Checklist (GAC) used in this study consists of 23 adjectives which are distributed fairly evenly across the nine scales. This study is using a revised version of the GAC, which was developed in 1996, and needs further testing. According to Gorsuch, the 23 adjectives measure Benevolent, Guiding, and Stable for the Traditional Christian Deity and Condemning and Wrathful for the Severe Deity. This study will look particularly at the concept of God as benevolent and the concept of God as condemning and wrathful. Moreover, pertinent to this study is Gorsuch's second independent factor, wrathfulness, which "he hypothesized to differentiate between fundamentalists and liberals" (Lawrence, 1991, p. 12). As stated in the literature review, this study also pays particular attention to the adjective "protective," in order to examine whether subjects who had experienced physical abuse as children hold an image of God as not being protective. In other words do adults who were corporally punished/physically-abused hold an image of God of simply not being there to protect them?

This study used the directions as suggested by Gorsuch:

> The term 'God' means different things to different people. We would like to know what it means to you. Below is a set of adjectives, which we would like for you to rate according to your personal concept of God. The ratings range from "Strongly disagree" to "Strongly agree" as to whether you might use that word to describe your

concept of God. If the term seems completely unrelated to your concept of God, then use the midpoint of the scale, 3. For each of the adjectives below, please place the number, which shows how much you agree or disagree that that particular word describes your concept of God on the line in front of the adjective.

Again Lawrence (1991) criticizes Gorsuch by suggesting that by using adjectives rather than sentences he measures peoples' cognitive concepts of God rather than their image of God. Building on Rizzuto (1979), Lawrence (1991) conceptualizes image of God to be based on a more emotional/experiential understanding of God (p. 7) coming from various sources (Lawrence, 1996, p. 1) or what Rizzuto (1979) calls a "compound memorial process" (p. 54). Furthermore, Lawrence (1991) expresses the viewpoint that only Gorsuch's second factor, wrathfulness, "appears to have a tinge of the God image about it,"(p. 13).

The Revised Conflict Tactics Scales (CTS2)

The revised Conflict Tactics Scales (CTS2) measures levels of physical violence in adults. The Conflict Tactics Scales (CTS1) upon which the (CTS2) is based is "the most widely used instrument for research on intrafamily violence" (Straus and Gelles, 1990, p. 49) and has a known quantitative history of "strong evidence of validity and reliability (summarized in Straus, 1990a)" (Straus, Hamby, Boney-McCoy, & Sugarman, 1996, p. 15). Since the CTS2 appears "in principle" (p. 15) to be a superior scale, this study uses it rather than the CTS1.

More specifically the revised Conflict Tactics Scales (CTS2) "measures psychological and physical attacks on a partner in a marital, cohabiting, or dating relationship; and also the use of negotiation" (Straus et al., 1996, p. 1). Like the original CTS, the theoretical basis for the CTS2 is conflict theory:

> This theory assumes that conflict is an inevitable part of all human association, whereas violence as a tactic to deal with conflict is not (Straus et al., 1996, p. 2).

The CTS2 has five scales: 1) negotiation, 2) psychological aggression, 3) physical assault, 4) sexual coercion and 5) injury. Each scale has subscales. The negotiation scale consists of an emotional and a cognitive subscale. The other four scales (psychological aggression, physical assault, sexual coercion and injury) consist of minor and severe subscales. For instance, the item "I beat up my partner" is part of the severe subscale of the physical assault scale.

The CTS2 is actually a revised version of the CTS1, which had three scales: violence, verbal aggression and reasoning. In the revised CTS2 the original violence scale has become the physical assault scale. The original verbal aggression scale has become the psychological aggression scale and the original reasoning scale has become the negotiation scale. The two new scales, which were added, are the injury and sexual coercion scales. This study has left out the sexual coercion scale.

I. The Negotiation Scale measures a person's ability to negotiate conflict. Its Cognitive Subscale measures a person's "actions taken to settle a disagreement through discussion" (p. 5). The Emotion Subscale measures "the extent to which positive affect is communicated by asking about expressions of feelings of care and respect for the partner" (p. 5). II. The Psychological Aggression Scale measures severity of verbal and non-verbal aggressive acts such as "stomped out of the room" (p. 5). III. The Physical Assault Scale measures severity of physical violence.[21] IV. The Sexual Coercion Scale measures severity of behavior (from verbal insistence to physical force) "which is intended to compel the partner to engage in unwanted sexual activity" (p. 5). V. The Injury Scale measures severity of physical injury.

Straus et al. (1996) argue that the psychological aggression and physical assault scales should be highly correlated. Their reasoning is in line with conflict-escalation theory of couple violence which "argues that verbal aggression against a partner, rather than being cathartic and tension reducing, tends to increase the risk of physical assault (Berkowitz, 1993)" (p. 11).

The CTS2 has 78 questions or 39 items. All items are repeated twice once for the participant and then for one's partner or the person one is dating. When possible it is suggested that the CTS2 be used with both partners of a couple. All the questions are asked in pairs of questions ascertaining what the subject did and what the partner did. Like the original CTS1, the CTS2 consists of a list of actions, which the participant might use, in a conflict with one's partner/date etc. The items begin with those that are low in coerciveness and gradually become more coercive and aggressive. The participants are asked to rank the number of times an action "occurred during the past year, ranging from 'Never' to 'More than 20 times'" (Straus et al., 1996). The six-item range goes from "Once in the past year" to "More than 20 times in the past year." Also "Not in the past year, but it did happen" and "This has never happened" are also options. In this research project the instructions were modified for students:

> No matter how well people get along there are times when they disagree, get annoyed with the other person, want different things from each other, or just have spats or fights because they are in a bad mood, are tired, or for some other reason. Couples also have many different ways of trying to settle their differences. This is a list of things that might happen when you have differences. Please circle how many times you did each of these things in the past year, and how many times your partner (or someone you were dating) did this in the past year. If you or your partner (or someone you were dating) did not do one of these things in the past year, but it happened before that, circle '7.'

---

[21] In this study when the term "violence" is used, it is used as Straus employs it: a "shorter synonym for 'physical assault by a partner'"(p. 5).

The CTS2 is almost twice as long as the original CTS1. The CTS2 was developed to facilitate self-administration and requires only a 6th grade reading ability (Straus et al., 1996, p. 11). It is estimated that it would take 10-15 minutes to complete.

When possible it is suggested that the CTS2 be used with both partners of a couple. All the questions are asked in pairs ascertaining what the subject did and what the partner did. Straus et al. (1996) write:

> In addition, men who engage in severe assaults tend to under-report their violence relative to their partner (see for example, Browning & Dutton, 1986; Szinovacz, 1983; but there are also exceptions such as Cascardi, Langhinrichsen & Vivian, 1992). (p. 12)

When the CTS1 or CTS2 is used with any group known not to be violent, Straus et al. (1996) recommend that a prevalence variable and a chronicity variable be created for the Physical Assault, Sexual Coercion, and Physical Injury scales:

> The prevalence variable is a 0-1 dichotomy, with a score of 1 assigned if one or more of the acts in the scale occurred. The chronicity variable is the number of times the acts in the scale occurred, among those who engaged in at least one of the acts in the scale. (p. 15)

As stated earlier, not only is the CTS the most widely used instrument in intrafamily violence research (Straus & Gelles, 1990) but it also has strong evidence of validity and reliability (Straus et al., 1996).

Even though (Straus et al., 1996) argue that the CTS2 is a superior scale to the CTS1, the drawback in using the CTS2 is that there is "only preliminary evidence of validity and reliability" (p. 15). The CTS1 has "established validity and reliability with national norms and an extensive body of literature," (p. 15).

Straus et al. (1996) give a number of reasons why it is better to use the new CTS2 rather than the established CTS:

❏   An increased number of items to enhance content validity and reliability

❏   Revised wording to increase clarity and specificity

❏   Better differentiation between minor and severe levels of psychological and physical aggression

❏   Replacement of the weakest of the original scales (Reasoning) by a new scale to measure cognitive and emotional aspects of negotiating conflict

❏   Simplified format to facilitate use as a self-administered questionnaire

❏   Interspersal of items from each scale to reduce response sets and demand characteristics

❏   Additional scales to measure two important aspects of abuse of a partner: sexual coercion and physical injury. (p. 15)

It is reported that the internal consistency reliability of the CTS2 scales range from .79 to .95, with preliminary evidence of construct validity and discriminate validity (p. 16). Because of the similarities between the CTS and CTS2 it is Straus et al.'s (1996) contention that "the extensive evidence supporting the validity of the CTS1 (Straus, 1990a) may also apply to the CTS2" (p. 16).

The preliminary psychometric findings of the CTS2 are based on college student couples (p. 16). Straus et al. (1996) stress the point that college students "are much more often violent than older couples" (p. 16).

The Test of Self-Conscious Affect (TOSCA)

Tangney's Test of Self-Conscious Affect (TOSCA) is a revised version of the Self-Conscious Affect and Attribution Inventory (SCAAI). It measures Shame-proneness, Guilt-proness, Externalization, Detachment/Unconcern, Alpha Pride, and Beta Pride. For purposes of this study the TOSCA will be used to measure guilt and detachment. TOSCA follows a situational format: a series of subject-generated scenarios and responses. There are 15 situational scenarios with four responses, "two of which are representative of 'shame-proneness' and 'guilt-proneness'"(Cook, 1994, p. 7). An example of a scenario is the following: "You break something at work and then hide it." One is then asked to rank four possible response-scenarios from "not likely" to "very likely." A typical guilt response-scenario would be: "You would think: 'This is making me anxious. I need to either fix it or get someone else to.'" A shame response would be: "You would think of quitting." A detached response would be: "You would think: 'It was only an accident.'"

A study by Harder et al. (1992) found that the TOSCA (Tangney et al., 1992) demonstrated construct validity (Harder, 1995, p. 379). TOSCA's situational format has excellent discriminant validity, meaning that there is a "clearly differentiated pattern between the measure of shame the measure of guilt" (Cook, 1996, p. 153):

> When Tangney et al. parceled out guilt from shame, only three of the 27 correlations with guilt were significant and only one of the 27 correlations with shame was not significant. (p. 153)

Tangney, Wagner, Barlow, Marschall & Gramzow (1994) in a recent cross-sectional developmental study reported that the reliabilities (Cronback's Alphas) "for the Shame and Guilt scales, respectively, were .74 and .61 for adults (TOSCA), .74 and .69 for college students (TOSCA), .77 and .81 for adolescents (TOSCA-A), and .78 and .83 for children (TOSCA-C)" (Tangney, 1994). Tangney (1994) notes that scenario-based reliabilities tend to be lower than those of adjective checklist measures. She further notes that these estimates of internal consistency are reasonably high given the fact that as a rule alpha coefficients tend to underestimate reliability in scenario-based measures (p. 11).

Cook (1996) points out the limitations of Tangney's situational format by stating that situational items are limited in that they only measure guilt or shame in a particular situation. Cook goes on to argue that the "trait" approach that he uses "gets at the more enduring or chronic results of frequent shame experiences over a lifetime" (p. 145).

Harder et al. (1992) have been highly critical of Tangney's TOSCA. Harder (1995) finds Tangney's operational definition of guilt too limited, meaning that she views "almost all negative self-evaluations as shame, and to restrict guilt to specific actions unconnected with negative self-judgements" (p. 382). Furthermore, Harder et al. (1992) have criticized her conviction that guilt plays a negligible role in psychopathology (p. 594). In fact, Harder et al. (1992) argue the case that "guilt is much more involved with symptomatology than the current clinical and theoretical emphasis on shame would imply" (p. 601). Cook (1996) criticizes Harder's viewpoint by arguing that Harder et al's (1992) belief in a relationship between guilt and psychopathology "is drawn from outdated psychodynamic theory that, from Freud forward, has neglected (with few exceptions) the study of shame in particular and affect in general" (p. 154).

In contrast to theorists such as Harder et al. (1992), Cook (1996) argues that "shame references the entire self while guilt is triggered by specific acts" (p. 154). Thus when guilt is measured situationally the overlap with trait shame disappears (Cook, 1996, p. 154). There is no correlation between the TOSCA guilt scale and Cook's Internalized Shame Scale (Cook, 1994, p. 150) which will also be used in this study to measure shame.

Perception of Parents as Cold and Uncaring Scales (PPCUS)

Two scales were created from the Demographics Questionnaire, which measured the respondents' perception of father and mother as cold and uncaring. The four items used in each of the scales were: "Seemed cold and uncaring," "Did not meet your emotional needs," "Was insensitive to your feelings," and "Seemed not to love you." For the father scale the four questions were asked in reference to the father; for the mother scale the four questions were in reference to the mother. Possible responses to each of the questions ranged from 0 (Never) to 6 (More than 20 times). Internal consistency reliability statistics were computed for each of the scales. For the mother scale the coefficient alpha was .91 and for father the coefficient alpha was .92. Thus, the internal consistency was quite satisfactory.

Demographics of the Research Sample

A summary of the major demographic characteristics of the sample obtained is shown in Table 1. The age range of the research participants was from 18 to 86, with the mean age of 39. The largest percentage of participants (68%) was between the ages of 18 and 49; 15% of the sample were under 20, 28% were in their 20's, 10% in their 30's, 15% in their 40's, 15% in their 50's, and 17% over the age of 60. Over a third of the respondents were male (37%) and the rest female (61%).

About half the sample (45%) were married and about half the sample (45%) were single, 2% of the sample were co-habiting, 1% were separated, 4% were divorced and 3% were widowed. The average numbers of years married was 22.7. About half of the sample (46%) had children, with 37% of the children being 18 or younger.

The ethnicity of the sample was predominantly White (87%), with 3% African American/Black, under 1% Native American, 2% Hispanic, 4% Asian, and with 2% from other ethnic backgrounds.

The sample tended overall to be well educated in that 66% of the sample were college graduates or had attended some years of college. Twenty-one percent of the participants held master's degrees and 4% had received doctorates. Sixty percent of their fathers and 70% of their mothers had not completed college. Nine percent of the sample did not graduate from high school.

Most of the participants described themselves as university or seminary students (45%) or as professionals (29%). Twenty percent of the participants described themselves as being employed either as semi-unskilled workers, farmers, or in clerical-sales.

The majority of sample was Protestant (64%), of various denominations, but with the largest participation coming from the United Church of Christ (26%) and the United Methodist Church (11%). The second largest group was Roman Catholic (24%). Three percent were Jewish, and 1% were Muslim or Hindu. The remainder of the sample was made up of participants who described themselves as Buddhist, Gnostic, Pagan and holding no religious affiliation (5%).

The demographics religious characteristics suggest that over 61% of the participants were affiliated with mainline Protestant denominations or were Roman Catholic. Only about 5% of the participants identified themselves as belonging to Evangelical/Fundamentalist churches. Research participants were asked if their current religion was the same as their religion during childhood. In response, 65% of the participants stated that their religion was the same as in childhood, while 34% indicated they had changed religious affiliation. Fifty-nine percent reported having attended religious services every week or more while growing up. They reported attending religious services more frequently than their parents did. They also reported that their father attended religious services every week or more about 38% of the time, while their mother attended religious services every week or more about 50% of the time. Currently they report attending religious services every week or more 54% of the time.

Table 1
Demographics

Demographic Characteristics of The Sample (n=277)		
Characteristic	n	%
Gender		
Male	107	39
Female	170	61
Age		
Under 20	41	15
20-29	77	28
30-39	27	10
40-49	41	15
50-59	43	15
60-69	29	10
70 or more	18	7
Marital Status		
Single—Never Married	127	45
Married	125	45
Single—Living With Partner	4	2
Separated	2	1
Divorced	10	4
Widowed	9	3

Table 1 (cont.)

Characteristic	n	%
<u>Education Level</u>		
Less than high school	3	1
High School graduate	2	8
Some College	120	43
College Graduate	63	23
Masters Degree	59	21
Doctoral Degree	11	4
<u>Occupation</u>		
Semi-Unskilled	12	4
Skilled	19	7
Farmer	2	1
Clerical-Sales	20	7
Proprietor	2	1
Professional	81	29
Student	92	33
Seminary	33	12
Retired	13	5
Don't know	1	0

Table 1 (cont.)

Characteristic	n	%
Ethnic Group		
White	244	87
African American/Black	8	3
Native American	1	0
Hispanic	7	2
Asian	12	4
Other	5	2
Religion		
Roman Catholic	67	24
Eastern Orthodox	4	2
Protestant	178	64
Jewish	7	3
Muslim	2	1
Buddhist	1	0
Hindu	2	1
Gnostic	1	0
Pagan	1	0
None	14	5

Note: Percents may not totally add up to 100 due to rounding

Data Analysis

To analyze the data relevant to the six research hypotheses and 13 exploratory questions a number of statistical techniques have been employed. The specific statistical techniques depended on the type of independent variable (categorical or continuous) and type of dependent variable (categorical or continuous). For example, Hypothesis 1 predicted a relationship between level of childhood corporal punishment (a categorical variable) and adult partner violence (a categorical variable). Thus for this hypothesis the Chi-square statistic was the appropriate statistical test and was therefore employed. Other statistical techniques used were F-tests, Pearson Correlation Coefficients, and t-tests. Table 2 summarizes all the statistical techniques employed the study.

Table 2
Summary of Statistical Techniques Employed

Hypothesis/ Question	Independent Variable (Type)	Dependent Variable (Type)	Statistical Technique Employed
H1	Level of Childhood Corporal Punishment (Categorical)	Violence (Categorical)	Chi-square test
H2	Level of Childhood Corporal Punishment (Categorical)	Internalized Shame (Continuous)	F-test
H3	Level of Childhood Corporal Punishment (Categorical)	Image of God (Continuous)	F-test
H4	Violence (Continuous)	Adult Shame (Continuous)	Pearson Correlation
H5a/H5b	Image of God (Continuous)	Violence (Continuous)	Pearson Correlation
H6a/H6b	Image of God (Continuous)	Adult Shame (Continuous)	Pearson Correlation
Q1	Level of Childhood Corporal Punishment (Categorical)	Role of Religion (Continuous)	t-test

Table 2 (continued)

Q2	Level of Childhood Corporal Punishment (Categorical)	Perception of Parent (Continuous)	F-test
Q3	Perception of Parent (Continuous)	Violence (Continuous)	Pearson Correlation
Q4	Level of Childhood Corporal Punishment (Categorical)	Child Spanking (Categorical)	Chi-square test
Q5	Level of Childhood Corporal Punishment (Categorical)	Suicidality/Depression (Categorical)	Chi-square test
Q6	Level of Childhood Corporal Punishment (Continuous)	Detachment (Continuous)	F-test
Q7	Perception of Parent (Continuous)	Adult Shame (Continuous)	Pearson Correlation
Q8	Gender (Categorical)	Violence (Categorical)	Chi-square test
Q9	Belief About Human Nature (Continuous)	Violence (Continuous)	Pearson Correlation
Q10	Gender (Categorical)	Times Spanked (Continuous)	t-test
Q11	Level of Childhood Corporal Punishment (Categorical)	Ever Hit With Object (Categorical)	Chi-square test
Q12	Suicidality/Depression (Categorical)	Age (Continuous)	t-test
Q13	Violence (Continuous)	Adult Guilt (Continuous)	Pearson Correlation

CHAPTER 4

Results

Introduction

The four sections of this chapter present the results of the data analyses. Sections I and II present the statistical results pertaining to the six hypotheses. Sections III and IV contain the results relative to the additional exploratory questions asked of the data.

In Section I the results pertaining to hypotheses one through three are presented. These hypotheses examined the relationship between levels of childhood corporal punishment and the following aspects of adult functioning: adult partner violence, images of God and shame. Section II looks at certain aspects of adult functioning; namely, the relationships among partner violence, shame and images of God. Sections III and IV explore certain additional questions.

Section I

Hypotheses Concerning Relationships Between Childhood Corporal Punishment, and Adult Partner Violence, Shame and Images of God.

Hypothesis 1 predicted that those who experienced higher levels of childhood corporal punishment will tend to display higher levels of adult partner violence. Table 3 presents the results relevant to that hypothesis. Two statistically significant relationships were found. Higher levels of childhood corporal punishment were associated with higher levels of physical injury (p<.009) in adult partner relationships enacted by the respondent. Higher levels of childhood corporal punishment were also related to the respondent being a victim of physical assault in an adult relationship (p<.02).

Table 3
Use of Adult Partner Violence by Level of Childhood Corporal Punishment (H1)

% Acknowledging Use

Level of Childhood Corporal Punishment

Violence Measure	None (n=52)	1-5 times (n=156)	6-10 times (n=37)	11 +times (n=20)	Chi-sq	p
Respondent's use of tactics to resolve conflict						
Negotiation	98	97	100	100	1.97	n.s.
Psychological Aggression	73	77	89	90	5.25	n.s.
Physical Assault	14	21	27	20	2.56	n.s.
Physical Injury	6	5	14	25	11.58	<.009
Partner's use of tactics to resolve conflict:						
Negotiation	98	97	100	100	1.97	n.s.
Psychological Aggression	73	73	84	90	4.33	n.s.
Physical Assault	12	17	35	30	9.70	<.02
Physical Injury	4	6	11	10	2.30	n.s.

In Hypothesis 2 it was expected that those who experienced higher levels of childhood corporal punishment would tend to display higher levels of adult shame.Table 4 shows that this relationship held approximately in this sample. That is, those whose level of childhood corporal punishment increased from

None to 6-10 times showed higher internalized shame, but at the highest level of childhood corporal punishment (11 +times) internalized shame leveled off.

Hypothesis 3 predicted relationships between childhood corporal punishment and images of God. For benevolent/loving images the relationships with level of childhood corporal punishment were expected to be negative (Hypothesis 3a): those who experienced higher levels of childhood corporal punishment would tend to display lower levels of benevolent/loving images of God. For wrathful/punitive images the prediction was that the relationships would be positive (Hypothesis 3b): those who experienced higher levels of childhood corporal punishment would tend to display higher levels of wrathful/punitive images of God.

From Table 5 it can be seen that no significant results were obtained. Thus, the hypotheses were not supported by the data.

Table 4
Adult Shame by Level of Childhood Corporal Punishment (H2)

Mean

Level of Childhood Corporal Punishment

Measure	None (n=52)	1-5 times (n=161)	6-10 times (n=39)	11+ times (n=20)	F	p
Internalized Shame	23.3	26.8	34.3	29.4	3.57	<.06

Table 5
Images of God by Level of Childhood Corporal Punishment (H3)

Mean

Level of Childhood Corporal Punishment

Image of God Measure	None (n=51)	1-5 times (n=157)	6-10 times (n=39)	11+ times (n=19)	F	p
Benevolent/Loving						
stable	3.8	4.0	3.9	4.0	.56	n.s.
benevolent	4.4	4.5	4.4	4.5	.28	n.s.
guiding	4.3	4.3	4.2	4.4	.36	n.s.
traditional deity	4.2	4.2	4.2	4.3	.56	n.s.
Wrathful/Punitive						
condemning	1.7	1.6	1.9	1.7	.05	n.s.
wrathful	2.5	2.5	2.5	2.5	.00	n.s.
severe deity	2.1	2.0	2.2	2.1	.02	n.s.

Traditional Deity: God as benevolent, stable and guiding
Severe Deity: God as wrathful and condemning
For all image measures: 1=strongly disagree with image /5=strongly agree

Hypotheses Concerning Relationships Among Adult Partner Violence, Shame and Images of God.

Hypothesis 4 anticipated that higher levels of the use of violence in adult partner relationships would be related to higher levels of adult shame. In Table 6 it can been seen that two significant correlations relative to this hypothesis were found. Those who experienced higher levels of psychological aggression tended to have higher levels of shame (p<.05). Similarly, those who experienced more physical assault tended to have more shame (p<.05).

In Hypothesis 5a it was predicted that there would be relationships between adult partner violence and images of God. For benevolent/loving images the relationships with adult partner violence were expected to be negative (Hypothesis 5a): those who experienced higher levels of adult partner violence would tend to display lower levels of benevolent/loving images of God.

Table 7 presents the results relevant to that hypothesis. Two statistically significant findings emerged from the data. Higher levels of psychological aggression were associated with lower levels of benevolent/loving images of God (p<.01) in adult relationships perpetrated by the respondent. Similarly, those who experienced higher levels of psychological aggression tended to have lower levels of benevolent/loving images of God (p<.01).

For wrathful/punitive images the relationships with adult partner violence were expected to be positive (Hypothesis 5b): those who experienced higher levels of adult partner violence would tend to display higher levels of wrathful/punitive images of God.

Table 8 presents data relevant to that hypothesis. Two statistically significant relationships emerged. Those who experienced higher levels of physical assault in an adult partner relationship tended to have higher levels of wrathful/punitive images of God (p<.01). Likewise, those who experienced higher levels of physical injury in an adult partner relationship also tended to have higher levels of wrathful/punitive images of God (p<.05).

Table 6

Relationship Between Adult Partner Violence and Adult Shame (H4)

Violence Measure	Correlation with Adult Shame
Respondent's Tactics to Resolve Conflict:	
Negotiation	-.10
Psychological Aggression	.10
Physical Assault	.05
Physical Injury	.11
Partner's Tactics To Resolve Conflict:	
Negotiation	-.10
Psychological Aggression	.12*
Physical Assault	.13*
Physical Injury	.07

*p<.05
(n=270)

Table 7
Relationship Between Adult Partner Violence and Benevolent/Loving Images of God (H5a)

Correlation with Benevolent/Loving Images of God As:

Violence Measure	Benevolent	Guiding	Stable	Traditional Deity
Respondent's Tactics to Resolve Conflict:				
Negotiation	-.10	-.02	-.03	-.05
Psychological Aggression	-.18**	-.16**	-.11	-.17**
Physical Assault	-.05	-.01	.06	.01
Physical Injury	-.08	-.05	-.02	-.05
Partner's Tactics To Resolve Conflict:				
Negotiation	-.10	-.02	-.03	-.05
Psychological Aggression	-.17**	-.15*	-.08	-.15*
Physical Assault	-.11	-.10	.04	-.05
Physical Injury	-.12	-.03	-.01	-.06

Traditional Deity: benevolent, guiding, stable
*$p<.05$
**$p<.01$
(n=265)

Shame, Images of God and the Cycle of Violence

Table 8
Relationship Between Adult Partner Violence and Wrathful/ Punitive Images of God (H5b)

Violence Measure	Correlation with Wrathful/Punitive Images of God As:		
	Condemning	Wrathful	Severe
Respondent's Tactics to Resolve Conflict:			
Negotiation	.05	-.04	.00
Psychological Aggression	.06	.01	.04
Physical Assault	.03	.09	.07
Physical Injury	.07	.10	.10
Partner's Tactics To Resolve Conflict:			
Negotiation	.05	-.04	.00
Psychological Aggression	.10	.04	.07
Physical Assault	.11	.16**	.15**
Physical Injury	.12	.12*	.14*

Severe Deity: God as condemning and wrathful
*p<.05
**p<.01
n=265

Hypothesis 6a predicted a relationship between adult shame and images of God. For benevolent/loving images the relationships with adult shame were expected to be negative (Hypothesis 6a): those who experienced higher levels of adult shame would tend to display lower levels of benevolent/loving images of God.

Table 9 presents the results relevant to that hypothesis. Statistically significant relationships were found between adult shame and the following images of God: benevolent (p<.05), guiding (p<.05), traditional deity (p<.05). Higher levels of adult shame were associated with lower levels of benevolent/loving images of God (p<.05).

Hypothesis 6b predicted a relationship between adult shame and images of God. For wrathful/punitive images the relationships with adult shame were expected to be positive (Hypothesis 6b): those who experienced higher levels of adult shame would tend to display higher levels of wrathful/punitive images of God.

Table 9 also presents the results relevant to that hypothesis. Statistically significant relationships were found between adult shame and wrathful/punitive images of God: condemning (p<.05), severe deity (p<.05). Higher levels of adult shame were associated with higher levels of condemning and severe deity images of God (p<.05).

Table 9

Relationship Between Benevolent/Loving (H6a)and Wrathful/Punitive Images of God (H6b)and Adult Shame

Image of God Measure	Correlation With Adult Shame
Benevolent/Loving	
stable	-.05
benevolent	-.15*
guiding	-.13*
traditional deity	-.12*
Wrathful/Punitive	
condemning	.13*
wrathful	.09
severe deity	.13*

Traditional deity: God as stable, benevolent and guiding
Severe deity: God as wrathful and condemning
*p<.05
n=272

Section II

Exploratory Questions Pertaining to Corporal Punishment, Religion, Parental Warmth, Attitudes Toward Spanking Children, Adult Suicidality and Depression and Adult Detachment

Question 1 asked whether there was a statistically significant relationship between level of childhood corporal punishment experienced as a child and the role of religion in current life. The means on Role of Religion did not vary in a systematic way with level of childhood punishment.

From Table 10 it can be seen that no significant result was obtained. Thus, no relationship was found between childhood corporal punishment and the role of religion in current life.

In Question 2 the relationship between shame in adults and perception of parent as cold and uncaring was explored. From Table 11 it can be seen that two significant findings emerged from the data. Higher levels of childhood corporal punishment were associated with higher levels of the respondent as a child having perceived father as cold and uncaring ($p < .001$). In addition, higher levels of childhood corporal punishment were associated with higher levels of the respondent as a child having perceived mother as cold and uncaring ($p < .0004$).

Table 10
Role of Religion in Current Life by Level of Childhood Corporal Punishment (Q1)

| | Mean | | | | | |
| | Level of Childhood Corporal Punishment | | | | | |
	None (n=52)	1-5times (n=162)	6-10times (n=39)	11+times (n=21)	F	p
Role of Religion	3.4	3.7	3.4	3.8	.82	n.s.

Role of Religion: 1=none/5=extremely strong

Table 11

Relationship Between Perception of Parent as Cold and Uncaring and Level of Childhood
Corporal Punishment (Q2)

	Mean					
	Level of Childhood Corporal Punishment					
Frequency of Perceiving Parent as Cold and Uncaring	None (n=50)	1-5 times (n=151)	6-10 times (n=37)	11 +times (n=20)	F	p
Father	1.4	2.0	2.8	3.3	11.08	<.001
Mother	1.1	1.3	2.2	3.0	16.02	<.0004

Frequency of Perceiving Parent as Cold and Uncaring: 0=never/ 6=more than 20 times at age 10

Question 3 asked whether there was a statistically significant relationship between adult partner violence and perception of parent as cold and uncaring. From Table 12 it can be seen that no significant results were obtained. Thus, according to the data of this study, there was no relationship between adult partner violence and perception of parent as cold and uncaring.

In Question 4 the relationship between attitudes toward spanking children and level of childhood corporal punishment was explored. Table 13 shows that no significant relationship was found. However, examination of the percentage of "yes" responses to the Question suggested a follow-up analysis in which level of childhood corporal punishment was collapsed into two categories: No Childhood Corporal Punishment (None in Table 13) and Yes—Childhood Corporal Punishment (1-5, 6-10 and 11+ in Table 13). The two groups were then compared, and the results are displayed in Table 14. In that table it can be seen that those who experienced at least some childhood corporal punishment were more than twice as likely (38% vs 16%) to endorse disciplining a child with a hard spanking than those who had not experienced childhood corporal punishment (p<.01).

Table 12
Relationship Between Adult Partner Violence and Perception of Parent as Cold and Uncaring
(Q3)

Correlation With Perception of Parent as Cold and Uncaring:

Violence Measure	Father (n=256)	Mother (n=263)
Respondent's Tactics to Resolve Conflict:		
Negotiation	-.04	.02
Psychological Aggression	.09	-.00
Physical Assault	-.01	.01
Physical Injury	.06	.07
Partner's Tactics To Resolve Conflict:		
Negotiation	-.04	.02
Psychological Aggression	.06	-.02
Physical Assault	.04	.02
Physical Injury	-.01	-.02

Table 13
Attitudes Toward Spanking Children by Level of Childhood Corporal Punishment (Q4)

		% Responding Yes				
		Level of Childhood Corporal Punishment				
Question	None (n=49)	1-5 times (n=160)	6-10 times (n=38)	11 +times (n=21)	Chi-sq	p
It is sometimes necessary to discipline a child with a good hard spanking	16	43	21	33	.30	n.s.

Table 14
Attitudes Toward Spanking Children by Whether or Not Respondent Was Corporally Punished (Q4)

	% Responding Yes			
	Whether or Not Respondent Experienced Childhood Corporal Punishment			
Question	No (n=49)	Yes (n=219)	Chi-sq	p
It is sometimes necessary to discipline a child with a good hard spanking	16	38	8.59	<.01

Question 5 asked if there was a statistically significant relationship between adult suicidality and depression and level of childhood corporal punishment. From Table 15 it can be seen that three statistically significant relationships emerged from the data. Higher levels of childhood corporal punishment were associated with higher levels of being suicidal (p<.002). Similarly, higher levels of childhood corporal punishment were also related to higher levels of trying to commit suicide (p<.001). In addition, higher levels of childhood corporal punishment were related to higher levels of depression (p<.001). The strong relationship between childhood corporal punishment and suicidality and depression demonstrated in this data will be discussed in the next chapter.

In Question 6 the relationship between adult detachment and level of childhood corporal punishment was explored. Table 16 shows that there was a statistically significant association between adult detachment and childhood corporal punishment (p<.008). Those who experienced higher levels of such disciplining tended to display greater levels of adult detachment and unconcern.

Question 7 asked if there was a statistically significant relationship between perception of parent as cold and uncaring and adult shame. Table 17 shows that two statistically significant findings were found. Higher levels of adult shame were associated with higher levels of the respondent as a child having perceived father as cold and uncaring (p<.001) and higher levels of adult shame were associated with higher levels of the respondent as a child having perceived mother as cold and uncaring (p<.001).

Table 15
Adult Suicidality and Depression By Level of Childhood Corporal Punishment (Q5)

% Responding Yes

Level of Childhood Corporal Punishment

Question	None (n=52)	1-5 times (n=162)	6-10 times (n=38)	11+times (n=21)	Chi-sq	p
Ever Been Suicidal	2	21	26	29	9.53	<.002
Ever Tried Suicide	0	4	8	19	10.83	<.001
Ever Suffered From Depression	29	39	51	67	10.75	<.001

Table 16
Adult Detachment by Level of Childhood Corporal Punishment (Q6)

Mean

Level of Childhood Corporal Punishment

Measure	None (n=51)	1-5 times (n=160)	6-10 times (n=39)	11+ times (n=20)	F	p
Detachment	28.9	28.5	29.7	33.0	7.20	<.008

Table 17
Relationship Between Perception of Parent as Cold and Uncaring and Shame in Adults (Q7)

Correlation with Perception of Parent as Cold and Uncaring

Measure	Father (n=262)	Mother (n=270)
Adult Shame	.27***	.26***

***p<.001

Section III

Questions Concerning Partner Violence, Gender and Beliefs About Human Nature

In Question 8 the relationship between adult partner violence and gender was explored. From Table 18 it can be seen that three statistically significant relationships emerged from the data. The use of negotiation to resolve conflict in an adult partner relationship was significantly related to gender (p<.002). Females tended to be more likely than males to use negotiation in adult partner relationships as a tactic to resolve conflict. Higher levels of psychological aggression were also related to gender (p<.05). Females tended to be more likely to use psychological aggression in adult partner relationships as a tactic to resolve conflict. In addition, women tended to be more likely as partners than men to use negotiation in adult partner relationships as a tactic to resolve conflict (p<.002).

Question 9 asked if there was a statistically significant relationship between beliefs about human nature (from good to perverse/corrupt) and adult partner violence. From Table 19 it can be seen that five statistically significant findings were found. Lower levels of the use of negotiation as a tactic to resolve conflict was associated with higher levels of belief about human nature as basically corrupt and perverse (p<.05). Higher levels of the use of psychological aggression as a tactic to resolve conflict were related to higher levels of belief about human nature as basically corrupt and perverse (p<.001). Lower levels of the use of negotiation by one's partner as a tactic to resolve conflict was associated with higher levels of belief about human nature as basically corrupt and perverse (p<.01). Higher levels of the use of psychological aggression by one's partner as a tactic to resolve conflict was associated with higher levels of belief about human nature as basically corrupt and perverse (p<.01). Finally, higher levels of the use of physical assault by one's partner as a tactic to resolve conflict were associated with higher levels of belief about human nature as basically corrupt and perverse (p<.05).

Table 18
Use of Adult Partner Violence by Gender (Q8)

Violence Measure	% Acknowledging Use			
	Gender			
	Male (n=104)	Female (n=164)	Chi-sq	p
Respondent's Use of tactics to Resolve conflict				
Negotiation	94	100	9.68	<.002
Psychological Aggression	72	83	4.44	<.05
Physical Assault	15	24	2.75	n.s.
Physical Injury	9	8	0.04	n.s.
Partner's Use of tactics To resolve conflict:				
Negotiation	94	100	9.68	<.002
Psychological Aggression	72	78	1.22	n.s.
Physical Assault	17	21	0.48	n.s.
Physical Injury	9	5	1.53	n.s.

Table 19
Relationship Between Beliefs About Human Nature (basically good to perverse and corrupt) and
Adult Partner Violence (Q9)

Correlation With Beliefs About Human Nature

Violence Measure

Respondent's
Tactics to Resolve
Conflict:

Negotiation	-.17*
Psychological Aggression	.22***
Physical Assault	.08
Physical Injury	.06

Partner's Tactics
To Resolve Conflict:

Negotiation	-.17**
Psychological Aggression	.16**
Physical Assault	.15*
Physical Injury	.03

Beliefs about human nature: 1=basically good/ 6=perverse and corrupt
*p<.05
**p<.01
***p<.001
(n=266)

Section IV

Further Questions

In Question 10 the relationship between number of times spanked or hit and parent gender was explored. Table 20 shows that one statistically significant relationship was found. Mothers spanked their children more often than fathers (p<.05).

Question 11 asked if there was a relationship between being hit with an object and level of childhood corporal punishment. From the first row of Table 21 it can be seen that higher levels of childhood corporal punishment were associated with being hit with an object, and this relationship was highly significant (p<.000001).

In Question 12 the relationship between age of being corporally punished (first time and last) and adult suicidality and depression was explored. From Table 22 it can be seen that no statistically significant relationships were found between age and whether or not the respondent had been suicidal and had tried to commit suicide. However, there was a statistically significant relationship between age and depression. The older the respondent had been when hit by his or her father the more likely he or she would be depressed (p<.03).

Question 13 asked if there was a statistically significant relationship between adult partner violence and guilt. From Table 23 it can be seen that no significant correlations were obtained.

Table 20
Number of Times Spanked or Hit By Parent Gender (Q10)

| | Mean | | | |
Measure	Father	Mother	t	p
Number of times spanked or hit	1.79	2.14	2.02	<.05

Table 21

Whether Hit by an Object by Level of Childhood Corporal Punishment (Q11)

% Responding Yes

Level of Childhood Corporal Punishment

Question	None (n=51)	1-5 times (n=161)	6-10 times (n=39)	11+ times (n=21)	Chi-sq	p
Were you ever hit with an object?	0	46	77	91	69.82	<.000001

Table 22

Age of Being Corporally Punished (first time and last) by Adult Suicidality and Depression (Q12)

Mean

Whether Suicidal or Not

Measure	Yes	No	t	p
Age first hit by father	5.8 (n=30)	6.4 (n=125)	.87	n.s.
Age first hit by mother	6.1 (n=37)	6.4 (n=130)	.49	n.s.
Age last hit by father	11.6 (n=28)	10.9 (n=124)	.77	n.s.
Age last hit by mother	11.8 (n=35)	11.4 (n=130)	.39	n.s.

Table 22 (cont.)

Whether Tried to Commit Suicide or Not

Measure	Yes	No	t	p
Age first hit by father	5.7 (n=9)	6.3 (n=146)	.60	n.s.
Age first hit by mother	5.3 (n=9)	6.4 (n=159)	.86	n.s.
Age last hit by father	11.5 (n=8)	11.1 (n=144)	.28	n.s.
Age last hit by mother	11.6 (n=9)	11.5 (n=157)	.10	n.s.

Whether Depressed or Not

Measure	Yes	No	t	p
Age first hit by father	5.9 (n=65)	6.5 (n=88)	1.09	n.s.
Age first hit by mother	6.1 (n=74)	6.5 (n=93)	.76	n.s.
Age last hit by father	11.9 (n=64)	10.5 (n=86)	2.18	<.03
Age last hit by mother	11.7 (n=71)	11.4 (n=94)	.51	n.s.

Table 23
Relationship Between Adult Partner Violence and Adult Guilt (Q13)

	Correlation with Adult Guilt
Violence Measure	

Respondent's
Tactics to Resolve
Conflict:

Negotiation	-.02
Psychological Aggression	-.00
Physical Assault	-.06
Physical Injury	.04

Partner's Tactics
To Resolve Conflict:

Negotiation	-.02
Psychological Aggression	.01
Physical Assault	-.02
Physical Injury	-.08

(n=268)

CHAPTER 5

Discussion

Introduction

The purpose of this study was to investigate factors which may promote as well as mitigate the expression of violence in adults. This research has built upon previous research that has indicated that shame, a history of childhood corporal punishment and certain religious beliefs may be factors in the intergenerational cycle of violence. It extends current literature to include an empirical examination of the interrelationships among adult violence and shame, images of God and childhood corporal punishment. Furthermore, using a theoretical research methodology this study has examined certain aspects of the shame/honor system and its relationship to violence in the ancient Mediterranean world with the intent of determining if there are clues that might be helpful in mitigating and preventing violence.

This study addressed one primary question: how is shame, images of God and childhood corporal punishment related to adult violence? As well as empirically exploring the relationships among these variables, this study also theoretically examined the shame/honor system in the ancient Mediterranean world and its relationship to the perpetuation and/or mitigation and prevention of violence. It was predicted that there would be relationships among a history of childhood corporal punishment, adult shame, wrathful/punitive and benevolent/loving images of God and violence.

Major findings in the literature suggest that shame, a history of childhood corporal punishment, certain religious beliefs and images of God, and adult violence are widespread in our society.

Historically, Sigmund Freud and orthodox psychoanalytic theory downplayed shame and viewed childhood abuse as a figment of the imagination. Erik Erikson also failed to examine a possible relationship between shame and childhood corporal punishment in his developmental theory. Relational/feminist theoretical models of human personality contextually see shame as an experience of human disconnection and as a weapon used by dominant cultures to control non-dominant groups of people. Nathanson suggests that not only are intense emotions such as shame the doorway to the dynamic unconscious, but shame can also be the primary engine that fuels anger and impedes joy.

Helen Block Lewis (1971) developed the theory of bypassed and unacknowledged shame, which stresses that it is the hidden, unconscious aspects of shame, which can be the most destructive and lead to what she calls "humiliated fury." Scheff and Rezinger (1991) described a shame/rage spiral in which unacknowledged shame leads to anger and then to aggression. Tangney (1995a) argues that shame-prone people tend to withdraw from others and display more difficulty in managing their anger. Gilligan (1996) argues that shame is the most deadly of all emotions and there is an intimate tie between violence and shame. Klein (1991a, 1991b) suggests a model for violence prevention in which humiliation-prone people learn psychologically to immunize themselves to the destructive impact of humiliation.

The literature suggests that there is a long history of societal denial regarding the detrimental impact of childhood corporal punishment. Greven (1990, 1992) and others argue that historically religion has been used in the Western world to legitimize the use of corporal punishment and other forms of violence. Social scientist Murray Straus (1994b) believes that corporal punishment is one of the major factors in the cycle of violence in our world today. Recent studies indicate a possible relationship between childhood physical abuse, dissociation and the cycle of intergenerational violence. In fact, current literature suggests that one is less likely to repeat the cycle of abuse if an adult cognitively and affectively remembers his or her own childhood abuse.

Fowler makes a major contribution to the literature by coining the term "shame due to enforced minority status" which is shame based on internalized social discrimination. Capps calls for a theology of shame to address the experience of isolation, disconnection and inner "wrongfulness" which he feels many experience in our society.

No theorist or theologian writes about the relationship between shame and early childhood corporal punishment. The detrimental effects of childhood corporal punishment are frequently not considered in the literature supporting Straus's contention that there is a "selective inattention or a conspiracy of silence" surrounding this issue.

However, the literature does note a relationship between childhood abuse and images of God. In fact, a severely traumatized child is likely to develop not only a self-concept as an innately bad person, but also an image of God as wrathful and/or punitive. Current research supports an assumption of this study that the behavior of one's parents is related not only to one's images of God but also ultimately to the intergenerational cycle of violence (Mihalie & Elliott, 1997).

This study acknowledges that biblical literature has been used by some Christians to justify the use of corporal punishment. Whereas biblical texts in the hands of some conservative Christians of more evangelical/fundamentalist persuasion justify corporal punishment by their prescriptive perspective, the descriptive perspective that is offered in this study provides an alternative approach to the cycle of violence. The descriptive approach shows that the bible can provide insight into violence prevention.

Some argue that the ancient Mediterranean world was based on a shame/honor system, which evolved around the axis of public opinion (Pitt-Rivers, 1966, 1974; Malina, 1981; Neyrey, 1994). Others caution against seeing shame/honor in every Mediterranean interactions at the expense of other important meanings and dynamics (deSilva, 1995, pp. 11-12). Nonetheless, this study argues that the cycle of violence is perpetuated by a belief within the Code of Honor system that when one is dishonored or shamed it is necessary for a person to find a way to save face or to restore his or her honor even if it means resorting to violence. By examining certain aspects of the early Christian community as presented by deSilva (1995) an alternative perspective is presented on how to break the cycle of corporal punishment and angry paternal images of God by urging "communities of encouragement" that counter cultural structures of shame and shaming.

The 277 men and women, ages 18 to 86, who volunteered to participate in this study completed the Cook Internalized Shame Scale (ISS), the Gorsuch Adjective Checklist (GAC), the Test of Self-Conscious Affect (TOSCA), the Revised Conflict Tactics Scales (CTS2) and the Perception of Parents as Cold and Uncaring Scales (PPCUS) which was created from the Demographics Questionnaire. The participants also completed a detailed Demographics Questionnaire, which yielded additional data pertaining to the participant's childhood disciplinary history, religious background and practices, and adult functioning. The instrument scores and demographic data were analyzed to determine relationships among shame, images of God, violence, and childhood corporal punishment. Data from additional exploratory questions were also analyzed: relationships between childhood corporal punishment and religion, parental warmth, attitudes toward spanking children, adult suicidality and depression and adult detachment; relationships between partner violence and gender and beliefs about human nature; and relationship between gender and times spanked, relationship between level of childhood corporal punishment and use of an object, relationship between suicidality/depression and age hit, and relationship between adult partner violence and guilt.

The major findings of this study were:

☐ There was a positive relationship between adult partner violence and level of childhood corporal punishment.

❑ There was a borderline positive association between adult shame and level of childhood corporal punishment.

❑ There was no relationship between images of God and level of childhood corporal punishment.

❑ There was a positive relationship between being a victim of adult partner violence and shame.

❑ There was a relationship between adult partner violence and images of God: higher levels of psychological aggression were associated with lower levels of benevolent/loving images of God. Higher levels of assault and injury were related to higher levels of wrathful/punitive (condemning and severe) images of God.

❑ There was a relationship between adult shame and images of God: higher levels of shame were related to lower levels of benevolent/loving images of God and higher levels of shame were related to higher levels of wrathful/punitive images of God.

❑ There was no association between role of religion in current life and level of childhood corporal punishment.

❑ There was a positive relationship between having perceived, as a child, parent as cold and uncaring and level of childhood corporal punishment. The more a child was corporally punished the more likely he or she would perceive mother and/or father as cold an uncaring.

❑ There was no relationship between adult partner violence and having perceived, as a child, parent as cold and uncaring.

❑ There was a positive association between adult attitudes toward spanking children and whether or not a person was corporally punished as a child. If a person was corporally punished in childhood it was more likely that he or she would believe that "it is sometimes necessary to discipline a child with a good hard spanking."

❑ There was a positive relationship between adult suicidality/depression and level of childhood corporal punishment.

❑ There was a positive association between adult detachment and level of childhood corporal punishment.

❑ There was a positive association between having perceived, as a child, parent as cold and uncaring and adult shame.

❑ There was a positive relationship between psychological aggression and gender. Women tended to be more likely to use psychological aggression in adult partner relationships as a tactic to resolve conflict.

❑ There was an association between adult partner violence and beliefs about human nature. The more a person viewed human nature as basically corrupt and perverse the more likely that person could be physically assaulted in an adult partner relationship.

❑ There was a relationship between gender of parent and likelihood of being hit: one is more likely to be hit by one's mother than by one's father.

❑ There is a positive association between being hit by an object as a child and level of corporal punishment. The more one is corporally punished the more likely that an object was used.

❑ There is a positive relationship between age hit by father and adult depression. The older a child was hit by one's father the more likely this person will experience adult depression.

❑ There was no relationship between adult partner violence and adult guilt.

Major Findings

Section 1

Hypotheses Concerning Relationships Between Childhood Corporal Punishment, and Adult Partner Violence, Shame and Images of God

Hypothesis 1

The first hypothesis predicted that there would be a positive correlation between adult partner violence as measured by the CTS2 and higher levels of childhood corporal punishment. As was seen from the data analysis, this hypothesis was supported by two statistically significant relationships. Higher levels of childhood corporal punishment were associated with higher levels of physical injury ($p<.009$) perpetrated by the respondent in adult partner relationships. Higher levels of childhood corporal punishment were also related to the respondent being a victim of physical assault in an adult relationship ($p<.02$). In other words, the more you were corporally punished as a child was, the more you are at risk of physically injuring your partner in an intimate relationship. Likewise, the more you were corporally punished as a child the more likely you will be a victim of physical assault in an intimate adult partner relationship. These results confirm what some previous studies have indicated: that corporal punishment of children is one of the major factors in the cycle of violence in our world today (Straus, 1994b).

As was discussed in the review of the literature, several researchers have suggested that childhood corporal punishment is related to the cycle of intergenerational violence. Miller (1983, 1984) early on theorized a link between childhood corporal punishment/abuse and intergenerational violence (p.x). Likewise, Greven (1990, 1992) has held the same conviction as Alice Miller (1983,1984) that the breeding ground for societal violence is found within our families of origin (p. 9). I will attempt to expand our understanding of the roots of intergenerational violence later in this chapter as I discuss the relationships among a history of childhood corporal punishment, adult dissociation and intergenerational violence.

Straus's (1994b) empirical research has shown that corporal punishment of children is related to the intergenerational cycle of violence. Being corporally punished as a child increases the likelihood that as an adult one will be in a violent marriage and approve of interpersonal violence (p. 96).

The findings in this investigation contribute to this area of research both by confirming theories such as Greven (1990, 1992) and Miller (1984) and empirical studies such as those of Straus (1994b). These findings suggests that the more one is corporally punished in childhood the more likely one will either physically injure an adult partner or be the victim of physical assault in an adult partner relationship. Specifically these findings suggest that the reduction or elimination of childhood corporal punishment would decrease the levels of violence in American society (Straus et al., 1997, p. 761).

The results of this study also challenge some research and societal beliefs that a good spanking of a misbehaving child will stop violent behavior. In fact, this study shows the opposite in that corporal punishment of children increases the likelihood of adult violence. Finally, this study confirms Straus's (1994b) findings that the harmful effects of childhood corporal punishment show up later in life (p. xi).

Hypothesis 2

The second hypothesis predicted that there would be a positive relationship between adult shame as measured by the ISS and higher levels of childhood corporal punishment. Results indicate that this relationship held approximately in this sample. This is, those whose level of childhood corporal punishment increased from None to 6-10 times showed higher internalized shame, but at the highest level of childhood corporal punishment (11+ times) internalized shame leveled off.

Further research is needed to understand this finding—specifically, what needs to be investigated is whether denial may be a major factor in accessing feelings around shame and acknowledging the detrimental effects of childhood corporal punishment. Furthermore, this sample had lower than average shame scores. The average shame score (27.3) of this sample was below the national norm (31.5) indicating that as a whole the participants of the study reported less internalized shame than the general population. A contributing factor in this sample's lower than average shame scores may have been its demographic nature. Overall this sample was well-educated; most of the participants were either university or seminary students (45%) and /or professionals (29%).

Gelles and Straus's (1988) classic study on family violence described abused children as having "a poor self-concept" as well as other characteristics (p. 125). Thus it follows that higher levels of childhood corporal punishment could be related to higher levels of internalized shame. Lewis's (1971) shame theory suggests that shame frequently remains unacknowledged and unconscious. Even David R. Cook (1994) author of the Internalized Shame Scale cautions researchers about their interpretation of the ISS: "low scores are not necessarily free of significant shame issues" (p. 54). In fact, he emphasizes that "some people can be so well defended against the recognition of shame feelings that they will not report their presence when responding to this scale" (Cook, 1994, p. 2). What needs to be emphasized is that Cook's (1994) Internalized Shame Scale measures only conscious aspects of shame. It does not take into account the unconscious, and the capacity to repress shame. It could be that those subjects at the highest level of childhood corporal punishment (11+times) emotionally coped by keeping their shame unacknowledged and unconscious. The Internalized Shame Scale simply does not measure unacknowledged and unconscious shame.

James Gilligan (1996) from his years of working with violent male prisoners theorizes a relationship between shame and corporal punishment stating that violence against the body is the ultimate humiliation (p. 54). Gilligan's theory especially suggests a relationship between childhood corporal punishment and shame. Just as Lewis (1971) emphasized that shame can be denied or bypassed when it is unacknowledged so too can the detrimental effects of childhood corporal punishment. Straus has argued (1994b) that not only does society ignore the detrimental effects of childhood corporal punishment but until recently there has been almost a "conspiracy of silence" surrounding the issue (p. 82). Thus it is conceivable that this sample under-reported their own histories of childhood corporal punishment.

What is most interesting in the results is the fact that at the highest level of childhood corporal punishment (11+times) internalized shame leveled off. Interestingly enough Straus (1994b) found a similar decline but with depression instead of shame:

> For the women in this sample (the upper line in Chart 5-1), the average Depressive Symptoms Index starts at 49 and goes up from there to about 61.

Then, for reasons that are not clear, it declines for the highest categories of corporal punishment. (Straus, 1994b, p. 72)

There may be several reasons for this. Subjects who experienced a history of severe childhood corporal punishment may have developed coping mechanisms, which enabled them to deny the level of hurt and shame they had experienced with the punishment. Some people almost develop a macho attitude pertaining to their abuse by saying, "Oh, yea, I was whacked a lot as a child, but it didn't hurt me a bit."

We also do not know from this data if these subjects were physically hit in front of other family members. We do not know whether subjects in the other three groups correctly reported their levels of corporal punishment. We do not know whether there was a supportive parent who eased the sense of internalized shame. There may have been others significant factors, which may have impacted the subjects' shame levels.

However, it is the contention of this author that further research is needed in the area of shame and childhood corporal punishment.

Hypothesis 3

The third hypothesis predicted that there would be relationships between childhood corporal punishment and images of God. Specifically it was predicted that those adults who had experienced higher levels of childhood corporal punishment would display lower levels of benevolent/loving images of God. Likewise it was predicted that those adults who had experienced higher levels of childhood corporal punishment would display higher levels of wrathful/punitive images of God. Finally it was predicted that those adults who had experienced higher levels of childhood corporal punishment would display lower levels of guiding/protective images of God. No significant results were obtained. In fact, this study showed no relationship between any of Gorsuch's levels of images of God and levels of childhood corporal punishment. Again it needs to be emphasized that the Gorsuch Adjective Checklist (GAC) only measures conscious images of God.

The literature on object relations and images of God and violence suggests a relationship between childhood abuse and images of God (Brokaw and Edwards, 1994; Doehring, 1993). Probably most pertinent to this study has been Doehring's (1993) research in which she examined the "inter-relationship between experiences of childhood and adolescent abuse, and the way women as adults consciously describe God" (p. 1). Contrary to this study, Doehring (1992) found that childhood and adolescent traumatization—whether it be sexual abuse, the witnessing of domestic violence and/or physical abuse (p.1) is only related to images of God (God representations) when it is severe (p. vi).

Thus, the findings of this study do not support the literature. These results suggest that adult images of God are not at all related to levels of childhood corporal punishment. In fact, this study suggests that a history of childhood corporal punishment does not impact one's images of God. It may be that some children who have been severely physically abused hold on to loving images of God and these loving images not only sustain and comfort but may also serve a protective function.

A recent study by Lawson, Drebing, Berg, Vincellette, and Penk (1998) had a surprising outcome which showed that child abuse (sexual, physical, or emotional) "was related to increased frequency of prayer and of 'spiritual experience'" in adulthood (p. 369). However, the severity of child abuse was not correlated with prayer and spiritual experiences (p. 378) only with whether one was abused or not. Thus the data from the Lawson et al. (1998) study as well as the data from this study suggests that childhood corporal punishment "may actually result in a multidimensional reaction toward God and spirituality" (p. 378) as well as toward images of God. Furthermore, instruments need to be developed that measure both conscious and unconscious images of God.

Hypotheses Concerning Relationships Among Adult Partner Violence, Shame and Images of God

Hypothesis 4

Hypothesis 4 anticipated a relationship between adult violence and shame, meaning that higher levels of adult partner violence would be associated with higher levels of adult shame. Two significant correlations were found. There was a relationship between psychological aggression and adult shame, meaning that those individuals who were more psychologically aggressive tended to display higher levels of adult shame. Similarly, those individuals who experienced more physical assault in adult partner relationships tended to display higher levels of shame.

In part these results are consistent with the psychological shame and violence literature (Lewis, 1971; Scheff and Retzinger,1991; Tangney, 1995a; and Gilligan, 1996).In her clinical case studies Helen Block Lewis (1971) observed a relationship between shame and anger. She called this relationship "humiliated fury," and stressed that when shame is not acknowledged it can turn into a shame/rage spiral exploding into "humiliated fury" (Lewis, 1971, p. 87), thus leading to aggression and acts of violence. Scheff and Retzinger (1991) have contributed to the literature by their non-empirical research on shame and violence. Building on Lewis (1971, 1976, 1981) they described a shame/rage spiral in which unacknowledged shame leads to anger and then to aggression (p. ix). Tangney (1995a, et al. 1992, et al. 1994) have found a relationship between shame, anger and hostility (p. 1140).

But the leading theoretical proponent of a relationship between shame and violence is Gilligan (1996). Based on his work with violent offenders he has argued that shame is the most deadly of all human emotions and is at the root of violence. Gilligan has developed what he calls the "germ" theory of violence, which holds as a central tenet the belief that a precondition for violence is overwhelming shame combined with an absence of love and or guilt. More specifically Gilligan views corporal punishment as a humiliating experience which not only "kills" a person's sense of self, but simultaneously increases a person's sense of shame while decreasing feelings of guilt.

It was predicted that higher levels of internalized shame would be related to higher levels of adult partner violence. However, in this sample there was no statistically significant association between internalized shame and being a perpetrator of violence in an adult partner relationship. Yet the results did demonstrate that being a victim of psychological aggression and physical assault in an adult partner relationship was related to higher levels of internalized shame.

It is evident that this sample was predominantly a non-violent sample, which makes it very different from Gilligan's population. Of the 277 participants only 19 % reported either having physically assaulted or having been the recipient of physical assault in an adult partner relationship. Moreover, only 8% reported having physically injured a partner in an adult partner relationship and only 6% reported having been physically injured in an adult partner relationship. Gilligan's (1996) theory is not based on a non-violent sample, but rather on his many years of work with violent prisoners. It is questionable whether his theory can be applied to the population in general. Nonetheless, it is evident from this sample of primarily non-violent subjects that there is a relationship between higher levels of internalized shame and the increased likelihood of being the victim of psychological abuse and or physical assault in an adult partner relationship.

Hypothesis 5

Hypothesis five predicted that there would be a relationship between adult partner violence and images of God. The specific images of God that this study analyzed were Gorsuch's benevolent and wrathful images of God. (a) Thus it was predicted that there would be a negative relationship between adult partner violence and images of God: those who displayed higher levels of adult partner violence would tend to display lower levels of benevolent/loving images of God. (b) There would be a positive relationship between adult partner violence and wrathful/punitive images of God: those who experienced higher levels of adult partner violence would also tend to display higher levels of wrathful/punitive images of God.

As was seen from the data analysis, part (a) of the hypothesis was supported by two statistically significant relationships. Higher levels of psychological aggression were associated with lower levels of benevolent/loving images of God ($p<.01$) in adult relationships perpetrated by the respondent. Similarly, those who experienced higher levels of psychological aggression tended to have lower levels of benevolent/loving images of God ($p<.01$). Basically these findings suggest that a person who maintains a benevolent/loving image of God is less likely to be either psychologically abusive and or to be psychologically abused in an adult partner relationship.

Similarly, as was seen from the data analysis, part (b) of the hypothesis was also supported by two statistically significant relationships. Those who were the victim of physical assault in an adult partner relationship tended to have higher levels of wrathful/punitive images of God (p<.01). Likewise, those who experienced higher levels of physical injury in an adult partner relationship also tended to display higher levels of wrathful/punitive images of God. In other words, those who were victims of physical assault and or physical injury in an adult partner relationship were more likely to have wrathful/punitive images of God.

These findings are consistent with certain aspects of the literature on object relations and images of God and violence. As stated earlier in this study there was no relationship between images of God and severity of childhood corporal punishment. However, hypothesis five suggests a relationship between adult partner violence and images of God. Brokaw and Edwards (1994) argue that a child's internal representation of self and others are formed within one's early interpersonal environment and "influence the creation and projection of God image in later life" (p. 354).

It may be that certain images of God only become manifest in later life in the midst of stressful situations: (i.e., being a victim or a perpetrator of psychological abuse and or a victim of physical assault and or injury). However, these findings clearly suggest that one is more likely to experience violence in an adult partner relationship if one holds a wrathful/punitive image of God. Lambert, Triandis, and Wolf's (1959) classic cross-societal study empirically documented a relationship between violence in the form of childhood corporal punishment and religious systems based on punitive deities (Straus, 1994b, p. 191).

Gorsuch's (1968) concept of a wrathful deity not only reflects an image of God as judgmental and punishing but also a "fundamentalistic approach to religion" (p. 61). It has been an assumption of this study that such a wrathful/punitive image of God would be related to adult partner violence.

Hypothesis 6

Hypothesis 6 predicted a relationship between adult shame and images of God. For benevolent/loving images of God the relationships with adult shame were expected to be negative: those who experienced higher levels of adult shame would tend to display lower levels of benevolent/loving images of God. For wrathful/punitive images the relationships with adult shame were expected to be positive: those who experienced higher levels of adult shame would tend to display higher levels of wrathful/punitive images of God. Higher levels of adult shame were associated with lower levels of benevolent/loving images of God (p<.05) and higher levels of adult shame were associated with higher levels of condemning and severe deity images of God (p<.05). In other words this means the lower the shame the more likely a person will hold a benevolent/loving image of God and the higher the shame the more likely a person will hold a condemning and severe deity image of God. According to Gorsuch the severe deity image of God is an image of God that combines the wrathful and condemning images of God.

Again these findings are consistent with the psychological literature. Lewis (1971), Scheff and Retzinger (1991), and Gilligan (1996) have theorized a relationship between shame and anger, rage and violence. It is consistent with this theory that the higher the internalized shame the more likely a person will hold an image of God as wrathful/punitive as opposed to benevolent/loving.

Theologically Donald Capps (1993) provides insight into why shame is correlated with wrathful/punitive images of God. For Capps shame is an experience of isolation, disconnection and inner "wrongfulness" and is the pastoral theological issue of contemporary society. Relying on Kohut, Capps (1993) views internalized shame as a result of faulty mirroring on behalf of a parent, meaning that the parent exhibits a lack of parental warmth and empathy toward the child. Again Spero (1992) and Doehring (1993) as well as other object relations theorists (Rizzuto, 1979; Meissner, 1977, 1978, 1984, 1987: McDargh, 1983) have acknowledged that images of God or God representations are frequently formed in early childhood and are correlated with a child's parental images(s). Thus it would be logical to conclude that if a person with heightened shame holds an image of parent as not being benevolent and loving there is a greater likelihood that they would also hold a similar image of God. Taken to its farthest extreme shame implies self-hatred and when a person is in such a self-loathing place it is easy to image a God that is wrathful and condemning.

Section II

Exploratory Questions Pertaining to Corporal Punishment, Religion, Parental Warmth, Attitudes Toward Spanking Children, Adult Suicidality and Depression and Adult Detachment

Question 1

Question 1 asked whether there was a relationship between level of childhood corporal punishment experienced as a child and the role of religion in current life. There was no statistically significant relationship. However, it is interesting to note that participants in this study who reported being the most involved in religion were those who reported being the most severely corporally punished. In a most recent study, Lawson et al. (1998) found that men who had been abused as children "reported a higher frequency of prayer and higher frequency of recent spiritual experience"(p. 378). Thus current thinking surrounding the role of childhood sexual abuse and adult religiosity is pointing to an ambivalent relationship, one which includes alienation from God and religion (Russell, 1986; Finkelhor, Hotaling, Lewis, & Smith, 1989), but also increased religious involvement (Lawson et al., 1998, p. 370). It is important to note, however, that Lawson et al. (1998) could not find any studies "examining the impact of physical or emotional abuse on spirituality" (p. 370).

Question 2

Question 2 examined the relationship between perception, as a child, of parent as cold and uncaring (parental image) and level of childhood corporal punishment. Two significant findings emerged from the data. Higher levels of childhood corporal punishment were associated with higher levels of having perceived, as a child, father as cold and uncaring (p<.001). In addition, higher levels of childhood corporal punishment were associated with higher levels of having perceived, as a child, mother as cold and uncaring (p<.0004).

These findings are important because they clearly demonstrate that the greater the severity of childhood corporal punishment the greater the likelihood that a child will perceive mother and or father as cold and uncaring. Some advocates of childhood corporal punishment argue that childhood corporal punishment is not harmful as long as there is parental warmth. Studies by Straus (1994b) and Larzelere (1986) "show that although the harmful effects, are reduced, they are not eliminated" (Straus, 1994b, p. 153). However, this study clearly demonstrates that the more one is hit the less likely a child will perceive his or her parent as warm and caring. Furthermore, this study destroys the myth that childhood corporal punishment is for the child's own good (Miller, 1983, 1984). Clearly, a child who ends up perceiving his or her mother or father as cold and uncaring does not share the perception that such punishment is actually for his or her own good. All 277 subjects in this study were asked to give their reactions to the "first time you can remember being hit by one of your parents" and the most recent incident. Nearly forty percent checked that they "hated him or her" from a list of reactions. This is similar to an unpublished study by Cohn and Straus (described in Straus, 1994b, p. 149) in which they asked 270 students at two New England Colleges for their reactions (Straus and Hill, 1997, p. 4). Straus reported that forty two percent checked that they "hated him or her" as opposed to this study's finding of nearly forty percent.

One of the most harmful effects of childhood corporal punishment according to Straus (1994b) is related to conscience formation. Furthermore, he argues that "children are more likely to do what the parents want if there is a strong bond of affection with the parent" (p. 153). If there is a weak parental bond, meaning that there is not a strong bond of affection such as is evident when a child perceives a parent as cold and uncaring, then the parent loses influence over the child (p. 153). This study clearly confirms Straus's assumption "that each spanking chips away at the bond between parent and child"[22] which is critical to the development of conscience (p. 154) even with parental warmth. Straus and Hill (1997) go a step further to argue that frequency of childhood corporal punishment not only weakens the child-to-parent bond but it also increases the likelihood of juvenile delinquency (p. 3). Obviously, children who perceive their parents as cold and uncaring may have a very intense intrapsychic relationship with parents. However, what Straus (1994b) is arguing is that children who are not corporally punished "tend to control their own behavior on the basis of what their own conscience tells them is right and wrong rather than to avoid being hit" (p. 155).

Question 3

This question asked if there was a relationship between adult partner violence and having perceived, as a child, parent as cold and uncaring. No significant results were obtained. Clearly the issue of whether a child perceived a parent or parents as warm and caring was not related to the increased likelihood that such a child would become a violent adult. This study did not look at the relationship between violence and adult partner relationships perceived as warm and caring. This could be an important step for further research.

Question 4

To explore the issue of the intergenerational cycle of violence, Question 4 examined the relationship between attitudes toward spanking children and level of childhood corporal punishment. When attitudes toward spanking were examined in light of level of childhood corporal punishment no significant relationship emerged from the data. However, in examining the number of yes "percentages" to the number of no "percentages" further analysis seemed warranted. The follow-up analysis examined the attitudes toward spanking children not by level of childhood corporal punishment, but rather by whether or not the subject was corporally punished. This follow-up analysis showed that those who experienced at least some childhood corporal punishment were more than twice as likely (38% vs. 16%) to endorse disciplining "a child with a good hard spanking" than those who had not experienced childhood corporal punishment ($p < .01$).

An early and still popular theory (Steele & Pollack, 1968) surrounding the intergenerational cycle of violence is that abusing parents were themselves

---

[22] Again when Straus uses the term "bond between parent and child," he means a positive bond of affection consisting primarily of feelings of love, care and parental warmth.

abused as children (Egeland and Susman-Stillman, 1996). It is estimated by Kaufman and Zigler (1987) that the "rate of transmission across generations to be 30%, which indicates that the majority of parents with a history of having been abused as children did not abuse their own children" (Egeland and Susman-Stillman, 1996, p. 1123). This study reports an attitudinal rate of transmission of 38%, which is 8% higher than the norm of 30%. In fact, it may be even higher in reality. The subjects answered theoretical questions about their attitudes concerning hitting a child. A parent who theoretically denies that he or she might hit a child could respond differently in a moment of passionate distress. Thus, conservatively we can estimate that 83 subjects in this study who were corporally punished as children are likely to perpetuate the intergenerational cycle of violence.

Question 5

One of the most important findings in this study pertains to Question 5. Question 5 explored the relationship between adult suicidality and depression and level of childhood corporal punishment. Three statistically highly significant relationships emerged from the data. Higher levels of childhood corporal punishment were related to higher levels of depression ($p<.001$). In addition, higher levels of childhood corporal punishment were related to higher levels of being suicidal ($p<.002$). Similarly, higher levels of childhood corporal punishment were also related to higher levels of trying to commit suicide ($p<.001$).

Straus (1994b) has theorized that childhood corporal punishment increases the chances that later in life one will be depressed and have suicidal thoughts (p. 67). Straus further argues that the relationship between depression and corporal punishment has been virtually ignored not only by sociologists but also by clinicians such as psychiatrists and psychologists (p. 68). Furthermore, Straus acknowledges that there has been a scarcity of research examining the relationship between childhood corporal punishment and adult depression.

Once more Straus attributes such a paucity of research to the issue of "selective inattention" which was discussed in more detail in the literature review. Greven (1990, 1992) attributes this societal avoidance of the harmful effects to the fact that most people were corporally punished as children. Thus Straus's notion of "selective inattention" is similar to Greven's (1990, 1992) notion of "perceptual blinders." According to their theory, because most adults were corporally punished as children there is a pervasive societal denial of its potential detrimental impact.

Straus (1994b) has emphasized that "social scientists have paid little attention to the possibility that hitting children causes depression in them as adults" (p. 68). Greven (1990, 1992) not only examined the theological roots that supported the use of corporal punishment especially among devout Protestants, he also hypothesized a relationship between childhood corporal punishment and adult depression. He emphasized that such a relationship was especially true for evangelicals, fundamentalists, Puritans and Pentecostals. According to Straus (1994b) Greven "provides extensive historical evidence on the frequency and severity of corporal punishment among these devout Protestants" (p. 69). However, Greven provides no statistical evidence to support his theory (Straus, 1994b, pp. 69-70). Furthermore, his research focuses almost solely on the relationship between evangelical/fundamentalists and childhood corporal punishment. However, in this study only 5% of the participants self-identified as evangelicals and fundamentalists. Contrary to Greven's thesis, this study suggests that corporal punishment of children is not just a theological issue of evangelicals and fundamentalists. The fact remains that 81.5% of the participants in this study experienced childhood corporal punishment even though very few (5%) self-identified as evangelicals and fundamentalists.

Using data from the second National Family Violence Survey, Straus (1994b) and others examined the relationship between being hit as an adolescent and adult depression. He found a statistically significant relationship between being hit as an adolescent and adult depression.

This present study shows that an adult is 10% more likely to experience depression even if he or she was spanked in childhood only (1-5 times) during the most frequently hit year. However, an adult is almost 40% more likely to be depressed if as a child he or she was hit 11 or more times.

Suicidal thoughts often accompany depression. Again Straus's (1994b) research found a relationship between level of corporal punishment and suicidal thoughts. He did not find any statistically significant difference between whether mothers or fathers were doing the hitting and suicidality. However, he did find that "the chances of being suicidal are double for women who were hit the most by their parents as adolescents compared to those who were not hit by their parents" (p. 77).

This study found that a person's chances of having suicidal thoughts increases 19% with even the lowest level of childhood corporal punishment (1-5 times) as compared to no corporal punishment. Furthermore, in this study there were 14 people who had tried to commit suicide. All of those individuals had been corporally punished as children.

Question 6

This question examined the relationship between adult detachment and level of corporal punishment. The intent of this question was to investigate in an exploratory fashion why some people continue the intergenerational cycle of abuse and others do not. Using Tangney's Test of Self-Conscious Affect (TOSCA) adult detachment/unconcern was measured. The results showed a statistically significant relationship between adult detachment and level of childhood corporal punishment. Thus, those who experienced higher levels of childhood corporal punishment tended to display greater levels of adult detachment/unconcern (p<.008).

This researcher had also hypothesized (Question 13) that there would be a relationship between guilt and adult partner violence. However, as will be noted this study showed no significant relationship. As a consequence this researcher building on current child abuse literature (Egeland and Susman-Stillman, 1996) asked if what needed to be explored was not so much adult guilt as adult dissociation/detachment in relationship to the cycle of violence.

The Egeland and Susman-Stillman (1996) study found that the dissociation process is a factor in the intergenerational transmission of abuse. They hypothesized such a relationship because of observed behavior:

> Anecdotally, it appeared that mothers who were abused as children and who abused their children dissociated or 'split-off' the abusive experience whereas mothers who broke the cycle integrated the abusive experience into their view of themselves. (p. 1124)

It appears that the notion "bypassed shame" (Lewis, 1971) is a similar process to dissociation. In a dissociative process "affect is separated from behavior and affect may be separated from the event," (p. 1124). Egeland & Susman-Stillman stress that an important aspect of the dissociative process "is the fact that experiences which to some degree are out of conscious awareness can nevertheless exert an effect on behavior" (p. 1130). Similarly, in "bypassed shame," affect is separated from cognition as well as from the event that may have stimulated the shame feelings. Likewise, "bypassed shame," in which, affect and cognition are not fully conscious can also exert an effect on behavior. A case in point is the experience of "humiliated fury" (Lewis, 1971). This author has coined the term "bypassed child abuse," to describe the intergenerational cycle of abuse in which an unconscious/dissociative process is at work. Bypassed child abuse is child abuse that was affectively repressed in childhood, and is overtly expressed emotionally and physically in the behavior of adults against their own children.

The literature notes that one of the possible manifestations of dissociation is "depersonalization, which may range from a mild sense of detachment from one's experiences to drastic alterations of mind-body perception (DSM-IV, American Psychiatric Association, 1994)" (p. 1124). The Egeland and Susman-Stillman (1996) study found that, indeed, individuals who were abused and continue this abuse with their own children display more dissociative symptomotology than those individuals who did not continue the cycle of abuse (p. 1125).

If one understands dissociative symptoms as on a continuum from detachment to drastic alternations in mind-body perception it is noteworthy that in this study higher levels of childhood corporal punishment were correlated with adult detachment. It would be interesting in a further study to examine how many of the severely corporally punished who scored higher on the detachment/unconcern scale actually repeated the cycle of physical abuse with their own children.

Question 7

Question 7 is similar to Question 2 which examined the relationship of having perceived, as a child, parent (parental image) as cold and uncaring and level of childhood corporal punishment and Question 3 which examined the relationship between adult partner violence and having perceived, as a child, parent as cold and uncaring.

Question 7 examines the relationship between having perceived, as a child, parent (parental image) as cold and uncaring and adult shame. The results show that there is a strong relationship between having perceived, as a child, parent as cold and uncaring (parental image) and the level of shame in adults ($p<.001$). This is important since the statistically significant relationship between parental image as cold and uncaring and adult shame may be an indirect factor in adult violence even though Question 3 did not find a statistically significant relationship between adult violence and having perceived, as a child, parent as cold and uncaring. In Hypothesis 4 this study found that the higher the level of adult shame the more likely that person would experience psychological aggression and physical assault in an adult partner relationship.

To explain the relationship between having perceived, as a child, parent as cold and uncaring (parental image) and adult shame again this study relies on the insights of pastoral theologian Donald Capps (1993) (see discussion under Hypothesis 6). Capps (1993) relying heavily on the works of Kohut sees internalized shame as a result of the lack of parental warmth. Thus one might argue that the more frequently a child is corporally punished as a child the more likely he or she will develop a parental image as cold and uncaring which will in turn contribute to heightened levels of shame. This study also indicates that people who have higher levels of shame are more likely to experience physical aggression and physical assault in an adult partner relationship.

Section III

Questions Concerning Partner Violence, Gender and Belief About Human Nature

Question 8

Question 8 examined the relationship between adult partner violence and gender. The results showed no relationship between physical assault and/or physical injury and gender. However, there was a significant difference between the use of negotiation to resolve conflict and gender. Women were more likely to use negotiation (p<.002) to resolve conflict. However, an interesting finding was that women also tend to use more psychological aggression in an attempt to resolve conflict. One might simply understand this finding by arguing that women generally are more verbal than men (i.e. the use of negotiation and psychological aggression). However, these findings are perhaps to be expected. For survival purposes women most likely became accustomed to expressing aggression verbally rather than physically.

Question 9

Theologically Question 9 is one of the most important questions of this study. Building on the Ellison and Sherkat (1993) study, this study asked if there was a relationship between a person's beliefs about human nature and violence (i.e., human nature is basically good versus human nature is basically corrupt and perverse)?

As stated in Chapter Four five statistically significant findings were found. People who tended to view human nature as corrupt and perverse were more likely to use less negotiation and more psychological aggression to resolve conflict in an adult partner relationship. Likewise, people who tended to view human nature as corrupt and perverse were more likely to be in a partner relationship in which less negotiation, more psychological aggression and more physical assault was used as a tactic by their partners to resolve conflict. These findings indicate that in our search to prevent violence, theological beliefs about human nature matter. In fact, a view of human nature as basically good is related to less violent behavior in an adult partner relationship.

The Ellison and Sherkat (1993) study focused on Conservative Protestantism and its support for corporal punishment. In fact, they hypothesized that "members of Conservative Protestant denominations are more supportive of the principle of corporal punishment than other individuals" (p. 134). Their reasoning was that Conservative Protestants not only tend to view human nature as sinful, but they also believe that sin needs to be punished (i.e., support for childhood corporal punishment).

However, this study had very few participants who identified themselves as Conservative Protestants (5%). In fact, most participants were either members of the more liberal United Church of Christ (26%) or were Roman Catholic (24%). Nonetheless, 81.5 % of the participants in this study reported that they had been corporally punished as children and 33.7% of this study agreed that "sometimes it is necessary to discipline a child with a good hard spanking."This study indicates that one of the ways to mitigate violence is by encouraging and promoting a theological view of human nature as good.

Section IV

Further Questions
Question 10

Question 10 simply examined which parent (mother or father) most frequently hit or spanked. This study showed that mothers hit more frequently than fathers. This finding not only is supported by the literature, but also it makes sense given the fact that in our culture mothers still spend more time with their children than fathers.

Question 11

Question 11 asked if there was a relationship between severity of childhood corporal punishment and use of an object. The results showed a highly significant relationship ($p<.000001$). In fact, those who were hit (11 +times) or more were nearly twice as likely to be hit by an object than those who were hit (1-5) times. Ninety-one percent of those in the most severely corporally punished category reported having been hit by an object.

It is important to wonder about the use of an object in punishing a child. Does the use of an object enable a parent to feel more detached from his or her action, less empathically attuned, then to say the use of a bare hand? Is the use of object similar to using a weapon as opposed to using one's physical body (i.e. hand) to punish?

Straus (1994b) for purposes of his research has classified the use of object as evidence of physical abuse (p. 5). Since the relationship between severity of corporal punishment and use of object was so strong, this study ultimately decided not to exclude those who were hit by an object, but rather to interpret the results.

Forty-four percent of this study reported having been hit with an object at least once. The objects listed were belts, sticks, wooden spoons, hairbrushes, razor straps, rulers, spatulas, shoes, flyswatters, switches, 2 x 4s, coat hangers, paddles, tennis rackets, yardsticks, belt buckles, and newspapers in order of frequency used. Again there was a direct relationship between frequency of corporal punishment and the use of an object.

Question 12

Question 12 similarly to Question 5 examined the relationship between adult suicidality and depression and childhood corporal punishment. But Question 12 specifically examined whether age of childhood corporal punishment was related to adult suicidality and depression. Straus's (1994b) research on childhood corporal punishment and adult depression was based on a sample of adolescents. Question 12 specifically asked the question of whether age made a difference in the relationship between childhood corporal punishment and adult depression. More precisely, the relationship between age of being corporally punished (first time and last) and adult suicidality and depression was explored. There were no statistically significant relationships found between age and whether or not the respondent had been suicidal and had tried to commit suicide. However, similarly to Straus (1994b) there was a statistically significant relationship between age and depression. The older the respondent had been when hit by his or her father the more likely he or she would be depressed (p<.03) as an adult.

Straus (1994b) surmises that a contributing factor to the relationship between adolescent corporal punishment and adult depression is because during adolescence, fathers hit girls less. He explains this phenomenon by wondering about the specific impact on female adolescents: "So it could be that the psychological consequences are greater when a father hits an adolescent girl because it violates cultural norms about how a 'young lady' should be treated by a father" (p. 71). Straus found in his study that for males who were hit a lot during adolescence there was a 23 percent greater likelihood that they would experience depressive symptoms (p. 71). However, as stated earlier, "the chances of being suicidal are double for women who were hit the most by their parents as adolescents compared to those who were not hit by their parents" (p. 77).

Overall, Straus (1994b) found that the greater the severity of corporal punishment experienced during adolescence the more it was correlated with higher average scores on the "Depressive Symptoms Index" (p. 72). In line with other national studies on depression Straus's (1994b) research showed more depression for women who were corporally punished as children than for men (p. 72). Straus (1994b) also found an association between frequent corporal punishment as an adolescent and suicidality as an adult (p. 74). This study did not replicate any such findings.

In this study the average age of last being hit—of those adults who were depressed later in life—was 11.9 in contrast to 10.5 for those who were not depressed later in life. Thus these results indicate that the detrimental impact of childhood corporal punishment is clearly related to being hit at a later age. However, it is questionable whether the subjects actually remembered the first time they were hit in view of the fact that it is believed most children are hit at age three. The average age of remembering first being hit in this study was 6.29 years old for being hit by father and 6.34 years old for being hit by mother.

The subjects were asked to describe their reaction to the first time they could remember being hit or spanked by one of their parents. The first five responses out of a pool of 31 possible options were: "cried," "fearful," "humiliated and hurt," "angry," and "stopped me from doing it again." Only seven participants put "depressed." When asked their response to the last time they were hit the first five responses were: "angry," "cried," "resentful," "humiliated, hurt," "hated him or her." Fourteen participants reported feeling "depressed." It is interesting that the number who reported "depressed," actually doubled in the later years.

Question 13:

Question 13 asked if there was a relationship between adult partner violence and guilt. Gilligan, a prison psychiatrist, had theorized from his clinical practice with violent male prisoners and the criminally insane that the central precondition for violence is overwhelming shame combined with the absence of love and or guilt (pp. 113-114). Thus this question examined whether there was a relationship between adult violence and guilt. The assumption was there would be a negative relationship between adult partner violence and guilt, meaning that those individuals who displayed higher levels of adult partner violence would have lower guilt scores on the Tangney's Test of Self-Conscious Affect (TOSCA).

It may be that this sample was too non-violent in make-up to show a relationship between adult partner violence and guilt. Fowler (1993, 1996) building on the works of Carl Schneider (1977) emphasized two crucial aspects of shame: disgrace and discretionary shame. Question 13, in essence, examined Fowler's notion of discretionary shame, meaning shame as a form of conscience. Thus what Question 13 was trying to examine in violent offenders was their level of conscience. Thus the assumption was that people who participate in violent acts are often lacking in the area of conscience, those deep seated feelings that can serve as an "early warning system" (p. 114) to prevent us from participating in certain actions that can be harmful to self and others.

Another important aspect of guilt and violence is the issue of empathy. As stated earlier in this study Tangney (1995a) has contributed to the literature on guilt and violence by examining the relationship between guilt and empathy. Her research has shown that guilt is related to empathy, meaning that those individuals who display higher levels of guilt are more likely to also exhibit higher levels of empathy. She stresses in her research that guilt like empathy is other oriented. Furthermore, her research as well as Wiehe's (1997) research has shown that empathy can inhibit interpersonal aggression (p. 1137).

Areas of Further Research

Even though shame and childhood corporal punishment were significant factors in this study, only a statistically borderline relationship ($p < .06$) between adult shame and childhood corporal punishment emerged from the data. Because this was a retrospective study relying on the historical memory of the participants, this author suggests in the future a longitudinal study examining in more depth a possible relationship between childhood corporal punishment and shame. An interesting finding in Hypothesis 2 was the fact that internalized shame increased with severity of childhood corporal punishment until the most severe category of childhood corporal punishment. In this last category of childhood corporal punishment—(11+ times)—there was actually a decline in the level of internalized shame. Straus (1994b) had a similar finding in relationship to severity of childhood corporal punishment but with depression rather than shame (p. 72). This surprising finding warrants more research.

Furthermore, a major hypothesis of this study was the relationship between adult violence and shame. The leading theoretical proponent of this relationship was Gilligan (1996). However, as stated earlier, Gilligan's theory comes out of his experience with violent prisoners. This study did not find a relationship between being a perpetrator of violence and adult shame. However, it did show that the higher a person's internalized shame the more likely that person could be a victim of psychological aggression and physical assault in an adult partner relationship. This sample was primarily a non-violent sample. Further research should look more specifically at these issues with a violent sample.

More research is necessary to examine why there was no relationship between childhood corporal punishment and any of Gorsuch's images of God. These results were not consistent with current literature on object relations and images of God and violence, which suggests a relationship between childhood abuse and images of God (Brokaw and Edwards, 1994; Doehring, 1993). Therefore, this author is of the opinion that these inconsistent findings warrant more research.

Lawson et al. (1998) in their research could not find any studies examining the impact of physical or emotional abuse on spirituality. However, in this particular research project it was the participants who had reported being the most severely abused as children who had also reported being the most actively involved in current religious behaviors as defined as "frequency of prayer and of 'spiritual experience'"[23] (p. 369). Because of this finding, more research is warranted examining the role of religious behavior and spirituality in adults who experienced severe childhood corporal punishment.

The results of this study linking a history of childhood corporal punishment and adult depression and suicidality agree with the findings of Straus (1994b). Likewise, these findings suggest the need for more definitive studies investigating the link between childhood corporal punishment and adult depression and suicidality. With such high rates of depression and suicide in our society it is pertinent to ascertain if childhood corporal punishment is a causal factor. Such a finding would have "far-reaching implications for preventing depression and suicide" (Straus, 1994b, p. 79).

This study found a highly statistically significant relationship between severity of childhood corporal punishment and adult detachment/unconcern as measured on the detachment scale of Tangney's Test of Self-Conscious Affect

---

[23] "Each subject completed the Spiritual Issues Assessment, a large survey which includes data about: (1) KASL Religiosity Index; (2) The Spiritual Injury Scale; and (3) Religious items from the Westberg Personal Health Inventory" (Lawson et al., 1998, p. 369).

(TOSCA). This finding warrants further research examining the relationships among being severely corporally punished in childhood, adult detachment/unconcern and the repetition of the cycle of physical abuse with one's own children.

This study showed that women tend to use negotiation as well as psychological aggression to resolve conflict more frequently than men do. More research could be done in this area. Straus's (1974) study indicated that those who use psychological aggression to resolve conflict are more likely to resort to physical violence. It would be interesting to explore a possible relationship between the use of psychological aggression with children and severity of corporal punishment. Are children who experience more psychological aggression from their mothers more likely to experience greater levels of childhood corporal punishment?

This study found a relationship between beliefs about human nature and violence (i.e., human nature is basically good versus human nature is basically corrupt and perverse). In essence, a view of human nature as basically good is related to less violent behavior in an adult partner relationship. As stated previously the theory behind this question was based on a sample of Conservative Protestants (Ellison and Sherkat, 1993). Yet only 5% of the participants in this study self-identified as such. Further research is warranted because it appears from the literature that Conservative Protestants are often blamed as "the only religious people who support childhood corporal punishment." This study has clearly indicated that even Protestants from more liberal traditions are supportive of the use of childhood corporal punishment. It would be interesting at some point to do a comparative study between Conservative Protestants and Liberal Protestants examining more in-depth the relationship between the use of corporal punishment on children, and theological views about human nature.

This study showed a highly significant relationship between severity of childhood corporal punishment and the use of an object. More research could be done in this area. Are certain objects more indicative of severe corporal punishment than others are? Do parents use objects to distance themselves from the act of corporally punishing their children? Would these parents score higher than non-abusing parents on a detachment scale or a dissociation scale such as the Dissociative Experience Scale (Bernstein & Putnam, 1986)?

This study showed that the older the respondent had been when hit by his or her father the more likely he or she would be depressed ($p<.03$) in adulthood. More research should be done on the impact of being hit as an adolescent in relationship to adult depression and suicidality and gender of parent. Furthermore, more longitudinal studies should also be done on the impact of early childhood corporal punishment. Because of memory/recall problems in retrospective studies on childhood corporal punishment it is virtually impossible for such a study to ascertain reliable data.

Tangney's (1995a) and Wiehe's (1997) research indicate that one of the most important areas of possible future research is examining the relationship between empathy and violence prevention. This researcher feels that another study is warranted that would examine the relationships among shame, violence, guilt and empathy. Perhaps a sample of violent offenders and or victims of violence would be necessary for such a study.

Implications of the Study

This study has shown that one is more likely to be both a perpetrator and victim of adult partner violence the more one was corporally punished as a child. Thus a major implication of this study would suggest—in keeping with Straus et al's (1977) research— that the reduction or elimination of childhood corporal punishment would decrease the levels of family violence in American society. Furthermore, this study challenges the societal belief that a good spanking of a misbehaving child will stop violent behavior. In fact, this study shows that the opposite is often the case, meaning childhood corporal punishment increases the likelihood that one will be the victim or perpetrator of adult partner violence. This study implies that on the short run parents might have the impression that a spanking was effective but it is the long-term consequences of childhood corporal punishment that must come to public attention such as the increase in adult violence, suicidality/suicide and depression.

This study with 277 participants showed that 38% or 83 participants felt it was "sometimes necessary to discipline a child with a good hard spanking." This was predominately a white, high functioning, non-clinical, religious, non-violent sample. Nonetheless, even this sample had over one-third of the participants who mostly likely would continue the intergenerational cycle of childhood corporal punishment.

Not a surprising finding was the fact that this study showed that mothers hit their children more frequently than fathers. However, this finding does have important implications for mothers. If the family is the "cradle of violence" (Straus, 1994b) mothers dedicated to stopping the use of corporal punishment on children could play a significant role in breaking the intergenerational cycle of violence.

Implications for Clinical/Pastoral Practice

From this study it is very clear that internalized shame puts a person more at risk of being a victim of both psychological aggression and physical assault. This has major implications for clinical/pastoral practices in that a client and or parishioner who suffers from high levels of internalized shame is at risk of being a victim of domestic violence. It is critical that clinicians and pastors understand that high levels of shame can be a marker for violence.

Equally important for clinical/pastoral practice is the relationship between shame and images of God. People who have more benevolent/loving images of God tend to have lower levels of shame. Likewise people who have more wrathful/punitive images of God tend to have higher levels of internalized shame. It is important as a clinician and pastor to be aware that wrathful/punitive images of God are not only a marker for interpersonal violence but also a marker for higher levels of internalized shame.

It is pertinent that the relationship between childhood corporal punishment and depression and suicidality be brought to the attention of clinicians and pastors. The suicide and depression rates are extremely high in our culture. A history of childhood corporal punishment should be viewed as a risk factor for adult depression and suicidality.

This study showed a highly significant relationship ($p<.000001$) between severity of childhood corporal punishment and the use of an object. There is such a direct relationship between severity of childhood corporal punishment and use of object that a clinician in taking a history of a client could simply ask whether or not a person had been hit with an object. This information could help the clinician determine the probability of a history of severe corporal punishment, which in turn is a risk factor for depression and suicidality.

Egeland and Susman-Stillman (1996) found that mothers who were able to break the cycle of abuse "were involved as adolescents and young adults in long-term, intensive psychotherapy that enabled them to come to grips with their early experience of abuse" (p. 1130). This is an important finding for clinicians and pastors as we seek ways to stop the cycle of intergenerational violence.

Implications for the Community of Faith

A major finding of this study which has major implications for the community of faith has to do with our images of God. This study has shown that wrathful/punitive images of God are correlated with increased violence whereas benevolent/loving images of God are correlated with lowered emotional violence. Basically these findings suggest that a person who maintains a benevolent/loving image of God is less likely to be either psychologically abusive and/or psychologically abused in an adult partner relationship. Furthermore, these findings suggest that a person who maintains wrathful/punitive images of God is more likely to be a victim of physical assault and/or physical injury in an adult partner relationship. These findings have major implications for faith communities concerned with interpersonal/ family and societal violence.

Furthermore, results from Gorsuch's God Adjective Checklist showed that people are less psychologically aggressive if they have a more supportive and encouraging image of God as encompassed in Gorsuch's guiding image of God. This is consistent with deSilva's (1996) thesis that the early Christian community as depicted in Hebrews was able to resist the violence of societal shaming by creating communities of encouragement.

This study showed that those individuals who reported being most involved in religion were also those individuals who had been most severely corporally punished as children. From this study it is incumbent upon faith communities to be sensitive to its population which may include high rates of adults who have experienced severe childhood abuse.

Furthermore, it is important that the community of faith understand the cycle of intergenerational abuse as a first step in learning how to mitigate violence. This study has shown that the more frequently a child is corporally punished, the more likely he or she will develop a parental image as cold and uncaring which will in turn contribute to heightened levels of shame and will most likely be related to wrathful/punitive images of God. This study also indicates that people who have higher levels of shame and wrathful/punitive images of God are more likely to experience psychological aggression, and/or physical assault and/or physical injury in an adult partner relationship. Moreover, this study has shown that a view of human nature as basically good is related to less violent behavior in adult partner relationships. A step in breaking the intergenerational cycle of violence in the community of faith would be by providing an affirming, encouraging and supportive environment for parishioners in which benevolent/loving images of God are emphasized as well as a vision of human nature as good.

Chris Schlauch (1995) emphasizes that empathy is at the heart of pastoral care. Recent research has shown that empathy can inhibit interpersonal aggression (Tangney, 1995a). An implication of this research for the community of faith in its desire to prevent violence would be teaching people how to be more empathic (Wiehe, 1997). Empathy training can also help parishioners reduce their reliance on corporal punishment as a disciplinary tactic with children. In fact, there seems to be a relationship between empathy, dissociation/detachment and the cycle of abuse:

> Not having access to past experience or having intermittent and inconsistent access may make the abused individual more vulnerable to abusing in the next generation. Compartmentalizing experiences and not associating thoughts, feelings, and actions may make it more likely that a parent could abuse his/her child without having empathy and feeling the pain. (Egeland & Susman-Stillman, 1996, p. 1130)

In fact, Egeland and Susman-Stillman (1996) note that the mothers who broke the intergenerational cycle of abuse "were very aware of the hurt they experienced as a child and made sure that this was not repeated with their children" (p. 1130).

Conclusion

This study began by investigating factors, which may promote as well as mitigate the expression of violence in adults. It concluded that shame, a history of childhood corporal punishment and certain religious beliefs and practices are major factors in the intergenerational cycle of violence.

This study stressed that the detrimental effects of childhood corporal punishment are frequently ignored and society at large participates in a kind of "selective inattention or a conspiracy of silence" surrounding this issue. A major focus in the Literature Review of this study was on shame. Until very recently both theologians and psychologists also participated in a kind of "selective inattention" regarding shame. This study showed that shame is intimately tied to violence and that the higher a person's internalized shame the more likely that person could be a victim of psychological aggression and physical assault in an adult partner relationship.

The literature suggests that it is the hidden aspects of shame that are most deadly. Empirical studies note that shame can kill and is a leading factor in violence turned inward, namely suicide. This study showed an irrefutable relationship between a history of childhood corporal punishment and adult suicidality/suicide and depression.

This study also showed that one is more likely to be both a perpetrator and victim of adult partner violence the more one was corporally punished as a child. Viewing the family as the "the cradle of violence" (Straus, 1994b), a logical conclusion of this study suggests that the reduction or elimination of childhood corporal punishment would decrease the levels of violence in American society.

This study in its investigation into factors, which may promote as well as mitigate the expression of violence, has identified several risk factors or markers for interpersonal violence. Higher levels of internalized shame places a person more at risk of being a victim of both psychological aggression and physical assault. People who hold more wrathful/punitive images of God are more at risk of being physically assaulted and/or injured in an adult partner relationship. A history of childhood corporal punishment puts an adult at greater risk of suicide/suicidality and depression. A history of childhood corporal punishment increases the chances that an adult will be either a perpetrator and/or victim of interpersonal violence. Finally this study has shown that a view of human nature as perverse and corrupt is related to more violent behavior in adult partner relationships.

It is the opinion of this author that future research should focus on the role of empathy in violence prevention. Finally, this study concludes that a major step in breaking the intergenerational cycle of violence would be to develop affirming, encouraging, empathy based non-shaming faith communities in which benevolent/loving images of God are emphasized as well as a vision of human nature as good. Then, perhaps, one day the nursery rhyme will read:

> There was a little girl, and she had a little curl
> Right in the middle of her forehead;
> When she was good she was very, very good,
> But when she was bad she was understood.
> She no longer screamed and squalled or yelled and bawled
> Or drummed her little heels against the winder.

REFERENCES

Adler, A. (1956). The individual psychology of Alfred Adler. New York: Basic Books.

Ainsworth, M. (1979). Infant-mother attachment. Am. Psychologist, 34, 932-937.

Albers, R.H. (1995). Shame: A faith perspective. New York: The Haworth Pastoral Press.

Alwin, D. F. (1986). Religion and parental child-rearing orientations: Evidence of a Catholic-Protestant convergence. American Journal of Sociology, 92, 412-40.

Alonso, A., & Rutan, S. (1988). The experience of shame and restoration of self respect in group therapy. Int J Group Psychotherapy, 38 (1), 3-14.

Anderson, R.S. (1990). Imago Dei. In R. J. Hunter (Ed.), Dictionary of pastoral care and counseling (pp. 571-572). Nashville: Abingdon Press.

Balcom, D. (1991). Shame and violence: Considerations in couples' treatment. In K. Lewis (Ed.), Family therapy applications to social work: Teaching and clinical practice (pp. 165-181). New York: Haworth.

Baroja, J.C. (1966, 1974). Honour and shame: A historical account of several conflicts. In J. G. Peristiany (Ed.), Honour and shame: The values of Mediterranean society(pp. 79-137). Chicago: University of Chicago Press.

Bellah, R.N., Madsen, R., Sullivan, W.M., Swidler, A., & Tipton, S.M. (1985). Habits of the heart—Individualism and commitment in American life. Berkeley: University of California Press.

Belenky, M., Clinchy, B., Goldberger, N., & Mattuck, J. (1986). Women's way of knowing: The development of self, voice, and mind. New York: Basic Books.

Bernardez, T. (1988). Women and anger—Cultural prohibitions and the feminine ideal. (Work in Progress, No. 31.) Wellesley, MA: Stone Center Working Paper Series.

Bernstein, E.M.; & Putnam, F.W. (1986). Development, reliability, and validity of dissociation scale. The Journal of Nervous and Mental Disease, 174(12), 727-735.

Blumenthal, D. (1993). Facing the abusing God: A theology of protest. Louisville, Kentucky: Westminster/John Knox Press.

Bonhoeffer, D. (1955). Ethics. London: SCM Press.

Bowlby, J. (1969). Attachment and loss (Vol. 1). New York: Basic Books.

Bowlby, J. (1973). Attachment and loss (Vol. 2). New York: Basic Books.

Braithwaite, J. (1989). Crime, shame, and reintegration. Cambridge:Cambridge
       University Press.

Braithwaite, J. (1993). Shame and modernity. British-Journal-of Criminology, 33
       (1), 1-18.

Bradshaw, J. (1988). Healing the shame that binds you. Deerfield Beach, Florida:
       Health Communications, Inc.

Breuer J., & Freud, S. (1955). In J. Strachey (Ed. And Trans.), The standard edition
       of the complete psychological works of Sigmund Freud (Vol. 2). London: The
       Hogarth Press.

Brock, R. N. (1988). Journey by heart: A Christology of erotic power. New York:
       Crossroad.

Brokaw, B.F.; & Edwards, K.J. (1994). The relationship of God image to level of
       object relations development. Journal of Psychology and Theology, 22(4),
       352-371.

Brown, J., & Bohn, C. (1989). Christianity, patriarchy and abuse. New York: The
       Pilgrim Press.

Brown, R. M. (1973). Religion and violence: A primer for white Americans.
       Philadelphia: The Westminster Press.

Browning, D. (1991). A fundamental practical theology. Minneapolis: Fortress
       Press.

Brueggemann, W. (1982). Genesis: Interpretation—A biblical commentary for
       teaching and preaching. Atlanta: John Knox Press.

Buber, M. (1973). Guilt and guilt feelings. In E.C. Nelson (Ed.), Conscience:
       Theological and psychological perspectives (pp. 224-237). New York:
       Newman Press.

Burton, L.A. (1988). Original sin or original shame? Quarterly review—A journal
       of scholarly reflection for ministry, 8(4), 31-41.

Burton, L.A. (1991). Respect: Response to shame in health care. Journal of Religion and Health, 30(2), 139-148.

Capps, D. (1983). Life cycle theory and pastoral care. Philadelphia: Fortress Press.

Capps, D. (1990). Bible, pastoral use and interpretation of. In R.J. Hunter (Ed.), Dictionary of pastoral care and counseling (pp. 82-85). Nashville: Abingdon Press.

Capps, D. (1992). Religion and child abuse: Perfect together. Journal for the Scientific Study of Religion, 31(1), pp.1-14.

Capps, D. (1993). The depleted self—Sin in a narcissistic age. Minneapolis: Fortress Press.

Capps, D. (1995). The child's song—The religious abuse of children. Louisville: Westminister John Knox Press.

Carson, B.A. (1986). Parents who don't spank: Deviation in the legitimization of physical force. Durham, NH: University of New Hampshire, Ph.D. dissertation.

Chopp, R. (1995). Saving work: Feminist practices of theological education. Louisville, Kentucky: Westminster John Knox Press.

Coleman, M. (1985). Shame: A powerful underlying factor in violence and war. Journal-of-Psychoanalytic-Anthropology, 8(1), 67-79.

Cook, D. R. (1987). Measuring shame: The internalized shame scale. Alcoholism Treatment Quarterly, 4(2), 197-215.

Cook, D. R. (1988). The measurement of shame: The internalized shame scale. Paper presented at the Annual Meetings of the American Psychological Association, Atlanta, August.

Cook, D.R. (1991). Shame, attachment, and addictions: Implications for family therapists. Contemporary Family Therapy, 13(5), 405-419.

Cook, D. R. (1994). The internalized shame scale manual. Menomonie, WI:Channel Press.

Cooley, C. H. (1902, 1970). Human nature and the social order. New York: Schocken Books.

Crossan, J.D. (1992). The historical Jesus—The life of a Mediterranean Jewish peasant. New York, New York: Harper Collins Publishers.

Daly, M. (1993). Beyond God the father. Boston: Beacon Press.

Daube, D. (1969). The culture of Deuteronomy. Orita, 3, pp. 27-52.

Davenport, D. S. (1991). The functions of anger and forgiveness: Guidelines for psychotherapy with victims. Psychotherapy, 28(1), 140-144.

Davis, P.W., & Kii, T. (1997, June). Naturalistic observations of 250 children hit in public settings. Paper presented at the 5th International Family Violence Research Conference, Durham, New Hampshire.

Dean, D. G. (1961). Alienation: Its meaning and measurement. American Sociological Review, 26, 753-58.

Dixon, S.L., Underwood, M., Hoeft, J., & Roth, H. (1996). Alice Miller's insightful, inadequate critique of religion. Religious Studies Review, 22(3), 191-196.

deSilva, D. A. (1995). Despising shame: Honor discourse and community maintenance in the Epistle to the Hebrews. Atlanta, Georgia: Scholars Press.

Doehring, C. (1992). An exploratory study of the relationship between traumatization and mental representations of God. Ann Arbor: University Microfilms International.

Doehring, C. (1993). Internal desecration:Traumatization and representations of God. Lanham, Maryland: University Press of American, Inc.

Doehring, C. (1995). Taking care: Monitoring power dynamic and relational boundaries in pastoral care and counseling. Nashville: Abingdon Press.

Doehring, C. (1998). (in press) A method of feminist pastoral theology. In Bonnie Miller-McLemore and Brita Gill-Austern (Eds.), Feminist and womanist pastoral theology: Implication for care, faith and reflection. Nashville:Abingdon Press.

Durkheim, E. (1905, 1951). Suicide. New York: Free Press.

Dutton, D. & Painter, S.L. (1981). Traumatic bonding: The development of emotional attachments in battered women and other relationships of intermittent abuse. Victimology, 6, 139-155.

Dutton, D.G. (1987). Wife assault: Social psychological contributions to criminal justice policy. In S. Oskamp (Ed.), Applied Social Psychology Annual(pp. 238-261). Newbury Park, Beverly Hills: Sage Publications.

Elias, Norbert. (1978, 1982, 1983). The civilizing process. Vols. 1-3. New York:Vintage.

Elissa, L. (1983). The group treatment of battered women. Women-and Therapy, 2(1), 51-58.

Ellison, C.G.; & Sherkat, C.E. (1993). Conservative Protestantism and support for corporal punishment. American Sociological Review, 58,131-44.

Egeland, B., & Susman-Stillman, A. (1996). Dissociation as a mediator of child abuse across generations. Child Abuse & Neglect, 16, 1123-1132.

Englander, E. (1977). Understanding violence. Mahwah, N.J.: Lawrence Erlbaum Associates.

Erikson, E. (1950,1963). Childhood and society. New York: Norton.

Erikson, E. (1958). Young man Luther: A study in psychoanalysis and history. New York: W.W. Norton.

Erikson, E. (1965). Psychoanalysis and ongoing history: Problems of identity, hatred and nonviolence. The American Journal of Psychiatry. 122, 241-250.

Erikson, E. (1968). Identity: Youth and crisis. New York: W.W. Norton.

Erikson, E. (1969). Gandhi's truth: On the origins of militant nonviolence. New York: W.W. Norton.

Fain, J. (1996, April 17). Dr. Gilligan's prison education. Boston Globe, pp.57,60.

Fergusson, D. M. & Lynskey, M.T. (1997). Physical punishment/maltreatment during childhood and adjustment in young adulthood. Child Abuse & Neglect, 21(7), 617-630.

Feshbach, N. (1989). The construct of empathy and the phenomenon of physical maltreatment of children.   In D. Cicchetti & V. Carlson (Eds.), Child maltreatment: Theory and research on the causes and consequences of child abuse and neglect (pp. 349-373). New York: Columbia University Press.

Finkelhor, D., Hotaling, G.T., Lewis, I.A., & Smith, C. (1989). Sexual abuse and its relationship to later sexual satisfaction, marital status, religion, and attitudes. Journal of Interpersonal Violence, 4, 379-399.

First, M.B. (1994). (Ed). Diagnostic and statistical manual of mental disorders-DSM-IV (4th ed.). Washington, DC: American Psychiatric Association.

Fonagy, P., Steele, M., Steele, H., Higgit, A., & Target, M. (1994). The theory and practice of resilience. Journal of Child Psychology and Psychiatry, 35(231), 231-257.

Foster, R.A., & Keating, J.P. (1992). Measuring androcentrism in the western God-concept. Journal for the Scientific Study of Religion, 31, 366-375.

Fossum, M.A., & Masson, J. (1986). Facing shame:Families in recovery. New York: W.W. Norton.

Fowler, J.W. (1993). Shame: Toward a practical theological understanding. The Christian Century, 110, 816-819.

Fowler, J.W. (1996). Faithful change: The personal and public challenges of postmodern life. Nashville: Abingdon Press.

Freire, P. (1973). Pedagogy of the oppressed. New York: Seabury Press.

Freud, S. (1950). A child is beaten. In E. Jones (Ed.) & J. Riviere (Trans.),Collected Papers, (Vol. 4, pp. 172-201). London: The Hogarth Press. (Original work published in 1919)

Freud, S. (1950). Fragment of an analysis of a case of hysteria. In E. Jones (Ed.), Sigmund Freud Collected Papers (Vol. 3, pp. 13-146). London: The Hogarth Press. (Original work published 1905)

Freud, S. (1957). The disillusionment of the war. In J. Strachey (Ed. And Trans.), The standard edition of the complete psychological works of Sigmund Freud (Vol. 14, pp. 275-288). London: The Hogarth Press. (Original work published in 1914)

Freud, S. (1957). Our attitude towards death. In J. Strachey (Ed. And Trans.), The standard edition of the complete psychological works of Sigmund Freud (Vol. 14, pp. 289-300). London: The Hogarth Press. (Original work published in 1914)

Freud, S. (1961). Civilization and its discontents. In J. Strachey (Ed. And Trans.), The standard edition of the complete psychological works of Sigmund Freud

(Vol. 21, pp. 64-145). London: The Hogarth Press. (Original work published in 1930)

Freud, S. (1964). Why war? In J. Strachey (Ed. And Trans.), Collected Papers (Vol. 22, pp. 199-215). London: The Hogarth Press.(Original work published in 1932)

Frude, N., & Goss, A. (1979). Parental anger: A general population survey. Child Abuse and Neglect, 3,331-33.

Gandhi, M. (1965). Selected texts from Mohandas K. Gandhi's non-violence in peace and war. In T. Merton (Ed.), Gandhi on non-violence (pp. 1-76). New York: New Directions Paperbook.

Gandhi, M. (1982). All men are brothers: Autobiographical reflections. New York: The Continuum Publishing Corporation.

Garfinkel, H. (1956). Conditions of successful degradation ceremonies. American Journal of Sociology, 61, 420-424.

Gay, P. (1988). Freud: A life for our time. New York & London:W.W. Norton & Company.

Gelles, R.J., & Straus, M.A. (1979). Determinants of violence in family: Towards a theoretical integration. In W. R.Burr, R. Hill, F. I. Nye, I.L. Reiss (Eds.), Contemporary Theories About the Family (Vol. 1, pp. 549-581). New York: Free Press.

Gelles, R. J., & Straus, M.A. (1988). Intimate violence. New York: Simon and Schuster.

Gilligan C. (1992). In a different voice. Cambridge, MA: Harvard University Press.

Gilligan, J. (1996). Violence. New York: G.P. Putnam's Sons.

Godin, A., & Hallez, M. (1964). Parental images and divine paternity. Lumen Vitae, 19, 253-284.

Goffman, E. (1956). Embarrassment and social organization. American Journal of Sociology, 62, 264-71.

Goffman, E. (1959). The presentation of self in everyday life. New York: Anchor.

Goldberg, C. (1991). Understanding shame. New York: Aronson.

Goleman, D. (1995). Emotional intelligence: Why it can matter more than IQ. New York: Bantam Books.

Gorsuch, R.L. (1968). The conceptualization of God as seen in adjective ratings. Journal For The Scientific Study Of Religion, 7,(1), 56-64.

Goudey, J. (1993). "Atonement imagery and Eucharistic praxis in the Reformed tradition: A feminist critique" (Ann Arbor: University Microfilms).

Glaser, J.W. (1973). Conscience and superego: A key distinction. In E.C. Nelson (Ed.), Conscience: Theological and psychological perspectives (pp. 167-188). New York: Newman Press.

Grasmick, H.G., Bursik, R.J., & Kimpel, M. (1991). Protestant fundamentalism and attitudes toward corporal punishment of children. Violence and Victims, 6, 282-98.

Greven, P. (1977). The Protestant temperament: Patterns of child-rearing religious experience, and the self in early America. Chicago: The University of Chicago Press.

Greven, P. (1990, 1992). Spare the child: The religious roots of physical punishment and the psychological impact of physical abuse. New York: Knopf.

Griffin, J.T. (1991). Racism and humiliation in the African-American community. Journal of Primary Prevention, 12 (2), 149-167.

Hall, T.W., Tisdale, T.C., & Browkaw, B.F. (1994). Assessment of religious dimensions in Christian clients: A review of selected instruments for research and clinical use. Journal of Psychology and Theology, 22 (4), 395-421.

Hammersla, J. F., Andrews-Qualls, L. C., & Frease, L. G. (1986). God concepts and religious commitment among Christian university students. Journal for the Scientific Study of Religion, 25, 424-435.

Harder, D. W. (1984). Character style of the defensively high self-esteem man. Journal of Clinical Psychology, 40, 26-35.

Harder, D. W. (1990). Additional construct validity evidence for the Harder personal feelings questionnaire measure of shame and guilt proneness. Psychological Reports, 67, 288-290.

Harder, D.W. (1990). Comment on Wright, O'leary, and Balkin's 'shame, guilt, narcissism, and depression: Correlates and sex differences.' <u>Psychoanalytic Psychology</u>, <u>7</u>(2), 285-289.

Harder, D.W. (1995). Shame and guilt assessment, and relationships of shame-and guilt-proneness to psychopathology. In J. P. Tangney (Ed.), <u>Self-conscious emotions: The psychology of shame, guilt, embarrassment and pride</u> (pp. 368-392). New York, New York: Guilford Publications, Inc.

Harder, D.W., & Zalma, A. (1990). Two promising shame and guilt scales: A construct validity comparison. <u>Journal of Personality Assessment</u>, <u>55</u> (3&4), 729-745.

Harder, D.W., Cutler, L., & Rockart, L. (1992). Assessment of shame and guilt and their relationships to psychopathology. <u>Journal of Personality Assessment</u>, <u>59</u>(3), 584-604.

Harlow, H. (1962). The heterosexual affectional system in monkeys. <u>Am Psychologist</u>. <u>17</u>: 1-9.

Hartling, L.M. (1995). "Humiliation: Assessing the specter of derision, degradation, and debasement" (Ann Arbor: University Microfilms).

Herman, J. (1992). <u>Trauma and recovery</u>. New York: Basic Books.

Holden, C. (1991). "Depression: The news isn't depressing." <u>Science</u>, <u>254</u>: 1450-52.

Hood, R. W., Spilka, B., Hunsberger, B., & Gorsuch, R. (Eds.). (1996). <u>The psychology of religion: An empiricl approach</u>. New York: The Guildford Press.

Howe, L. (1995). <u>The image of God: A theology for pastoral care and counseling</u>. Nashville, Abingdon Press.

Hordern, W. (1976). Conscience. In A. Richardson (Ed.), <u>A dictionary of Christian theology</u> (p. 71). Philadelphia: The Westminster Press.

Hordern, W. (1976). Doctrine of man. In A. Richardson (Ed.), <u>A dictionary of Christian theology</u> (pp. 202-205). Philadelphia: The Westminster Press.

Horney, K. (1945). <u>Our inner conflicts</u>. New York: W.W.Norton.

Horney, K. (1950). <u>Neurosis and human growth</u>. New York: Norton.

Huber, L. B. (1983). "The biblical experience of shame/shaming: The social experience of shame/shaming in biblical Israel in relation to its use as religious metaphor" (Ann Arbor: University Microfilms).

Hyman, I.A. (1997). The case against spanking—How to discipline your child without hitting. San Francisco: Jossey-Bass Publisher.

Irwin, H.J. (1996). Traumatic childhood events, perceived availability of emotional support, and the development of dissociative tendencies. Child Abuse & Neglect, 20(8), 701-707.

James, W. (1910). Psychology. New York: Henry Holt.

James, W. (1980). The self. In C. Gordon & K. Gergen (Eds.), The self in social interaction (pp. 41-49). New York: John Wiley and Sons.

Johnson, E. L. (1992). A place for the Bible within psychological science. Journal of Psychology & Theology, 20(4), 346-355.

Johnson, L. T. (1986). The writings of the New Testament. Philadelphia: Fortress Press.

Johnson, L.T. (1996) The real Jesus. New York, New York: Harper San Francisco.

Jones, E. (1929). Fear, guilt, and hate. International Journal of Psychoanalysis, 10, 304-319.

Jones, E. (1945). Psychology and war conditions. The Psychoanalytic Quarterly, 14, 1-27.

Jones, D.P.H. (1996). Editorial: Dissociation, and cycles of abuse across generations. Child Abuse & Neglect, 20(11), 1121-1122.

Jonge, J. (1995). On breaking wills: The theological roots of violence in families. Journal of Psychology and Christianity, 14(1), 26-37.

Jordan, J. (1984). Empathy and self-boundaries. (Work in Progress, No. 16.) Wellesley, MA: Stone Center Working Paper Series.

Jordan, J. (1986). The meaning of mutuality. (Work in Progress, No. 23.) Wellesley, MA: Stone Center Working Paper Series.

Jordan, J. (1989). Relational development: Therapeutic implication of empathy and shame. (Work in Progress, No. 39.) Wellesley, MA: Stone Center Working Paper Series.

Jordan, J.V.,Kaplan, A.G., Miller, J.B., Stiver, I.P., & Surrey, J.L. (1991). Women's growth in connection. New York: The Guilford Press.

Jordan, J.V. (Ed.). (1997). Women's growth in diversity. The Guilford Press: New York, N.Y.

Kaplan, A. (1990). Women and suicide: The cry for connection. (Work in Progress, No. 46.) Wellesley, MA: Stone Center Working Paper Series.

Kaplan, H.I., Sadock, B.J., Grebb, J.A. (Eds.). (1994). Synopsis of psychiatry: Behavioral sciences clincial psychiatry—seventh edition. Baltimore: Williams & Wilkins.

Katz. J. (1988). Seductions to crime. New York: Basic Books.

Kaufman, G. (1992). Shame: The power of caring (3rd ed.). Cambridge, MA:Schenkman.

Kaufman, J., & Zigler, E. (1987). Do abused children become abusive parents? American Journal of Orthopsychiatry, 57, 186-192.

Kendall-Tackett, K., Williams, L., & Finkelhor, D. (1993). Impact of sexual abuse on children: A review and synthesis of recent empirical studies. Psychological Bulletin, 113, 164-180.

Kirkpatrick, L.A.(1986). Developmental psychology and religion: Potential application of attachment theory for the psychology of religion. Paper presented at the annual meeting of the Society for the Scientific Study of Religion, Washington, DC.

Klein, Donald. C. (1991a). Introduction to special issue. Journal of Primary Prevention, 12 (2), 87-91.

Klein, Donald. C. (1991b). The humiliation dynamic: An overview. Journal of Primary Prevention, 12 (2), 93-121.

Klein, Donald C. (1992). Managing humiliation. Journal of Primary Prevention, 12 (3), 255-268.

Kleinbaum, D., Kupper, L., & Muller, K. (1988). Applied regression analysis and other multivariable methods. Duxbery Press: Belmont, California.

Klopfenstein, M. (1972). Scham und schande nach dem alten testament. Zurich: Theologischer Verlag.

Koch, Sigmund E. (1992). Forward: Wundt's creature at age zero—and as centenarian; some aspects of the institutionalization of the 'new psychology.' In S. Koch and D. E. Leary, (Eds.), <u>A Century of Psychology As Science</u>(pp.7-35).Washington, DC: American Psychological Association.

Kohut, H. (1971a). <u>The analysis of the self: A systematic approach to the psychoanalytic treatment of narcissistic personality disorders</u>. New York: International Universities Press, 1971.

Kohut, H. (1977). <u>The restoration of the self</u>. New York: International Universities Press.

Kohut, H. (1978a). Thoughts on narcissism and narcissistic rage. In P.H. Ornstein (Ed.),<u>The search for the self: Selected writings of Heinz Kohut, 1950-1978</u> (Vol. 2, pp. 615-658). International University Press: New York.

Kohut, H. (1978b). The psychoanalyst in the community of scholars. In: P. Ornstein (Ed.), <u>The search for the self: Selected writings of Heinz Kohut, 1950-1978</u> (Vol. 2, pp. 685-724). New York: International Universities Press.

Kohut, H. (1984). <u>How does analysis cure</u>? Chicago, IL: University of Chicago Press.

Kolb, B., & Whisham, I. (1990). <u>Fundamentals of human neuropsychology</u>. New York: W. H. Freeman and Company.

Lezak, M. (1983). <u>Neuropsychological assessment</u>. New York: Oxford University Press.

Labov, W., & Fanshel, D. (1977). <u>Therapeutic discourse</u>. New York: Academic Press.

Lambert, W., Triandis, L., & Wolf, M. (1959). Some correlates of beliefs in the malevolence and benevolence of supernatural beings: A cross-societal study. <u>The Journal of Abnormal and Social Psychology</u>, 58(2),162-169.

Lansky, M. R. (1984). Violence, shame, and the family. <u>International-Journal-of-Family-Psychiatry</u>, 5(1), 21-40.

Lansky, M. (1987). Shame and domestic violence. In D. Nathanson (Ed.), <u>The many faces of shame</u>(pp.335-362). Guilford: New York.

Lansky, M. (1992). <u>Fathers who fail: Shame and psychopathology in the family system</u>. Hillsdale, NJ: Analytic Press.

Lansky, M. (1993). Family Genesis of aggression. Psychiatric-Annals, 23(9),494-499.

Larzelere, R.E. (1986). Moderate spanking: Model or deterrent of children's aggression in the family? Journal of Family Violence, 1, 27-36.

Lawrence, R.T. (1987). God image and self image: The need for a psychometric instrument. Paper presented at annual meeting of the Society for the Scientific Study of Religion, New York, NY.

Lawrence, R. T. (1991). "The God image inventory: The development, validation and standardization of a psychometric instrument for research, pastoral and clinical use in measuring the image of God" (Ann Arbor:University Microfilms).

Lawrence, R.T. (1996). Measuring the image of God: The God image inventory and the God image scales. Paper presented at the annual meeting of the American Psychological Association, Toronto, Canada.

Lawson, R., Drebing, C., Berg, G., Vincellette, A., & Penk, W. (1998). The long term impact of child abuse on religious behavior and spirituality in men. Child Abuse & Neglect, 22(5), 369-380.

Lehmann, Paul (1973). The decline and fall of conscience. In E.C. Nelson (Ed.), Conscience: Theological and psychological perspective(pp. 28-45). New York, Newman Press.

LeTourneau, C. (1981). Empathy and stress: How they affect parental aggression. Social Work, 26, 383-389.

Lewis, E. (1983). The group treatment of battered women. Women-and-Therapy, 2(1), 51-58.

Lewis, H. (1971). Shame and guilt in neurosis. New York: International Universities Press.

Lewis, H. B. (1976). Psychic war in men and women. New York: New York University Press.

Lewis, H.B. (1981). Freud and modern psychology (Vol. 1). New York: Plenum Press.

Lewis, H. (1987a). The role of shame in symptom formation. Hillsdale, NJ: Lawrence Erlbaum Associates.

Lewis, H. (1987b). Shame and the narcissistic personality. In D. L. Nathanson (Ed.),The many faces of shame(pp. 93-132). New York: Guilford Press.

Lewis, H. B. (1987c). The role of shame in depression over the life span. In H.B. Lewis (Ed.), The role of shame in symptom formation(pp. 29-50). Hillsdale, NJ: Lawrence Erlbaum Associates.

Lewis, M. (1992). Shame: The exposed self. New York: Free Press.

Lifton, R.J. (1979). The broken connection. New York: Simon & Schuster.

Lifton, R.J. (1986). The Nazi doctors. New York: Basic Books, Inc.

Linehan, M. (1993). Cognitive-behavioral treatment of borderline personality disorder. New York: The Guilford Press.

Lister, E.D. (1982). Forced silence: A neglected dimension of trauma. American-Journal-of-Psychiatry, 139(7), 872-876.

Loder, J. (1990). Theology and psychology. In R.J. Hunter (Ed.), Dictionary of pastoral care and counseling (pp.1267-1270). Nashville: Abingdon Press.

Lowenfeld, H. (1976). Notes on shamelessness. Psychoanalytic Quarterly, 45, 62-72.

Lynd, H. (1958). On shame and the search for identity. New York: John Wiley and Sons.

Malina, B. J. (1981). The New Testament world: Insights from cultural anthropology. John Knox, Atlanta.

Malina, B.J. (1991). Reading theory perspective: Reading Luke-Acts. In J.H. Neyrey (Ed.), The social world of Luke-Acts(pp. 3-23). Peabody, MA: Henrickson Publishers.

Malina, B. J. (1997). Despising shame: Honor discourse and community maintenance in the Epistle to the Hebrews. Journal of Biblical Literature, 116(2), 378-379.

Malina, B.J., & Neyrey, J.R. (1991a). Honor and shame in Luke-Acts: Pivotal values of the Mediterranean world. In J.H. Neyrey (Ed.), The social world of Luke-Acts(pp. 25-65). Peabody, MA: Henrickson Publishers.

Malina, B.J., & Neyrey, J.R. (1991b). First century personality: Dyadic, not individualistic. In J.H. Neyrey (Ed.), The social world of Luke-Acts(pp. 67-96). Peabody, MA: Henrickson Publishers.

Malina, B.J., & Neyrey, J.R. (1991c). Conflict in Luke-Acts:Labelling and deviance theory. In J.H. Neyrey (Ed.), The social world of Luke-Acts(pp. 97-122). Peabody, MA: Henrickson Publishers.

Malina, B.J., & Rohrbaugh, R. (1992). Social-science commentary on the synoptic gospels. Minneapolis: Fortress.

Malinosky-Rummell, R., & Hansen, D. (1993). Long-term consequences of childhood physical abuse. Psychological Bulletin, 114, 68-79.

Manning, M. (1997, November 2). Intimacy and stuff. The New York Times Book Review (Vol. CII, No. 44).

Marino, M. (1992). Empathy levels and depression in physically-abusive adolescent mothers and nonphysically-abusive adolescent mothers. Dissertation Abstracts International, 53, 3378A.

Marx, K. (1964). Economic and philosophic manuscripts of 1944. New York: International Publishers.

McDargh, J. (1983). Psychoanalytic object relations theory and the study of religion: On faith and the imaging of God. New York: University Press of America.

McFarland, W.G. (1992). A multitrait-multimethod validation and factor analysis of an experimental shame-proneness scale. Doctoral Dissertation, The University of New Mexico.

Mead, M. (1937). Cooperation and competition among primitive peoples. New York: McGraw-Hill Book Company.

Meeks, W. A. (1986). The moral world of the first Christians. Philadelphia: The Westminster Press.

Meissner, W.W. (1977). The psychology of religious experience. Communion, 4, 36-59.

Meissner, W.W. (1978). Psychoanalytic aspects of religious experience. Annual of Psychoanalysis, 6, 103-141.

Meissner, W.W. (1984). Psychoanalysis and religious experience. New Haven, CT: Yale University Press.

Meissner, W.W. (1987). Life and faith: Psychological perspectives on religious experience. Washington, DC: Georgetown University Press.

Meissner, W.W. (1992). Religious thinking as transitional conceptualization. The Psychoanalytic Review, 79, 175-196.

Menniger, K. (1938). Man against himself. New York: Harcourt, Brace and Company.

Menniger, K. (1942). Love against hate. New York: Harcourt, Brace and Company.

Mihalie, S.W.; Elliott, D. (1997) A social learning theory model of marital violence. Journal of Family Violence, 12(1), 21-47).

Miller, A. (1981). The drama of the gifted child. New York: Basic Books.

Miller, A. (1983, 1984). For your own good. New York: Farrer, Strauss and Giroux.

Miller, A. (1984). Thou shalt not be aware. New York: Farrer, Strauss and Giroux.

Miller, A. (1990). Banished knowledge. New York: Doubleday.

Miller, A. (1991). Breaking down the wall of silence. New York: Dutton Books.

Miller, D. (1990). Violence. In R.J. Hunter (Ed.), Dictionary of pastoral care and counseling, (pp.1303-1305), Nashville: Abingdon Press.

Miller, J.B. (1984). The development of women's sense of self. (Work in Progress, No. 12.) Wellesley, MA: Stone Center Working Paper Series.

Miller, J.B. (1987). Toward a new psychology of women. Boston: Beacon Press.

Miller, J.B. (1988). Connections, disconnections, and violations. (Work in Progress, No. 33.) Wellesley, MA: Stone Center Working Paper Series.

Miller, J.B., & Surrey, J. (1990). Revisioning women's anger: The personal and the global. (Work in Progress, No. 43.) Wellesley, MA: Stone Center Working Paper Series.

Miller, J.B., Jordan, J.V., Kaplan, A.G., Stiver, I. R., & Surrey, J.L. (1997). Some misconceptions and reconceptions of a relational approach. In J.V. Jordan

Ed.),Women's Growth in Diversity(pp.25-49). New York, New York: The Guilford Press.

Miller, S. B. (1988). Humiliation and shame. Bulletin of Menninger Clinic, 52 (1), 40-51.

Miller, S. B. (1996). Shame in context. Hillsdale, NJ: The Analytic Press.

Milner, J., Halsey, L., & Fultz, J. (1995). Empathic responsiveness and affective reactivity to infant stimuli in high-and low-risk for physical child abuse mothers. Child Abuse & Neglect, 19, 767-780.

Mount, E. (1960). Conscience and responsibility. John Knox Press. Richmond, Virginia.

Morrison, A. P. (1983). Shame, the ideal self, and narcissism. Contemporary Psychoanalysis, 19, 295-318.

Morrison, A. P. (1989). Shame, the underside of narcissism. Hillsdale, NJ: The Analytic Press.

Morrison, A. P. (1996). The culture of shame. New York: Ballantine Books.

Moscarello, R. (1992). Victims of violence: Aspects of the "victim-to-patient" process in women. Canadian-Journal-of-Psychiatry, 37(7) 497-502.

Moxnes, H. (1991). Patron-client relations and the new community in Luke-Acts. In J.H. Neyrey (Ed.), The social world of Luke-Acts(pp. 241-268). Peabody, MA: Henrickson Publishers.

Nathanson, D. (1987). The many faces of shame. New York: Guilford Press.

Nathanson, D. (1992). Shame and pride: Affect, sex, and the birth of the self. New York: Norton.

Nathanson, D. (1996). Knowing feeling: Affect, script and psychotherapy. New York: W.W. Norton and Company.

Neyrey, J.H. (Ed.). (1991). The social world of Luke-Acts: Models for interpretation. Peabody, MA: Henrickson Publishers.

Neyrey, J.H. (1994). Despising the shame of the cross: Honor and shame in the Johannine passion narrative. Semeia, 68, 113-137.

Niebuhr, R. (1941). The nature and destiny of man (Vol.1). New York: Charles Scribner's Sons.

Niebuhr, R. (1949). The nature and destiny of man: A Christian interpretation. New York: Charles Scribner's Sons.

Opie, I., & Opie, P. (Eds.). (1963). A family book of nursery rhymes. New York: Oxford University Press.

Ornduff, S. R. (1997). Implications for child abuse. Bulletin of the Menniger Clinic, 61(1), 1-15).

Osgood, C.E., Suci, G.J., & Tannenbaum, P.H. (1957). Measurement of meaning. Urbana, Ill: University of Illinois Press.

Owens, D.J., & Straus, M.A. (1975). The social structure of violence in childhood and approval of violence as an adult. Aggressive Behavior,1, 193-211.

Painter, S. L., & Dutton, D. (1985). Patterns of emotional bonding in battered women: traumatic bonding. International Journal of Women's Studies, 8(4), 363-375.

Pais, J. (1991). Suffer the children: A theology of liberation by a victim of child abuse. New York: Paulist Press.

Patton, J. (1985). Is human forgiveness possible? A pastoral care perspective. Nashville: Abingdon Press.

Pedersen, J. (1926). Israel: Its life and culture. London: Oxford University Press.

Peristiany, J.G. (Ed.). (1966, 1974). Honour and shame: The values of Mediterranean society. Chicago:University of Chicago Press.

Petrik, N.D. (1994). The reduction of male abusiveness as a result of treatment: Reality or myth? Journal-of-Family-Violence, 9(4), 307-316.

Piaget, J. (1952). The origins of intelligence in children. New York: W.W. Norton.

Pierce, C.A. (1955). Conscience in the New Testament. London: SCM Press.

Piers, G., & Singer, M.B. (1953, 1971). Shame and guilt. New York: W.W. Norton and Company, Inc.

Pitt-Rivers, J. (1966, 1974). Honour and social status. In J.G. Peristiany (Ed.), Honour and shame: The values of Mediterranean society(pp. 19-77). Chicago:University of Chicago Press.

Pitt-Rivers, J. (1968). Honor. International Encyclopedia of Social Science, 6, 503-511.

Poling, J. (1991). The abuse of power: A theological problem. Nashville: Abingdon Press.

Pontius, A.A. (1997). Homicide linked to moderate repetitive stresses kindling limbic seizures in 14 cases of limbic psychotic trigger reaction. Aggression and Violent Behavior, 2(2), 125-141.

Potvin, R. H. (1977). Adolescent God images. Review of Religious Research, 19, 43-53.

Proulx, J., Aubu, J., McKibben, A., & Cote, M. (1994). Penile responses of rapists and nonrapists to rape stimuli involving physical violence or humiliation. Arch-Sex-Behav, 23(3), 295-310.

Prothrow-Stith, D. (1996). Violence—A public health crisis. Healthcare Forum Journal, 39(5), 18-21.

Rado, S. (1960). Rage, violence and conscience. Comprehensive Psychiatry,1,327-330.

Retzinger, S.M. (1985). The resentment process: Videotape studies. Psychoanal. Psychol, 2, 129-153.

Retzinger, S. M. (1987). Resentment and laughter: Video studies of the shame-rage spiral. In H.B. Lewis (Ed.), The role of shame in symptom formation(pp. 151-181). Hillsdale, NJ: Lawrence Erlbaum Associates, Publishers.

Retzinger, S. M. (1989). A theory of mental illness: Integrating social and emotional aspects. Psychiatry, 52, 325-335.

Retzinger, S. M. (1989). Marital conflict: The role of emotion. Presented at the Annual Meetings for the American Sociological Association, San Francisco, CA.

Retzinger, S. M. (1991a). Shame, anger, and conflict: Case study of emotional violence. Journal of Family Violence, 6(1), 37-59.

Retzinger, S. M. (1991). Violent emotions: Shame and rage in marital quarrels. Newbury Park, California, Sage Publications Ltd.

Ricoeur, P. (1971). The model of the text: Meaningful action considered as a text. Social Research. 38 (3), 529-562.

Ricoeur, P. (1973). Guilt, ethics and religion. In E.C.Nelson (Ed.), Conscience: Theological and psychological perspectives(pp. 11-27). New York: Newman Press.

Ricoeur, P. (1978). Listening to the parables of Jesus. In C.E. Reagan, & D. Stewart (Eds.), The philosophy of Paul Ricoeur—An anthology of his work(pp. 239-245). Boston: Beacon Press.

Rizzuto, A.M. (1970). Critique of the contemporary literature in the scientific study of religion. Paper presented at the annual meeting of the Society for the Scientific Study of Religion, New York, NY.

Rizzuto, A.M. (1979). The birth of the living God: A psychoanalytic study.Chicago: University of Chicago Press.

Rohrbaugh, R.L. (1991). The pre-industrial city in Luke-Acts: Urban social relations. In J.H. Neyrey (Ed.), The social world of Luke-Acts(pp.125-149). Peabody, MA: Henrickson Publishers.

Rosenberg, M. (1965). Society and the adolescent self-image. Princeton, NJ: Princeton University Press.

Rosenstein, P. (1995). Parental levels of empathy as related to risk assessment in child protective services. Child Abuse & Neglect, 19, 1349-1360.

Rossi, E.L. (1993). The psychobiology of mind-body healing—New concepts of therapeutic hypnosis. New York: W.W. Norton & Company, Inc.

Russell, D. E. (1986). The secret trauma: Incest in the lives of girls and women. New York: Basic Books.

Rybak, C.J. (1991). A validational study of the internalized shame scale: Theoretical origins and implications. Masters Thesis, Southern Illinois University.

Saiving, V. (1960). The human situation: A feminine view. The Journal of Religion, 40,100-112.

Sartre, Jean Paul. (1956). Etre et le neant. New York: Philosophical Library.

Sandler, J., & Rosenblatt, B. (1962). The concept of the representational world. Psychoanalytic Study of the Child, 17, 128-145.

Saunders, E.A., & Arnold, F. (1991). Borderline personality disorder and childhood abuse: Revisions in clinical thinking and treatment approach. (Work in Progress, No. 51.) Wellesley, MA: Stone Center Working Paper Series.

Schar, H. (1973). Protestant problems with conscience. In E.C. Nelson (Ed.), Conscience: Theological and psychological perspectives(pp. 79-94). New York: Newman Press.

Schlauch, C. (1995). Faithful companioning: How pastoral counseling heals. Minneapolis: Fortress Press.

Scheff, Thomas J. (1966). Being mentally ill. Chicago: Aldine.

Scheff, T. (1968). Negotiation of reality: Notes on power in the assessment of responsibility. Social Problem, 76, 3-17.

Scheff, T. (1984). The taboo on coarse emotions. Review of Personality and Social Psychology, 5,146-69.

Scheff, T. (1985). The primacy of affect. Review of Personality and Social Psychology, 5, 146-69.

Scheff, T. (1987). The shame-rage spiral: A case study of an interminable quarrel. In H.B.Lewis (Ed.), The Role of Shame in Symptom Formation(pp.109-149). Hillsdale, NJ: Lawrence Erlbaum Associates, Publishers.

Scheff, T. (1990). Microsociology: Discourse, emotion and social structure. Chicago, University of Chicago Press.

Scheff, T. J. (1995). Conflict in family systems: The role of shame. In J.P. Tangney & K.W. Fischer (Eds.), Self-conscious emotions: Shame, guilt embarassment, and pride(pp. 393-412). New York: Guilford.

Scheff, T. J., & Retzinger, S. M. (1991). Emotions and violence: Shame and rage in destructive conflicts. Lexington, MA: Lexington Books.

Schneider, C. (1977). Shame, exposure, and privacy. Boston: Beacon Press.

Schneider, C. (1990). Shame. In R.J. Hunter (Ed.), Dictionary of pastoral care and counseling (pp. 1160-1163). Nashville: Abingdon Press.

Scubla, L. (1988). The Christianity of Rene Girard and the nature of religion. In P.D. Dumouchel (Ed.),Violence and truth—On the work of Rene Girard(pp.160-178). Stanford, California: Stanford University Press.

Schneidman, E. (1996). The Suicidal Mind. New York: Oxford University Press.

Sears, R., Macoby, E., & Levin, H. (1971). How conscience is formed. In E.C. Nelson (Ed.), Conscience: Theological and psychological perspectives(pp. 292-309). New York: Newman Press.

Seebass, H. (1970). In G. J. Botterwick & H. Ringgrin (Eds.) & G.W. Bromiley (Trans.), Theological Dictionary of the Old Testament (Vol. II, 50-60). Grand Rapids, Michigan: William B. Eerdmans Publishing Company.

Sennett, R. (1980). Authority. New York: Alfred A. Knopf, Inc.

Shreve, B. W., & Kunkel, M.A. (1991). Self-psychology, shame and adolescent suicide: Theoretical and practical considerations. Journal of Counseling & Development, 69, 305-311.

Spero, M. (1974). Shame: An object-relational formulation. The Psychoanalytic Study of the Child, 39, 381-389.

Spero, M. (1992). Religious objects as psychological structures: A critical integration of object relations theory, psychotherapy, and Judaism. Chicago: The University of Chicago Press.

Stendahl, K. (1976). Paul among the Jews and gentiles. Philadelphia: Fortress Press.

Spies, R.G. (1975). War, sport and aggression: An empirical test of two rival theories. American Anthropologist, 75, 64-86.

Spilka, B., Addison, J., & Rosensohn, M. (1975). Parents, self, and God: A test of competing theories of individual-religion relationships. Review of Religious Research, 16, 154-165.

Spilka, B., Armatas, P., & Nussbaum, J. (1964). The concept of God: A factor analytic approach. Review of Religious Research, 6, 28-36.

Stiver, I. (1984). The meanings of "dependency" in female-male relationships. (Work in Progress, No. 11.) Wellesley, MA: Stone Center Working Paper Series.

Spitz, R. A. (1956). Anaclitic depression: An inquiry into the genesis of psychiatric conditions in early childhood. Psychoanalytic Study of the Child, 2: 313-332.

Stearns, C., & Stearns, P. (1986). Anger: The struggle for control in American history. Chicago: University of Chicago Press.

Steele, B., & Pollack, C. (1968). A psychiatric study of parents who abuse infants and small children. In R. Helfer & C. Kempe (Eds.), The battered child syndrome (pp. 103-145). Chicago, IL: University of Chicago Press.

Straus, M.A. (1974). Leveling, civility, and violence in the family. Journal of Marriage and the Family, 36(1), 13-29.

Straus, M.A. (1991). Discipline and deviance: Physical punishment of children and violence and other crimes in adulthood. Social Problems, 38, 101-123.

Straus, M.A. (1994a). Corporal punishment of children and depression and suicide in adulthood. In J. McCord (Ed.), Coercion and punishment in long-term perspective(pp.59-77). New York: Cambridge University Press.

Straus, M.A. (1994b). Beating the devil out of them. Corporal punishment in American families. New York, New York: Lexington Books.

Straus, M.S., & Gelles, R.J. (1988). How violent are American families? Estimates from the national family violence resurvey and other studies. In G. Hotaling, D. Finkelhor, J. T. Kirkpatrick and M. A. Straus (Eds.), Family abuse and its consequences: New directions in research (pp. 14-36). Newbury Park, CA: Sage.

Straus, M.A., & Gelles, R.J. (1990). Physical violence in American families: Risk factors and adaptations to violence in 8,145 families. New Brunswick, NJ: Transaction Publishers.

Straus, M. A., & Donnelly, D.A. (1993). Corporal punishment of teen age children in the United States. Youth and Society, 24, 419-442.

Straus, M.A., Hamby, S.L., Boney-McCoy, S., & Sugarman, D.B.(1996). The revised conflict tactics scales (cts2): Development and preliminary psychometric data. In M.A. Straus (Ed.) Manual for the conflict tactics scales (cts) and test forms for the revised conflict tactics scales(pp. 1-16). Durham, NH: University of New Hampshire.

Straus, M.A., & Hill, K.A. (1997, July). Corporal punishment, the child-to-mother bond, and delinquency. Paper presented at the 5th International Family Violence Research Conference, Durham, NH.

Straus, M.A., Sugarman, D.B., & Giles-Sims, J. (1997). Spanking by parents and subsequent antisocial behavior of children. Arch Pediatr Adolesc Med, 151(8), 761-767.

Suchocki, M. (1995). The fall to violence. Original sin in relational theology. New York: Continuum.

Sullivan, H. (1953). The interpersonal theory of psychiatry. New York: W.W. Norton.

Surrey, J. (1985). Self-in-relation: A theory of women's development. (Work in Progress, No.13) Wellesley, MA: Stone Center Working Paper Series.

Tangney, J.P. (1993). Shame and guilt. In C.G. Costello (Ed.), Symptoms of depression(pp. 161-180). New York: John Wiley.

Tangney, J.P. (1995a). Recent advances in the empirical study of shame and guilt. American Behavioral Scientist, 38(8), 1132-1145.

Tangney, J.P. (1995b). Shame and guilt in interpersonal relationships. In J.P. Tangney & K.W. Fischer (Eds.), Self-conscious emotions: Shame, guilt, embarrassment, and pride (pp. 114-139). New York: Guilford.

Tangney, J.P. (1996). Assessing shame and guilt. Behaviour Research and Therapy,34(9), 741-754.

Tangney, J.P., Wagner, P., & Gramzow, R. (1992). Proneness to shame, proneness to guilt, and psychopathology. Journal of Abnormal Psychology, 103, 469-478.

Tangney, J. P., Wagner, P.E., Barlow, D.H., Marschall, D.E., & Gramzow, R. (1994). The relation of shame and guilt to constructive versus destructive responses to anger across the life span. Journal of Personality and Social Psychology,70(4), 780-795.

Tangney, J.P., Marschall, D.E., Rosenberg, K., Barlow, D.H., & Wagner, P.E. (1994). Children's and adults' autobiographical accounts of shame, guilt and pride experiences: An analysis of situational determinants and interpersonal concerns. Manuscript submitted for publication.

Tangney, J.P., Miller, R.S., Flicker, L., & Barlow D.H. (1995). Are shame, guilt and embarrassment distinct emotions? A quantitative analysis of participant ratings. Manuscript submitted for publication.

Thompson, J.E. (1996). Shame in pastoral psychotherapy. Pastoral Psychology, 44(5), 311-320.

Tillich, P. (1951). Systematic Theology (Vol. 1). Chicago: The University of Chicago Press.

Tillich, P. (1952). The courage to be. New Haven: Yale University Press.

Tillich, P. (1973). A conscious above moralism. In E.C. Nelson (Ed.), Conscience: Theological and psychological perspectives(pp. 46-61). New York: Newman Press.

Tillich, P. (1973). The nature of a liberating conscience. In E.C. Nelson (Ed.), Conscience: Theological and psychological perspectives(pp. 62-71). New York: Newman Press.

Tomkins, S. (1962). Affect, imagery, consciousness: The positive affects (Vol.1). New York: Springer.

Tomkins, S. (1963). Affect, imagery, consciousness: The negative affects (Vol.2). New York: Springer.

Tomkins, S. (1987). Shame. In D. Nathanson (Ed.), The many faces of shame(pp. 133-161). New York: Guilford Press.

Tracy, D. (1983). Foundations of practical theology. In D. Browning (Ed.), Practical Theology(pp. 61-82). San Francisco: Harper and Row.

van der Kolk, B.A. (1987). The psychological consequences of overwhelming experiences. In B.A. van der Kolk (Ed.), Psychological trauma: The effects of overwhelming experience on mind, body, and society(pp. 1-30).Washington, DC: American Psychiatric Press.

van der Kolk, B. A., McFarlane, A. C., (1996). The black hole of trauma. In B.A. van der Kolk, A.C. McFarlane, & L. Weisaeth (Eds.), Traumatic Stress. New York, NY: The Guilford Press.

van der Kolk, B.A., Weisaeth, L., & van der Hart, O. (1996). History of trauma in psychiatry. In B.A. van der Kolk, A.C. McFarlane, & L. Weisaeth (Eds.), Traumatic Stress. New York, NY: The Guilford Press.

Vergote, A., & Tamayo, A. (Eds.). (1981). The parental figures and the representations of God: A psychological and cross-cultural study. The Hague: Mouton Publishers.

Wallace, B., & Nosko, A. (1993). Working with shame in the group treatment of male batterers. International-Journal-of-Group-Psychotherapy, 43 (1), 45-61.

Weed, M.R. (1978). "Conscience in Protestant ethics" (Ann Arbor: University Microfilms).

West, C. (1994). Race matters. New York: Vintage Books.

Wiehe, V. (1997). Approaching child abuse treatment from the perspective of empathy. Child Abuse & Neglect, 21(12), 1191-1204.

Wiesel, E. (1995). Memoirs: All rivers run to the sea. New York: Alfred A. Knopf.

Winnicott, D. W. (1971). Playing and reality. London:Tavistock Publications.

Wootton, R.J. (1990). God-representation and its relation to object relations and defensive functioning. Ann Arbor: University Microfilms International (9105385).

Wright, F., (1987). Men, shame and antisocial behavior: A psychodynamic perspective. Group, 11(4), 238-246.

Wurmser, L. (1981). The mask of shame. Baltimore: Johns Hopkins University Press.

Yamagugchi, M. (1988). Towards a poetics of the scapegoat. In P. Dumouchel, (Ed.), Violence and truth—On the work of Rene Girard(pp. 179-191). Stanford, California: Stanford University Press.

You, G.Y. (1997). Shame and guilt mechanisms in east Asian culture. Journal of Pastoral Care, 51, 57-64.

AUTHOR INDEX

SUBJECT INDEX